4/97

About Island Press

Island Press is the only nonprofit organization in the United States whose principal purpose is the publication of books on environmental issues and natural resource management. We provide solutions-oriented information to professionals, public officials, business and community leaders, and concerned citizens who are shaping responses to environmental problems.

In 1994, Island Press celebrated its tenth anniversary as the leading provider of timely and practical books that take a multidisciplinary approach to critical environmental concerns. Our growing list of titles reflects our commitment to bringing the best of an expanding body of literature to the environmental community throughout North America and the world.

Support for Island Press is provided by Apple Computer, Inc., The Bullitt Foundation, The Geraldine R. Dodge Foundation, The Energy Foundation, The Ford Foundation, The W. Alton Jones Foundation, The Lyndhurst Foundation, The John D. and Catherine T. MacArthur Foundation, The Andrew W. Mellon Foundation, The Joyce Mertz-Gilmore Foundation, The National Fish and Wildlife Foundation, The Pew Charitable Trusts, The Pew Global Stewardship Initiative, The Rockefeller Philanthropic Collaborative, Inc., and individual donors.

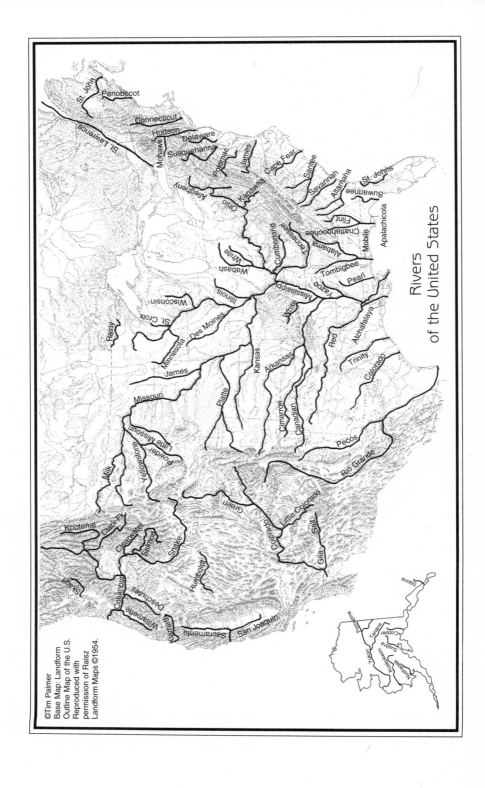

Rivers
of the United States

©Tim Palmer
Base Map: Landform
Outline Map of the U.S.
Reproduced with
permission of Raisz
Landform Maps ©1954.

America
by
Rivers

Also by Tim Palmer

Lifelines: The Case for River Conservation

Yosemite: The Promise of Wildness

The Wild and Scenic Rivers of America

California's Threatened Environment: Restoring the Dream

The Snake River: Window to the West

The Sierra Nevada: A Mountain Journey

Endangered Rivers and the Conservation Movement

Youghiogheny: Appalachian River

Stanislaus: The Struggle for a River

Rivers of Pennsylvania

America
by
Rivers

T i m   P a l m e r

ISLAND PRESS

Washington, D.C. ● Covelo, California

Photographs are by Tim Palmer
Photographs copyright © 1996 by Tim Palmer

Front cover photograph: Middle Fork of the Salmon River

Library of Congress Cataloging-in-Publication Data
Palmer, Tim
    America by rivers/Tim Palmer
        p.   cm.
    Includes bibliographical references and index.
    ISBN 1-55963-263-1 (cloth).
    1. Rivers—United States. I. Title.
    GB1215.P285   1996
    551.48'3'0973—dc20   96-14421
                                                           CIP

Printed on recycled, acid-free paper ✪

Manufactured in the United States of America

10 9 8 7 6 5 4 3 2

*to Ann, my companion
on all the rivers of life*

Contents

Acknowledgments

America by Rivers benefited from the help of many people. My wife, Ann Vileisis, has been a constant companion since 1992, providing not only wonderful company throughout the journeys on water but also a storehouse of bright ideas, a passion for rivers, and helpful critiques stemming from her background studying environmental history and leading educational river trips. My fieldwork in the East dovetailed well with Ann's as she researched *From Wastelands to Wetlands,* a history of wetlands in America, to be published in 1997.

I'm a fortunate writer in having not only a supportive wife but also a supportive publisher. Editor Barbara Dean and the entire staff of Island Press have been excellent working partners in the development of *America by Rivers.* Bill LaDue and Christine McGowan led the book through production, and Pat Harris copyedited the manuscript with great care and exceptionally fine judgment.

The Compton Foundation provided important financial assistance as I worked full-time on the book for two years. Backing important groups nationwide, Jim Compton stands as one of the great heroes of river protection today. American Rivers, the nation's principal river conservation group, helped through administration of the grant. In 1990,

Yvon Chouinard of Patagonia also contributed by paying for my new van, essential to my work and nomadic lifestyle.

Principal among my guides to the rivers of America have been the DeLorme atlases, available for twenty-five states at last count. Essential tools to my travel, these volumes are better than gold to anyone on the road, the river, or the trail. The DeLorme Mapping company of Freeport, Maine, graciously provided review copies of their atlases for my use. Payson Kennedy of the Nantahala Outdoor Center generously raided his bookstore to send me a box of guides to rivers of the Southeast.

My family helped with moral support and nuts-and-bolts assistance. My mother, Jane May, and her husband, Chuck, forwarded mail, messages, and confidence. My sisters, Becky Schmitz and Brenda Murray, provided space for storage of my books, files, photographs, and tools while I remained in the field. My brother, Jim Palmer—as fine a river companion as I can imagine—has joined me on rivers for years. Continuing a pattern of comforting security that goes back a long time, Jim has towed me ashore more than once and, I'm sure, will continue to do so.

I have not desired much in terms of living space, but for winter shelter in a place conducive to writing, I can think of no better base than the Teton Science School in Grand Teton National Park, Wyoming. As in my other recent books, I again thank Jack Shea and the staff of that excellent school for providing a cabin for Ann and me in the snowy months. It was a pleasure for us to offer a writing seminar to the graduate students at the school in the winter of 1994–1995 while we crafted our books. The Colorado Outward Bound School in Jensen, Utah, where Ann leads whitewater courses in the summer, also provided room and support. Julie Holding of Jackson, Wyoming, showed great generosity in sharing her home with Ann and me, and Beth Jacobi offered similar hospitality at her home in Portland, Oregon. Jamie and Florence Williams in Steamboat Springs, Colorado, provided a parking spot for our van, and we offer special thanks to Margo and Alan Hunt. More important, these people all provided close friendship.

For reading the full manuscript and suggesting improvements—a substantial gift of time—I thank Ann Vileisis; geography professors John Harper and Ben Bennion of Humboldt State University, who offered their professional expertise; Kevin Coyle and Peter Lavigne of River Network; and Mike Fremont of Rivers Unlimited. For their reading of individual chapters I appreciate the time and insight of Ken Cline, Tammis Coffin, John Kauffmann, Drew Parkin, Don Shields, Jim

Cummins, Lloyd Baldwin, Barry Beasley, Arthur Benke, Suzi Wilkins, Jack Griffith, Jamie Williams, Steve Harris, Mark DuBois, David Bolling, Doug Finlayson, Doug North, and Jack Hession. Bruce Thompson took my map drawings and applied skill and care on his computer to make them camera-ready. Mark Anderman and the staff of Terry Wild Studios printed the photos. The base map for Rivers of the United States and for the ten regional maps is the Landform Outline Map of the United States by Erwin Raisz—a classic in American cartography.

Scores of people granted interviews for this book and shared information, perspectives, and stories; some of them appear on the pages that follow. My thanks go to all for their time and their commitment to homelands along rivers, with special thanks to Rebecca Wodder of American Rivers. Geographer Peirce Lewis of The Pennsylvania State University extended help with his knowledge of sources regarding his science. Jim McClure provided good suggestions for the maps and, years ago, inspired me to travel on rivers with observant eyes and an open mind.

Introduction

The Way to the Water

This book began with an obsession for escape. Not that I really ran from anything. It's just that—who doesn't need to get away now and then? Like most people, I lived in a house and drove to work. It was time to see, to learn, to do something else.

With the seed of restlessness and yearning ready to germinate, I drove one day across the bridge spanning the broad West Branch of the Susquehanna River in Pennsylvania. As my car's wheels sang on the steel grate, I gazed a long way down from that airy space above the riffling water and wondered: Where does it come from? Where does it go? Why am I stuck here on this highway through Commercial Strip, U.S.A., when I could be down there seeing the *real* America? Of course, it's all real, but down *there* lay the world of bullrushes and beavers, whitewater and glassy calms, sleek canoes and rattletrap houseboats. Down there were Huck Finn and John Coulter, along with footpaths, water trails, greenways, floodplains, and lifelines through nearly every ecosystem and peopled community, coast to coast. That was where I wanted to be. I felt it so strongly I could almost have gone down and jumped in.

Beyond the Susquehanna—a big river whose acquaintance posed no small challenge—I wondered even more about the continent's *network* of rivers. I had established a certain intimacy with streams by way of short trips in my canoe, but now I longed to grasp a vision of the whole. My home river, after all, appeared as one of thousands, and life is so short. Why know only one river? I wanted to know them all, in every mood and season. Mindful of the human equation in the system, I desired to learn of the rivers' influence on people and of people's influence on the rivers. Not fitting into any one category, streams resemble, rather, a box of jewels, each of different color, size, shape, and origin. And each region of rivers possesses its own character, as variable as the entire greenhouse of life, as diverse as all that creeps underfoot or soars overhead. Rivers, indeed, constitute corridors of life, their differences defining what grows there, what swims out of sight, what browses and dabbles along the shore. Rivers have done more than any other agent of change to chisel North America from raw rock into the face we know and love today. They carve the country into canyons and lowlands. They are central to our history, to our way of living, to life on earth.

Yet rivers have been orphaned and lost from the day-to-day thoughts of many, the operative phrase being "Out of sight, out of mind." Some people don't know the name of their closest river. If they dump a bucket of water on their lawn or driveway, they don't know what river it will end up in. They don't know where the water in the tap comes from or where the water in the toilet goes. They don't think of traveling in anything but a car, even when a full-bodied river flows right by.

Learning that such a major feature of the American landscape lacked even a basic primer describing what exists, I saw justification for my odysseys on rivers, and my passion for exploring and traveling grew into a habit of disciplined curiosity, aggressive investigation, and conscientious reporting based on experience and on other knowledge from thousands of sources. This book is the result. While my living and researching along rivers spans, so far, a twenty-five-year window of my life, much of the work for *America by Rivers* was done during continuous travels from 1992 to 1995. The chapters present the rivers as if I visited them in succession from east to west, though some of the river trips occurred earlier and were updated where necessary. I undertook much of the exploration with my wife, Ann Vileisis, in our Ford van, equipped for comfortable living. The van has enabled us to tour all the roaded regions of the country over a period of years. Ann and I carried two canoes, a kayak, and a raft with a rowing frame—equipment enabling us to run rivers of all sorts. We carried skis for winter travel on the ice and bicycles for exploration on riverbank roads in the summer.

Each chapter of *America by Rivers* addresses the spectrum of rivers in one particular region. In the first part of every chapter I discuss the character of that region's rivers, its system of streams and how they fit together, the roster of major rivers in the area, the biology of the waters, and the cultures that surround and affect them. An overview of environmental problems and conservation efforts is followed by quick sketches of the principal streams. The second part of each chapter explores one of the region's rivers in more detail by describing a voyage on the water and through the river's basin. For these highlighted rivers, I avoid both the most-developed waterways and the best-preserved rivers, seeking instead streams distinguished in quality but typical of their regions. Though it is important to a full understanding, the history of the rivers discussed in these chapters is not included. Much has been written elsewhere, and with a shortage of space and an abundance of information, I focus on the rivers as they exist.

America by Rivers provides the geographic underpinning for a number of my other books, which address various interests people might have in rivers. More information on the environmental history of rivers can be found in *Endangered Rivers and the Conservation Movement*. The conservation issues of modern times are more fully discussed in *Lifelines: The Case for River Conservation*. Detailed coverage of the National Wild and Scenic Rivers System and sketches of each of 223 rivers and major tributaries so designated as of 1992 are contained in *The Wild and Scenic Rivers of America*. In *America by Rivers,* I repeat little of the information found in these earlier books. Further, this book offers information regarding boating but is not a guide; those planning float trips should consult good guidebooks.

A few additional details: I use the term "cubic feet per second" (cfs) to describe the volume of flow. My intent is not to overload the book with technical information but rather to describe the volume of flow so that the reader can understand the size of one river compared with another. Flows of up to 300 cfs make streams or creeks, flows of up to 5,000 cfs make small or medium-sized rivers, and anything more than that defines a large waterway. *The Water Encyclopedia* was my main source for flow data. My figures for lengths of rivers came from a variety of sources but most often from my own scaling of miles in the DeLorme atlases or on U.S. Geological Survey maps. For both cfs and mileage figures, various sources differ slightly because of ambiguity regarding diversions from the rivers and locations of headwater sources as well as other complications. I often found that other published mileage figures fail to adequately reflect meanders of rivers, especially in headwater areas. I look forward to the day when the Geological Survey publishes a gazetteer of American rivers, standardizing the flow and length figures.

The underlying theme of this book is that rivers are important, essential, vital to America as we know it and to life on earth. Obviously, we need water to live. Less obvious but just as important, a vast biological community requires healthy rivers. And beyond all that, who we *are* relates to *where* we are and to what we *see*. What our communities and landscapes become relates to our vision of them, and the enspiriting view from the water frames the portrait of civilization in a way that puts the life of the earth first.

While seeing America by rivers, perhaps we will find a new view that embraces the entire landscape, one in which we recognize that the health of our streams and land reflects the health of our society. To care for one, we must care for the other.

Finally and irresistibly, seeing America from the rivers offers a new avenue to adventure, a way to enjoy a new and healthy experience without even going far from home. At the water's edge—even the waterfront out the back door—a whole new world awaits!

Many Americas

Imagine America. Not some abstraction involving the flag or the Statue of Liberty, but the real thing—the land and water that make up this country. When we say "New England," "the South," or "the Northwest," the names carry the images of landforms and cities, but they also carry the twisting shine of rivers, which lie at the heart of the regional differences. Though wide bridges with guardrails block the view, who cannot be impressed when crossing the Mississippi as it bisects the Midwest? Here, one river and its lore define the whole heartland of the country. Other streams likewise say volumes about their regions: the legendary Rio Grande at the Mexican border, the Greenbrier as an idyll of the Appalachians, the Yukon across the tundra of the north, and on and on.

The rivers offer an avenue to America, each region with its own repertoire of streams, its own character of waterfront, its own attitudes that adhere to the waterways. With a goal of knowing the country better, of understanding it by understanding its river systems, where would one begin among the nation's 3.8 million square miles of land?

The country is divided into states—useful boundaries because people know them well—but these political lines fail to reflect important differences. The truer nature of the landscape that molds the rivers estate of America can be seen in another short series of maps. The most fundamental of these shows precipitation, including rain and snow, which determines the nature of rivers and more (see Average Annual Precipitation Map). From roughly the 100th longitudinal meridian, running from North Dakota through Texas, precipitation falls plentifully to the east but sparsely to the west, where twenty inches or less per year results in a semiarid climate and where less than ten inches produces a true desert. Notable exceptions are the Pacific coast and high mountains of the West with their plentiful moisture which delivers water to rivers and thus makes the West inhabitable. Southern and central California enjoy a Mediterranean climate—searing, dry summers contrasted with wet winters. The Pacific frontage of northern California through Washington has a marine West Coast climate, soggy with rain in winter. Alaska's wet south gives way to a dry interior. While precipitation in America varies from east to west, temperature gradients slice the land into northern and southern tiers of cool and warm weather, and the streams reflect the climate around them. In the wet Cascades of the Northwest, green, bubbly rapids burst from well-watered mountains. In the deserts, brown flows carry little local runoff because little rainfall occurs; rather, these rivers carry snowmelt from the faraway Rocky Mountains. Rivers of the South teem with life, breaking all records for biological diversity, in part owing to their ice-free winters, which encourage many families of species to breed, multiply, adapt, and diversify.

A portrait of America thus begins to jell: rainy in the East, dry in much of the West, cool in the North, hot in the South, with rivers responding to all this in their flow, in their runoff patterns, and in the life they support. Yet climate paints only part of the picture. The other part, separating one region of rivers from another, involves the lay of the land.

If you live in the Appalachians you may not be a hillbilly, but you are certainly a mountain person, Maine to Alabama. The Appalachians cross state and climatic lines. Similarly, the other great mountain chains link their landscapes together: the Rockies through the heart of the West; the Cascades, crowning the Northwest in snow; the Sierra Nevada

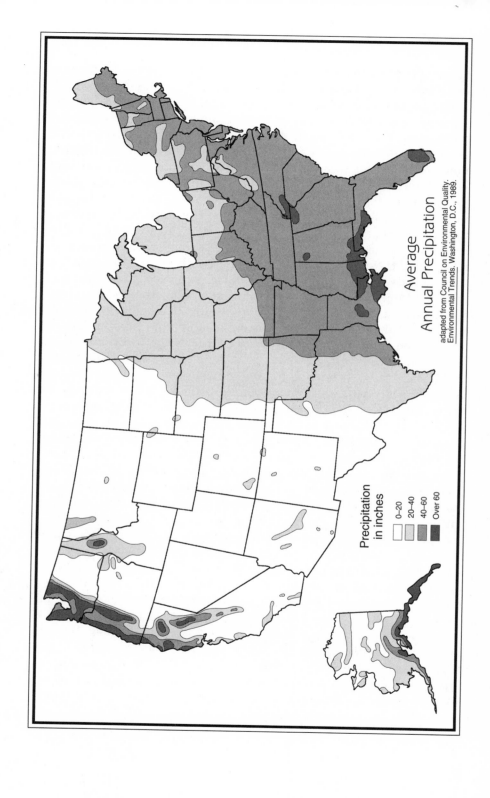

Average
Annual Precipitation

adapted from Council on Environmental Quality.
Environmental Trends. Washington, D.C., 1989.

Precipitation
in inches

0–20
20–40
40–60
Over 60

in California; and the Coast Range, which plummets to the Pacific with its fault-block shoreline stretching from the Santa Monica Mountains to Kodiak Island. Other landforms likewise cross state and climatic lines, for example, the Coastal Plain of the East and the Great Plains of the interior.

Using landforms as a guide, geographer N. M. Fenneman mapped the regions of the United States in 1928. His boundaries remain the standard. Not including Alaska, he named eight physiographic divisions and subdivided them into provinces—families of landforms that serve as an important basis for the regions of rivers delineated in this book (see Landform Regions of the United States).

Climate and landforms together determine what is most important on earth: what will grow in a given place. All organisms need a habitat—a place suitable for their survival. On the definitive map of ecological zones, Robert G. Bailey of the U.S.D.A. Forest Service identified fifty-six provinces. These can be simplified (see Vegetation of the United States), and the different ecosystems are delightfully evident from the rivers. Spruces and birches of the northern forest frame the Allagash River in Maine. In the central hardwoods region, silver maples crowd the Susquehanna, and sycamores lean out over the Gasconade in Missouri. Baldcypresses and tupelos tightly overhang the St. Johns River in the southeastern forest of Florida. Cottonwoods shade the grassland rivers of the Great Plains. Immense firs signify the Pacific Coast forest along the Hoh River on the Olympic Peninsula. Open tundra surrounds the Noatak in Alaska.

Some rivers, including most of the smaller ones, flow entirely within single regions, but large rivers cut across the boundaries. The Colorado, for example, begins in the peaks of the Rockies, carves its fabulous canyons into the Colorado Plateau, then discharges through the desert into Mexico. The James materializes high in the Appalachians, transects the rolling hills of the Piedmont, and winds past the tidal swamps of the Coastal Plain. The many Americas of varied climate, landform, and ecoregion are laced, crossed, and interconnected by a network of rivers.

The Rivers Estate of America

The estate of American waterways ranks as one of enormous size, intricate biology, stunning beauty, and fascinating variety. Fifteen enormous rivers flow with a volume of more than 50,000 cubic feet per sec-

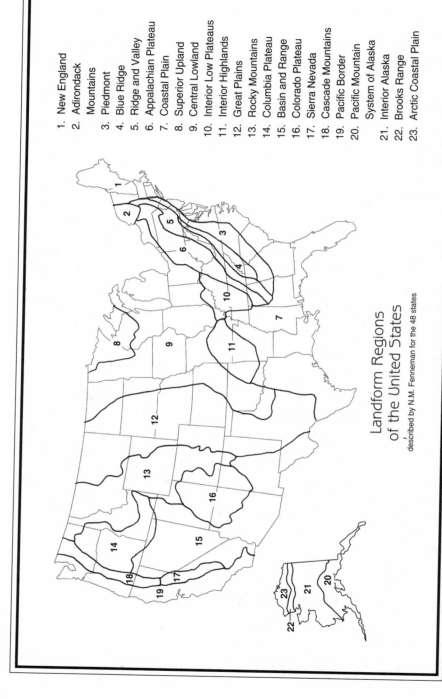

Landform Regions
of the United States

described by N.M. Fenneman for the 48 states

1. New England
2. Adirondack
   Mountains
3. Piedmont
4. Blue Ridge
5. Ridge and Valley
6. Appalachian Plateau
7. Coastal Plain
8. Superior Upland
9. Central Lowland
10. Interior Low Plateaus
11. Interior Highlands
12. Great Plains
13. Rocky Mountains
14. Columbia Plateau
15. Basin and Range
16. Colorado Plateau
17. Sierra Nevada
18. Cascade Mountains
19. Pacific Border
20. Pacific Mountain
    System of Alaska
21. Interior Alaska
22. Brooks Range
23. Arctic Coastal Plain

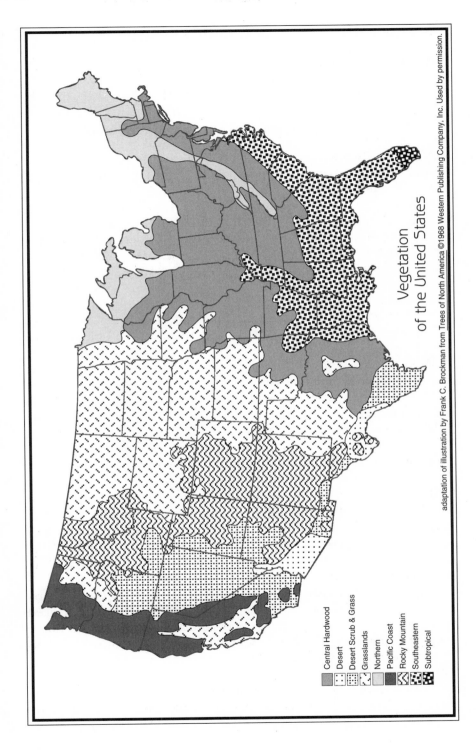

Vegetation
of the United States

Central Hardwood
Desert
Desert Scrub & Grass
Grasslands
Northern
Pacific Coast
Rocky Mountain
Southeastern
Subtropical

adaptation of illustration by Frank C. Brockman from Trees of North America ©1968 Western Publishing Company, Inc. Used by permission.

ond (cfs) on average at their mouths and account for most of the country's runoff (see Large Rivers of the United States). The Mississippi, far and away the nation's largest river, carries 593,000 cfs. Others, in descending order by volume, are the St. Lawrence, shared with Canada; the Ohio, larger than the Mississippi where the two join; the Columbia, largest river of the West Coast; the Yukon of Alaska and Canada; the Missouri; the Tennessee; and the Mobile (see appendix 1). Next to the St. Lawrence, the giant river of Canada is the Mackenzie, carrying 280,000 cfs and draining one-fifth of the country.

The ranking in length and watershed area is quite different from the ranking by volume, owing to climatic variations. The Missouri, including its upper tributaries, runs longer than any other river—2,540 miles—yet it ranks sixth in volume because less rain falls in the Missouri basin than in other large watersheds. The Mississippi is the second-longest river. The Yukon, third-longest, begins in Canada and flows all the way across Alaska. Next, in descending order by length, are the St. Lawrence, if its headwaters and the Great Lakes are counted as a unified system, the Rio Grande, the Arkansas, the Colorado, and the Ohio (see appendix 1).

Based on data obtained from the U.S. Geological Survey, the Water Resources Council, and the National Park Service, it appears that about 10,000 rivers are greater than 25 miles in length, totaling perhaps 320,000 miles. All rivers greater than 5 miles in length amount to about 1,100,000 miles. The bulk of total river mileage lies in small streams. Rivers and streams of all sizes total about 3.6 million miles.

To organize these thousands of streams that seem to flow in every direction, I looked at the boundaries of watersheds or basins. These land masses are defined by all the acreage that drains into a particular river or ocean. In the broadest sense, three divisions exist: rivers that flow into the Atlantic, the Pacific, and the Arctic Ocean. Within these divisions twelve major basins are found (see Drainage Basins of the United States). Most of the large basins drain portions of several climatic zones, landform divisions, ecosystems, and cultural regions.

In this book, each region of rivers is defined as a group of rivers having similar features and character (see River Regions of the United States). All six of the previously mentioned maps help determine where the river regions begin and end, but the regions adhere most closely to Fenneman's landform divisions, as those are the most important in determining the character of the river.

The waters, of course, don't exist in a vacuum; they reflect everything we do to the land. With tens of thousands of dams blocking nearly

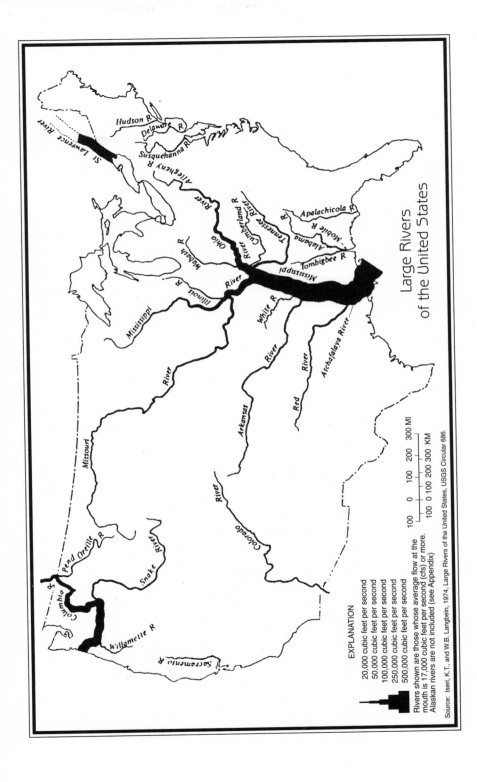

Large Rivers
of the United States

EXPLANATION

20,000 cubic feet per second
50,000 cubic feet per second
100,000 cubic feet per second
250,000 cubic feet per second
500,000 cubic feet per second

Rivers shown are those whose average flow at the
mouth is 17,000 cubic feet per second (cfs) or more.
Alaskan rivers are not included (see Appendix)

Source: Iseri, K.T., and W.B. Langbein, 1974, Large Rivers of the United States, USGS Circular 686.

100   0   100   200   300 MI

100 0 100 200 300 KM

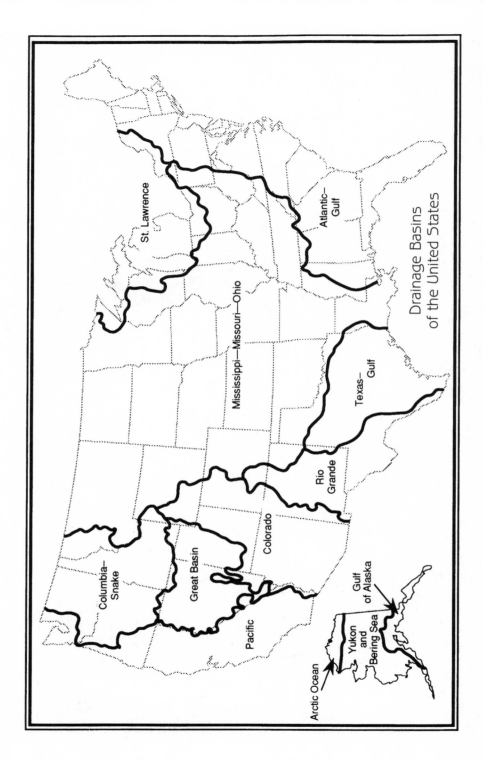

Drainage Basins
of the United States

St. Lawrence

Atlantic—
Gulf

Mississippi—Missouri—Ohio

Texas—
Gulf

Rio
Grande

Colorado

Columbia—
Snake

Great Basin

Pacific

Arctic Ocean

Yukon
and
Bering Sea

Gulf
of Alaska

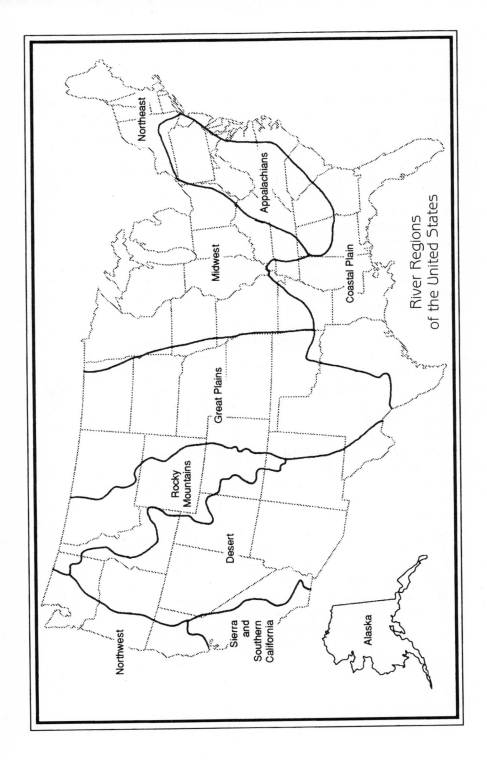

River Regions of the United States

Northeast

Appalachians

Midwest

Coastal Plain

Great Plains

Rocky Mountains

Desert

Northwest

Sierra and Southern California

Alaska

every major river in America outside Alaska, the rivers are not what they used to be. Well over 200,000 miles have been channelized; 25,000 miles are dredged for navigation. One-third of our surveyed stream mileage suffers acute pollution, and half fails to support the full range of native plants and wildlife. Most remaining miles are affected by lesser water quality problems; by diversions that leave rivers depleted, if not bone dry; by waterfront development; by overgrazing of cows; and by manipulated flows that result in damaged streambeds and allow invasion of alien species that crowd the native plants out. Because rivers represent an accumulation of all we do to the land, they provide a warning. They are the canary in the coal mine; dead fish indicate that trouble for people is not far behind.

By describing each region as a system of rivers, I hope to convey a greater awareness of this important part of America. Much of the damage done to rivers has occurred because people have regarded rivers and pieces of them as isolated parts, making their demise more palatable. It's easier to ruin something if it appears to be alone and isolated from everything else of importance. Even conservation efforts have been directed at segments of rivers—often tiny segments. This is understandable given the political difficulties of protecting even a small fragment of anything, yet knowledge of whole river systems is important if we are to make wise decisions about the future of these places.

As I crossed the country in the chapters that follow, the flow of water was the main force for me, much as it was for the Indians along the magnificent rivers of California's northern coast; the Yurok tribe had no names for the cardinal directions of north, south, east, and west and instead used "upstream" and "downstream." Going upstream and down, I experienced America's geography of water. I tried to stop the chatter that normally goes on in my mind and learn something new, see something new, feel something new without the day-to-day expectations that so often color our view of the world. Looking out to the rivers of the continent and to the travels ahead of me, I was reminded of John Wesley Powell when he explored the unknown wonders of the Colorado River and the mysterious depths of its canyons. He wrote, "We have an unknown distance yet to run, an unknown river to explore."

Chapter 1

—◆—

Rivers of the Glaciated Northeast

O n a striking palette of topography, the rivers run out from moun- tains to ocean in a remarkably short space. Exceptional variety and scenery result, most of it easily accessible, making the Northeast a fine place to begin a tour of American rivers.

New England is a northern extension of the Appalachian Mountains, but glaciers thoroughly groomed this area as they crept down from the north to cover the land. They churned up the surface, rounded off the peaks, and left a sculptured earth, as though a busload of artists had come to work after the first shift of mountain builders went home. Glaciers likewise swept across New York, and while people consider that state culturally separate from New England, its rivers possess ample similarities owing to the effects of ice.

Though the glaciers of the ice ages buried more than half the conti- nent, most of that expanse lies in Canada. Among the regions of the United States, ice completely covered only the Northeast and the Su- perior Uplands of the Midwest (even Alaska and the Rockies were glaciated only in certain places). The ice left its signature all over the northeastern riverbeds, which in higher country are paved with

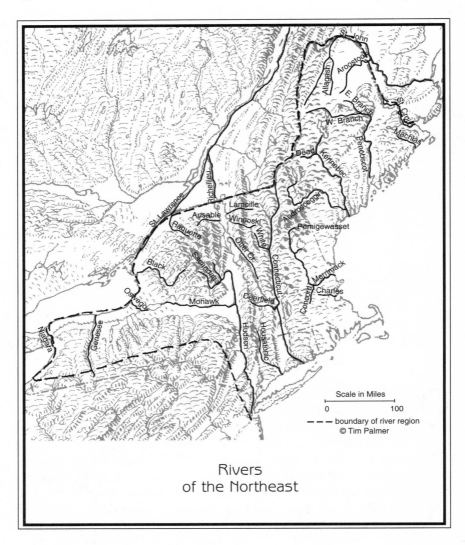

Rivers
of the Northeast

rounded, gray cobbles and boulders pushed south. Because of the glaciers' effectiveness in bulldozing soil, bedrock in New England rarely lies more than twenty feet underground and often juts up to the surface. Where rivers intersect these ledges and veins of resistant rock, sharp rapids occur. The ice also blocked entire passages of rivers and forced them into new routes—circuitous paths avoiding the advance of the glaciers. After the ice receded, many rivers remained in their new paths, which haven't been worn down to a uniform gradient. Instead the rivers drop over waterfalls of bedrock, force themselves through unexpected constrictions, and sometimes lack the usual orderly progression from narrow to wide valleys as the water moves downhill. This interesting legacy of the ice ages lends a special beauty from the Canadian border to the Appalachians of Pennsylvania.

In longitude, the region extends farther east than any other in the country, while the latitude corresponds to that of central Minnesota and extends south to that of southern Iowa. Though this region, consisting of the New England states plus New York, is small compared with other regions of rivers, it holds importance beyond its acreage. As regional journalist Neal Peirce wrote about the area, "The visitor feels transported back over time, into the milieu that makes New England such a precious part of America."

Rivers here flow out from six mountain ranges and a clutch of other intriguing natural features. At the far west, the glaciated land of New York eases down to the plain of Lake Ontario and the St. Lawrence Valley. Ice-sculpted hills ascend to the Adirondack Mountains in the northeastern part of the state. Although separate from the Appalachians in geologic origin, the Adirondacks share the common feature of glaciation. To the east, the Taconic Mountains rise from the Hudson River along the boundary of New York and Connecticut. Farther north, Lake Champlain lies in a north-south trough at the New York–Vermont border. Farther east, the Green Mountains run north to south—Vermont's backbone stepping down to become the Berkshires of western Massachusetts and the rolling Litchfield Hills of Connecticut. East of the Green Mountains, the White Mountains puncture the clouds of northern New Hampshire, and the arching jumble of the Longfellow Mountains angles northeastward into Maine. At its southern and far eastern edges, New England unambiguously ends at the Atlantic Ocean.

While all the Northeast eventually drains into the Atlantic, the river routes starting from central high points drop off to the full sweep of the compass. In northern New York, streams flow northward to Lake Ontario and the St. Lawrence River; streams of western Vermont likewise flow to the St. Lawrence via Lake Champlain and Québec's Rivière Richelieu. Part of the Adirondack Mountains and central New York drains westward and then northward to the St. Lawrence, but part drains oppositely, to the Hudson River and New York Bay. In the New England states, one set of streams, with the Connecticut River as midrib, flows southward from the mountains and empties into Long Island Sound. A second set filters in circuitous routes to the north and northeast and flows to the coasts of Massachusetts and Maine. Thanks to deeply incised embayments carved by glaciers and rivers, the coastline of Maine alone measures 3,500 miles—a greater distance than from New York to San Francisco. Only one river system in the entire East transects the Appalachians: the Hudson's palisaded valley slices the great range in two. The Mohawk River, a tributary, reaches across central New York lowlands almost to the Great Lakes.

Creating the regionwide character of rivers, a lot of rain and snow falls on rugged topography and produces many streams. Much of the river mileage lies in mountainous or rolling terrain, and an archetypal view shows rapid waters with the startlingly white trunks of paper birch in front of somber green hemlock or spruce. Streams here generally run clear rather than silty. Villages, towns, roads, and industries crowd waterfronts in an old, eastern style, yet many short reaches and a few long ones remain wild. These are the hallmarks of northeastern rivers, yet diversity abounds.

Seven distinct types of river or river reach exist in the Northeast. Moving from west to east, I see that the Lake Ontario streams wind northward through rolling farmland, but in their upper reaches many cut deep, fern-clad gorges. Quite different from the Great Lake tributaries, the Adirondack rivers run clear or amber and flow over steep rapids between plentiful lakes in a region densely wooded by conifers and hardwoods. The St. Lawrence is a waterway behemoth, tidal for hundreds of miles in its lower reaches, and to the south the lower Hudson shares characteristics of a big sea-level river, with steep mountains flanking its sides (the Hudson, in fact, once carried the heavy volume of Great Lakes runoff to sea, as the St. Lawrence does today). As a fourth type of river, the mountain streams of New England tumble over ice-carved landscapes and create the most photogenic mountain-and-river scenes in the East. Farther downstream, valley rivers turn in graceful bends through forests and farms and pass more waterfront villages than do the rivers of any other region. Lower yet, coastal streams meander out through marshes to embayments at Long Island Sound or the ocean; many of these streams cross the sandy and rocky expanses of moraines that mark the southern advance of the continental ice. Finally, the rivers of Maine begin in a system of interconnected lakes with low divides where only a few feet separate headwater sources. They flow as dark waters across ancient granite, similar to Adirondack rivers. The black or copper-colored water results from plentiful dissolved organic matter flowing into the river from wetlands, including those created by beavers. Waterfalls or rapids separate placid reaches, and farther down the Maine rivers traverse hilly country and enter deep inlets of the sea.

Flowing quickly into saltwater, most of the rivers of the Northeast are small or medium in size. But reaching west with headwaters in the heartland of the United States and Canada, the St. Lawrence is the great exception—the only northeastern river drawing water from another region. As the second-largest river on the continent, it averages 243,000 cubic feet per second where it leaves the New York boundary and 348,000 cfs at its mouth at Canada's Gaspé Peninsula on the Atlantic. Second-largest in the region, the St. John of Maine and Canada carries 9,730 cfs where it leaves the border of Maine and 17,945 at its mouth in New Brunswick. As the largest northeastern river entirely in the United States, the Connecticut runs with 16,400 cfs. The Penobscot in Maine empties with 14,210 cfs at tidewater, and the Hudson carries 13,700 but seems larger because it flows through a massively deep and wide trench subject to tidal flows from New York City to Albany. The sixth-largest river in the region, the Merrimack in Massachusetts delivers 7,530 cfs to the Atlantic. The Oswego runs to Lake Ontario with 6,690 cfs, and the Androscoggin runs to the coast of Maine with 6,140. The Mohawk contributes 5,750 cfs to the Hudson, and the Kennebec of Maine averages 4,450. High flows in the Northeast typically come in early spring, with a flood season that combines rain and the chill snowmelt of the mountains. As in most of the United States, low flows come in late summer and early fall.

The northeastern rivers were among the first in America to be explored by Europeans. Jacques Cartier sailed up the St. Lawrence in 1534—only forty-two years after Columbus's landing in the Caribbean. Though the first white settlements lay elsewhere, New England is often regarded as the birthplace of European civilization in America—the place where the white culture fully launched its eastern invasion, expelled or killed the Indians, and got its grip on the continent. Early immigrants flocked to the coast and the Connecticut River valley and, later, to the Hudson-Mohawk corridor of the Erie Canal. All these areas now show intense development as the rivers of this region meet the needs of 60 million people. The Northeast capitalized so heavily on waterpower that mills everywhere determined where the towns sprang up—almost always along a stream, where a rapid or waterfall provided a good head for mechanical and, later, hydroelectric power. Though storms have washed out decrepit old dams, 10,000 impoundments remain—certainly more per river mile and square mile than in any other region. Dams block single streams again and again. The Kennebec alone has thirteen dams on its main stem. The original Glens Falls of the Hudson, renowned in *The Last of the Mohicans,* is now unimaginable amid industrial development. Most of the dams, however, are small, owing to their early origins. The immense water projects of the West, Midwest, and South are unknown here, partly because they would have required elimination of many already settled communities—anathema to the New England political tradition.

The Mayflower landed here, and New England boasts the birthplace of Anglo influence in America, but the cultural mainstream bypassed the far Northeast as soon as other routes to the interior opened, beginning with the Erie Canal, made possible by the Hudson and Mohawk Rivers in 1825. Railroads later moved migration routes farther south, and trends conspired to move settlers out. While 60 percent of New England had been cleared for agriculture by 1830, the average farmer took his first opportunity to abandon the rocky, glacier-scarred ground and emigrate west. Woodlands now cover 83 percent of New England.

While the land has partly reclaimed itself as a result of simple neglect, rivers have enjoyed active restoration efforts that transformed industrial sewers to clear waters again (though they lack the biological health they once had). Efficient development of rivers once symbolized Yankee ingenuity and ambition, but now protection and restoration of streams exemplifies a new northeastern persona. Here, perhaps more than anywhere else in the country, local groups work to protect the natural pieces that remain and to reclaim some of what was lost. Chiefly used to transport logs and pollution only twenty years ago, the rivers now transport canoes, and the culture of this craft is nowhere else so evident. One might occasionally see canoes on cartops in other regions, but Maine is full of them.

As one might expect of a region where extraction of resources began with the Pilgrims, all the northeastern states show a "mature" economy; commodity goods available for the picking were long ago exhausted, except for timber in Maine, which continues to be recut and recut. Reflecting the Northeast's 300-year history of settlement, development straddles the rivers in town centers, but the streams remain pastoral or wooded idylls across much of the countryside, especially to the north. In much of the region, however, the quality of life now attracts large influxes from the nearby megalopolis, which threaten to destroy the same qualities that attract people. In all these respects, the Northeast may offer a window to the future of other regions in America. Ultimately, the Northeast may be more of a pacesetter than the much-touted California, whose endless boom and hype have turned into a sourness that few regions seek to emulate.

In this bastion of conservatism, as traditional as a field of Vermont Holsteins, some northeastern states have pioneered steps to manage their water and land progressively. The Maine legislature in 1971 required that municipalities zone property within 250 feet of rivers and other water bodies and created a commission to review large developments in unincorporated areas. The governor and legislature adopted a list of sixteen streams for protection in 1983. Vermont—a national leader in environmental legislation—enacted a state land-use planning law in 1970. The *Green Index* rated Vermont and Hawaii as having the finest environmental conditions in America; New York, Connecticut, Massachusetts, Rhode Island, and Maine all ranked among the top twelve states.

Though much of the Northeast's original river life has been overrun, the current rate of loss is probably less than in any other region but Alaska, and the restoration rate is probably the highest in America. Yet substantial threats and degradation continue from new development on floodplains, water pollution, dams, and introduced species that decimate native life.

For an overview of some of the Northeast's most interesting rivers, I begin in the southwestern corner of the region. A large set of New York rivers drains north to Lake Ontario and the St. Lawrence basin, some of them flowing from surprising gorges and lakes. The Genesee River, for example, cuts a deep trench in Letchworth State Park and eventually flows into Lake Ontario with 2,780 cfs. Just to its east, waters that once flowed south to the Susquehanna during the ice ages now flow north. Eleven of these streams drain the glacial Finger Lakes into the flat shore of Ontario. The Seneca River is the largest and flows into the sizeable Oswego River. Northward, the Black River drops from whitewater in the western Adirondacks and carries 4,020 cfs to Lake Ontario. Nearing the St. Lawrence, the Grass, Raquette, and St. Regis Rivers, all with sizeable flows, run in unusual parallel routes within one 7-mile-wide corridor—in effect, a single valley with four rivers in it.

The St. Lawrence system infiltrates deep into the northern Midwest and includes all the Great Lakes and the extraordinary short interconnecting rivers between them. The Niagara is the best known of these, linking Lake Erie and Lake Ontario. This river is unique not only as a honeymooners' hot spot but also for its shortness and volume; its 33 miles flow with an average of 200,000 cfs. Carrying far more volume than any other waterfall in America, Niagara is about 160 feet high, 1,060 feet across one portion on the American side, and 2,200 feet across another section in Canada, the two pitches separated by Goat Island. The Falls draws 10 million tourists per year, more than any other natural attraction in America, but the cataract is not the spectacle it once was. Utility companies divert half its volume of water in summertime daylight hours and three-quarters at night and in winter. Through erosion of its bedrock, the Falls has migrated 7 miles upriver in a process that will in geologic time drain Lake Erie—quite an event for the imagination to grapple with. Below the Falls, thunderous flows persist through the 200-foot-deep, 7-mile-long Niagara Gorge, one of the most awesome pieces of turbulent water on the continent.

When the water of the Great Lakes leaves Lake Ontario, it is called the St. Lawrence River, which for 112 of its 750-mile length defines the international border. It lumbers past the Thousand Islands, which total about 1,700, counting all the rocky outcrops. Dammed twice, the river enters the province of Québec where it is known as Fleuve St. Laurent. Farther down, wide tidal flows run more than 400 miles from below Montreal to the Atlantic—one of the first routes used by European explorers to reach the interior of America. Though it provides habitat for 120 species of fish, the St. Lawrence is heavily degraded by its role as a seaway, with all the dredging, pollution, and industrial development that function entails. Oceangoing ships are carriers for exotic species that menace native life, not just here but all over the East. The pestilent zebra mussel, for example, likely escaped from a freighter and made its way into the Erie Canal and hence into the Hudson and other eastern streams, where it may doom native species to extinction. At the end of the oceanic St. Lawrence, which is 90 miles wide, the northernmost of the Appalachian Mountains tower as the Gaspé Peninsula, 4,000 feet above the sea.

In northeastern New York, the Adirondack Mountains house one of the premier enclaves of natural rivers in the East. New York State has protected fifty-five of these—the largest number in any state scenic rivers system. The superb Black, Boreas, Moose, and Sacandaga flow with steep rapids; the excellent trout waters of the Ausable flow to Lake Champlain; the famously clear Opalescent joins the Hudson.

With its pristine source in the Adirondacks, the upper Hudson offers one of the classic whitewater rafting, canoeing, and kayaking trips of the East. This was one of the first rivers to be regularly paddled as whitewater travel caught on in the 1960s. The 315-mile artery picks up the Sacandaga (2,230 cfs), known for its mountain lakes. Though the Hudson is free-flowing for 108 miles, fifteen dams block its course down below, and just above Albany the historic, industrialized Mohawk River joins it from a route that once linked with today's Oswego River and served as a massive outlet for the Great Lakes during the ice ages—

an outlet that was blocked as the landmass rose or rebounded following the melting of the heavy ice cap. Below its confluence with the Mohawk, the Hudson is tidewater for about 150 miles. The Hudson here defined the route of the Erie Canal, the primary transportation artery to the West in the early 1800s. The lower river was immortalized in the mid-1800s by painters of the Hudson River school but in the 1960s became known as a sewer of PCBs and other toxins. Pollution here was one of the crises that caught people's attention and helped launch the environmental movement of the 1970s. Sustaining its scenic grandeur as it nears New York City, the Hudson includes the 40-mile-long Palisades, a stretch of rocky cliffs between Newburgh and Peekskill—the deepest cut through Appalachian slopes in the Northeast, making the Hudson one of few eastern rivers with mountains so close to its mouth.

The Hudson is exceptional, but to sample the flavor of a typical New England river, the 142-mile Housatonic is a good choice. Tightly hugged by the Berkshire Hills to the east and the Taconic Range to the west, the river flows southward from Massachusetts and through western Connecticut. Hydropower dams and diversions cut the river into pieces, but some whitewater and canoeing sections remain. The lower reach, flowing at 2,600 cfs, pools into three reservoirs and finally eases into Long Island Sound. The Shepaug—a choice tributary—endures as a stream of green, wooded shores and clear riffles, the finest natural river remaining in Connecticut.

Down through whitewater and woodlands, the Westfield and Deerfield flow through western Massachusetts, and the Farmington crosses forests, fields, bedrock rapids, and cobbled riffles as it nears the Connecticut River. These streams persist with much of nature intact, even amid a landscape inhabited for 250 years and at the doorstep of eastern cities.

Prominent in the geography and history of New England, the 410-mile Connecticut River rises at the international boundary in New Hampshire, separates that state from Vermont, and then runs down through Massachusetts and Connecticut to Long Island Sound. One can clearly see the river's route as seismic in origin—something rare in the East. The straight nature of the Connecticut's course is attributable to a fault on the eastern side of the valley. Ice-age lakes then flooded the Connecticut but eventually drained away, leaving silty plains that would become New England's best farming area, settled by large numbers as early as 1635.

Like most other major American waterways, the Connecticut long ago ceased to function as a natural river. Eighteen dams silence the water in a chain of bank-full reservoirs, leaving only short, isolated sections of current. By blocking migration paths, these waterpower dams of the 1800s eradicated teeming runs of Atlantic salmon, American shad, and other anadromous species, which spawn in the rivers after living at sea. Hydropower plants dewater sections where the river is sluiced through turbines. The nearly total damming of the Connecticut is one of the more significant river losses, not just for the Northeast but for America.

More than a hundred villages, towns, and cities nestle into the Connecticut's corridor, though much of the valley retains a pastoral charm and land-use regulations seek to limit new building on the floodplain. Now capitalizing on its riverfront as an urban amenity, the city of Hartford straddles the Connecticut at the head of tide, 50 miles above Long Island Sound. From his house near this central waterway of New England, Mark Twain wrote America's quintessential river novel, *Huckleberry Finn*. Unusual in the Northeast, the mouth of the Connecticut has no port and therefore escaped industrialization.

A unique experiment in protection, the Silvio Conte Fish and Wildlife Refuge was designated by Congress in 1991. Covering much of the Connecticut's length, the refuge highlights efforts to bring back the Atlantic salmon. A reintroduced population clings to life with the possibility of flourishing again if problems of passage around the dams can be solved. Most wildlife refuges are reserves of publicly owned land, but in this case the federal government owns almost no property. The Fish and Wildlife Service is seeking support from the 2 million people in the valley by drafting a plan that will emphasize not federal acquisition but local land-use regulation and private initiative for protection. The Nature Conservancy has privately acquired seventy sites to be preserved as open space, including one at the river's estuary—one of the most productive ecosystems in New England.

Eastward in Massachusetts the Charles River, which flows by Boston, was the subject of a pathbreaking case in wetlands protection. Though developers had drained and filled many of its tidal marshes, the Army Corps of Engineers agreed to save the upper basin's spongelike floodplains as natural reservoirs for high water instead of building dams.

The Merrimack draws water from the White Mountains to become the largest river of Massachusetts and one of the nation's outstanding examples of water quality improvement. The subject of Henry David Thoreau's *A Week on the Concord and Merrimac Rivers*, the Merrimack and its southern tributary, the Concord, were prominent in the American Revolution and later were the birthplace of the industrial revolution. Red brick factories still populate Lowell, Lawrence, and Manchester, where manufacturing began with the use of waterpower and proliferated with 900 mills and factories along the Merrimack. Rated one of America's ten most-polluted streams in the 1960s, the 116-mile river now runs clear, with 300,000 people tapping it for drinking supplies. Its tributary, the Nashua, has similarly been cleaned up.

The Merrimack's main source is the 70-mile Pemigewasset, crowded by roads and riprap down low but flowing from the scenic Franconia Notch. Before the 1970s its lower reaches stank with sulfite, acid, and toxins, but most of the river is now clean. The East Branch is New England's exemplar of a mountain river: crystal-clear water, boulder-cobbled bottom, and banks of birch, hemlock, and beech in the heart of the White Mountains.

Other than the Connecticut River at the state's eastern border, Vermont's largest river is the Winooski (1,706 cfs). It bisects not only the state capital of Montpelier but also the whole of the Green Mountains before emptying into Lake Champlain. Brook trout have returned following urban and industrial cleanups.

The only other river cutting all the way across the 170-mile-long Green Mountains is the Lamoille (1,239 cfs), which flows through a beautifully working landscape of farmland and villages. An early cartographer misspelled the name of this river, which had actually been designated La Mouette (The Sea Gull) by a Frenchman accompanying Champlain as he journeyed near the river's mouth. With views dominated by 4,393-foot-high Mount Mansfield, the river meanders with stretches of whitewater interrupted by eight dams in an 87-mile course. The Lamoille, Winooski, and upper Androscoggin in New Hampshire illustrate antecedent rivers established on a flat peneplain before today's mountains existed. Cutting away the resistant granite as it arose, these rivers hung on to their winding courses, resulting in scenic gorges and deep valleys.

The White River, flowing southeast off the Green Mountains to the Connecticut River, foams into some of New England's best whitewater. In an oddity of riverine linguistics, the White's tributaries are called First Branch, Second Branch, and Third Branch rather than being termed forks or north, south, and middle branches. Another quirk of Vermont's river résumé, Otter Creek winds for 100 miles and destroys the myth that rivers don't flow north—some do. Blocked by six small dams, the creek crosses a panorama of Holsteins in pasture. The Middlebury and four other rivers join as rare examples of "rivers" that flow into a "creek."

Maine can be praised as a land of northeastern rivers inscribed throughout by a dendritic pattern of many-branched streams that flow and curve in different directions. The Saco (2,710 cfs) spills in difficult whitewater from the White Mountains' Crawford Notch and then gently crosses the hills of southern Maine. During the 1970s, local governments pulled together to save open space along the 124-mile stream—a protection program that remains a model of what communities can do when they work together. More people tour the Saco by canoe than any other river in Maine. The rapid Androscoggin tumbles through steep country that links the White and Longfellow Mountains and takes a roundabout course caused by glaciers blocking its earlier, more direct route to sea. Partly reclaimed from vile waste discharged at a pulp mill in Berlin, New Hampshire, the valley still stinks with the flatulence of sulfur compounds below the Boise-Cascade paper mill at Rumford, Maine.

Farther to the east, the Kennebec flows from the splendid northwoods country at Moosehead Lake, charges through some of the Northeast's heaviest whitewater in a wild, 10-mile-long gorge, incomparable in New England, then drifts through gentle water before confronting a series of hydroelectric reservoirs. The river meets the tide at the state capital of Augusta, a city of stolid, brick industrial buildings and old frame homes tucked into hillsides. Here the state has supported the removal of Edwards Dam and its antiquated hydroelectric plant, which blocks salmon and nine other anadromous fish species while providing a minuscule 3.5 megawatts of power. A Kennebec tributary, the Dead River, is anything but dead, with some of the liveliest whitewater in Maine. The Arnold Trail, bound for Québec, passes along the North Branch of the Dead and commemorates Benedict Arnold's 1775 expedition to attack the English-held Québec City during the Revolutionary War. The army's river journey is vividly described in Kenneth Roberts's novel *Arundel*. Farther "down east"—meaning northeast along the coast—the Penobscot enters tidal waters at Bangor.

The Machias, one of the finest undeveloped rivers in the Northeast, supports the largest of only seven self-sustaining populations of Atlantic salmon. The stream's 76 miles of rapids and deep, glassy amber calms are interrupted by natural lakes with no impoundments; two antiquated dams were removed in 1974. The river enters an embayment of the ocean directly at the base of a sea-level waterfall and rapid in the picturesque town of Machias.

At the boundary between Canada and eastern Maine, the St. Croix (2,760 cfs) grows in boggy country and offers an excellent canoe run along the New Brunswick border. The only international river designated for protection in the Canadian Heritage Rivers System (Canada's

Hudson River near Storm King, NY

Connecticut River at Turner's Falls, MA

Housatonic River at West Cornwall, CT

Shepaug River above Washington Depot, CT

Allagash River above Round Pond, ME

East Branch Penobscot at Grand Pitch, ME

West Branch Penobscot at Cribwork Rapid, ME

Penobscot River estuary below Bucksport, ME

version of a wild and scenic rivers system), it empties into Passamaquoddy Bay, where twenty-six-foot-high tides surge in and out.

In the crown of Maine, which pushes up into Canada, the Allagash ranks as a premier wild river of the East with the most famous of all Maine canoe trips, flowing into the St. John River near the international border. Canoeists travel 92 miles, half of the distance through lakes reinforced by some small dams. The state designated the river as the Allagash Wilderness Waterway in 1965 in one of the earliest actions to protect a free-flowing river from a proposed dam, riverbank logging, and development. The section was added to the National Wild and Scenic Rivers System in 1970.

Farther down the St. John, the Aroostook River flows in after beginning in remote country, followed by potato fields and hardscrabble small towns, finally ending its 149 miles with a flow of 2,670 cfs in New Brunswick. A 126-mile reach of the Aroostook is the Northeast's second-longest undammed section of river. As in much of Maine, the wealth of timber in its watershed has vanished in clearcuts just behind the "beauty strip" of trees buffering the roads and waterways. The farm economy of spuds has lost out to big potato growers in western states who reap the benefits of taxpayer-financed subsidies for federal dams.

Wilder than the Allagash, the St. John begins in a remote northwoods empire and then traverses developed reaches, altogether 470 miles long in the United States and Canada. In this end of the state settled by French Canadians, radio broadcasts are in French. Only logging roads penetrate the St. John's upper watershed, and 200 miles flow with no dams or reservoirs to Grand Falls, New Brunswick. Several dams then block its lower reaches before the river ends in the Bay of Fundy. Industrial pulp operators mow the basin as if it were their lawn, but a magnificence endures in untrammeled reaches, and the St. John remains the least-developed big watershed in the East and has one of the longest undammed and unroaded lengths.

From the banks of the St. John, Canada tempted me to enter its seemingly endless network of waters, but to see a northeastern stream in detail, I returned to the Penobscot.

The Penobscot River

Ken Cline, a teacher of environmental studies at the College of the Atlantic in Bar Harbor, Maine, introduced this river to me by saying, "It's a privilege to paddle the East Branch of the Penobscot." I managed to catch him at home at ten P.M. the night before he was to embark on a five-day trip. The late hour and knee-deep unsorted gear failed to detract from Ken's enthusiasm. "Look at this," he said, tracing the river's route in the DeLorme atlas. "Floating down this river, you get a sense for the wilderness and for the conflicts. The East Branch was manipulated for years with dams and logging but has recovered a great deal. Few people go there because of four portages. But I take my class on the trip every other fall."

Following Ken's advice, my wife, Ann, and I later drove through Maine's backwoods and launched our boats with great anticipation below a twenty-foot-tall dam that embayed water in Grand Lake Mattagamon. Though a New England native, Ann has lived in the Rocky Mountains for years, leading whitewater trips for the educational organization Outward Bound. In September, with her summertime work in Utah, Colorado, and Alaska completed, she flew to Maine to join me. As we traveled, she worked on her own book about the history of wetlands.

For this Penobscot voyage we needed sturdy, maneuverable craft. Ann paddled her kayak, with waterproof gear bags jammed into both tapered ends. I paddled my Mad River canoe, a model called the M-E with lots of rocker turning up the ends so that it pivots in whitewater and buoys up on threatening waves. Though this canoe is usually employed as a "play boat" for one-day fun in rapids, it worked remarkably well when loaded with gear for multiday adventures on steep-gradient rivers.

We dipped our paddles into cold water that looked as clean as collected rain but in a few feet of depth turned amber with dissolved organics from swamps. While this watershed wears a cape of dusky green spruce, the riparian embroidery is red maple, a plentiful and pretty tree of eastern waterfronts from here to Florida. Its gray trunk and limbs overhang the water; its leaves turn maroon in fall, and the flowers resemble red constellations of stars in early spring. Though found elsewhere, the red maple excels as a riverfront species and in wet areas. The Penobscot's melting-pot mosaic of mixed forest included three other maple species, northern red oak, eastern cottonwood, white ash, mountain ash, white spruce, white cedar, yellow birch, slippery elm, and witch hazel. On a quarter-mile portage I counted nineteen tree species—more than I see for weeks at a time in Wyoming. Here rose the king of the forest—the eastern white pine—a limber-needled giant with a diameter of two feet and growing, a reminder of whole mountainsides of skyscraper softwoods that whistled in the breeze before the logger's axe, several rounds of cutting ago.

We curved through a marsh that seemed Alaskan in scale, then abruptly encountered the living bulk of a moose, symbolic of the north. She dunked her head and resurfaced, jowls dripping with strings of aquatic salad. Once a riverfront resident from northern Canada southward to Pennsylvania, the moose is now limited to America's far north and the northern Rockies. We hugged the right shore, and our queen of the Penobscot held her ground midstream with a suspicious, white-eyed glance as we retreated.

When evening descended, the rounded summit of Billfish Mountain popped into view to the northwest: luminous, green, high, airy, and vast in softening light. John Kauffmann, a seasoned river man and author of *Flow East,* called the upper Penobscot "easily Maine's most beautiful river."

Like kids in a watery playpen, Ann and I danced our boats through the rapid of Stair Falls, drifted out of it, and tilted our heads to the rumble of Haskell Rock Pitch. Our attention seized, we noticed a house-sized chunk of conglomerate looming like a stern doorkeeper halfway down the "pitch," as Mainers call some waterfalls—textbook examples of rapids formed by bedrock. We decided to carry around the drop, but running out of daylight, we camped at the top of the rapid and fired up dinner on the shore. The backdrop of velvet conifers faded to blue-gray as the light died and the sound of whitewater intensified. Great horned owls hooted in the dark.

After a misty sunrise we carried around the first plunge of the rapid, loaded our boats, cinched our gear down as if the knots counted, and kicked off into immediately squirrelsome water. Brace! Left of the rock! Right of the rock! Over the waves! Into the eddy! Glossy black in deep pools, the river contrasted with juicy green shores and gleaming white rapids outlined as if by chalk. Jagged, teethy lichen-covered rocks stuck up above the waterline. Gray-brown with prolific lichens, the stony surfaces were unbrushed and unflossed. We beached, swam, gobbled lunch, and scouted a sharp drop with a center sluice that challenged us with our full bellies.

Fun water followed to the eight-foot cascade of Pond Pitch, which we portaged. In another mile and a half we made certain to exit before Grand Pitch sucked us into oblivion. This fabulous drop of twelve feet knocks its water to smithereens in a splash pool, bubbles awhile, then hammers down another six feet. We camped at the top and had the warm autumn evening to become acquainted with this corner of the universe. While I searched for photographic angles, standing at arm's length and checking the whole scene, Ann's natural curiosity led her to the heart of the place. I spotted her climbing down to an unlikely swimming hole. By the time I arrived at her ledge, she was slipping into the enticing Penobscot, more air than water here. Bubbles surged where the first plunge of the falls bottomed out and sculpted a deep pool that sloshed up against a cliff in a surprisingly protected alcove—imagine a baby pool of uncorked champagne in such a north-woods paradise. The fireball of sunset angled in across the waterfall's blizzard and onto Ann, who was almost immersed in the bubble-mass. Just seeing it all was a thrill, and jumping in was almost too much. I held my breath and sank into the wet and airy foam.

Returning to the river the next day and again facing the issue of nuts-and-bolts survival, we were stopped a mile below Grand Pitch at Hulling Machine, named for its effect on logs but certainly capable of hulling a canoe in no time. This nasty rapid required the final portage of the trip. Lugging our gear, we enjoyed an aromatic forest, sweet with autumn rot. A long section of gentle water overhung by girthy silver maples led us to Lunksoos Stream—many creeks and small rivers are called streams in Maine—and to a campsite, where we quickly dove inside the tent for shelter from bugs.

That night we heard not drops of rain but open floodgates of it, water dumped on the tent by the bucketful. Under clear skies the next day, the utterly flat Lunksoos Deadwater awaited us. The name fit so well that we've used it since then for any long reach of flatwater: "a lunksoos." As the water began moving again, a garden of aquatic plants waved in the flow like a mass of hair; another crop resembled yellow-tinted ten-foot-long, half-inch-wide noodles. Moose had poked fist-sized holes in the mud where they stepped. Blue-winged teal joined our bird list, which included the common merganser, great blue heron, and spotted sandpiper—all common birds along eastern rivers.

Also common, though we couldn't see them, bass thrive in the East Branch, and the river is a choice spawning ground for reintroduced Atlantic salmon. Along with its other wild qualities, the salmon were one reason Department of the Interior officials in the 1970s considered the Penobscot as one of twenty-seven initial "study" rivers for the National Wild and Scenic Rivers System. They recommended 295 miles on the East and West Branches but hit a roadblock of state opposition. The governor and legislature later named the East Branch in a Maine rivers program, and the state's Land Use Regulation Commission subsequently banned logging within 125 feet of the water.

Chain saws whined nearby, causing us to appreciate the protection afforded the corridor but making obvious the shortcomings of anything less than a full-watershed perspective. After pitching our tent at Whetstone Falls in a north-woods campsite that N. C. Wyeth might have painted for *The Deerslayer,* we strolled down to a dirt logging road and up the road to a sliced sea of clearcuts. A log truck thundered through with a toppling load of skinny spruce.

Highway 11 began to parallel the river at Grindstone, where tempered rock crossed the river in a notched pattern exactly like a giant sawblade. We ended our East Branch trip in a few more miles, near Butch Barker's house.

Having lived all his life along the upper Penobscot, Barker is president of the Northern Penobscot Salmon Club and agitates for better treatment of the river. He works for improved water quality and dislikes the massive clearcuts that are now a hallmark of the industrial forest. "They get what they can and to hell with the next generation," he remarked. Trees are on a rotation for cutting every fifteen or twenty years.

Butch worked as a mechanic for Great Northern paper company for twenty-five years. Now grizzly, he builds cedar strip canoes—sleek, smooth-crafted works. "Up until the 1960s it was great up here," he recalled. "Out in the woods it was a long way between two people. But with unbelievably large equipment, the logging operators have opened it up. Now there are more roads and people everywhere—even on the upper West Branch."

The Penobscot's West Branch carries about four times the flow of the East Branch, and the Bowater Corporation, succeeding Great Northern, owns most of the watershed and controls access to it. At a gate on the highway, Ann and I paid eight dollars for our out-of-state licensed vehicle, plus six dollars to park in the bush overnight.

For that price we wanted to do more than drive around on logging roads, so to see the most turbulent part of the West Branch close up, we joined Eastern River Expeditions. Our raft guide had grown up in Colorado but emigrated to Maine because he liked the water, the weather, and the lower cost of land. Having worked on this body-battering section of river for fourteen years, Greg was a master of big whitewater and promised to coach us on a 12-mile plunge through some of the more fearsome runnable rapids in the East. Not far below Ripogenus Dam, with which the logging industry had turned three natural lakes into one big reservoir for hydroelectric power, we set our rafts into the cold water and took a great leap of faith into them.

Not fooling around, the river presented us with a rapid called Exterminator about twenty yards downstream from where we circled around doing practice strokes. A screamer of a drop with boat-sized holes—

and these were big boats—it demanded that all of us strangers pull together. Plastered by a wall of Penobscot, we burst through the rapid's
other end upright, shaking off water like dunked dogs, just in time for
the next challenge. Big Heater further chilled us on the drizzly day.
This rapid cuts both sides of a granite island that grows conifers on its
top like potted plants.

At a pool below, Orvis-dressed anglers waded into shallows. The
West Branch's stock of landlocked Atlantic salmon, introduced here in
the 1920s, became a self-sustaining fishery, and this spot is now one of
the more famous angling retreats in the East.

More rapids erupted, building to a climax at the Cribwork. We vise-
gripped our paddles and didn't say much as we approached the blank
horizon line that hid the rapid below. We threaded through a slot in the
center, powered right of a sinister horn rock that wanted to snag us,
then barreled, semicontrolled but in Greg's capable hands, through a
forty-five-degree incline of water-veneered boulders eight feet high.
The thrills kept coming, but the scenery stole the show: clear water
backed by foliaged shores, foaming rapids shoveled up against black
rock. Paddling hard, then holding on, we zinged through the ten-foot
incline of Nesowadnehunk Falls and into a blue-green sea below.
North of us, Mount Katahdin ascended, godlike, to the highest point in
Maine—5,267 feet of the rockiest mountain in the East.

As owners of Eastern River Expeditions, John Connelly and Sandy
Neily had years ago adopted the West Branch Penobscot as home. In
1977 John had been operating a rafting business in West Virginia and
took to the road looking for better year-round flows. Pushing the edges
of geography known to boaters, he arrived at the West Branch,
kayaked the hair-raising river by himself, recognized an excellent
whitewater descent for what it was, and established one of the first two
rafting companies in these north woods while living out of his truck.
"Was it risky," I asked Sandy, "setting up business in the middle of
nowhere and expecting people to come?"

"Risk?" she responded. "I don't think John ever thought about that at
all."

A Mainer by birth, Sandy had traveled in wild reaches of the West,
then decided to explore her own backyard. A no-nonsense, fast-moving woman, she thought back through the years after I asked how she
had arrived precisely here. "I looked for green on the map and saw that
no place else in the East has this feeling of huge territory. Then I bor-
rowed $60 one day to take my first raft trip, and that's when I met
John."

Connelly and Neily had married and built the business up to a survival level about the time the pulp company proposed Big Ambejackmockamus Dam. "Then," Sandy said with emphasis and an intense, blue-eyed stare, "then the business got *very* serious." Not only would Big A Dam wipe out the most famous landlocked salmon fishery in the country, but it would also slice in two this great whitewater run that meant home and livelihood to the Connelly–Neily couple.

"In college in the late 1960s, we had talked about the misuse of corporate power. It always sounded bad enough, but seeing it was something else. Only through the courage of one state biologist—Matt Scott—was it publicly known that the water quality in the reservoir wouldn't meet state standards. The state senator from up here in Millinocket said that the problem could be 'fixed.' That night the Maine legislature passed a bill reclassifying the West Branch so that it wasn't a 'river' anymore—that's how they intended to meet the water quality standards."

The event recalled what Duane Lockard had written in *New England State Politics* back in 1959: "In few American states are the reins of government more openly or completely in the hands of a few leaders of economic interest groups than in Maine." Meanwhile, the paper company laid off 1,300 people in 1986. This was problematic to corporate credibility because the corporation had said all along it needed the dam in order to save jobs. "It became obvious that jobs would be lost anyway," Sandy said, noting the automation that revolutionized the pulp and lumber business nationwide. The industry tried to shrug off this public relations fiasco, but after the legislature's reclassification of the river by redefining it as something unknown in the discipline of geography, media that had supported the dam started to use the word "corruption."

"The dam was stopped," Sandy concluded, "but it wasn't a clear victory because I'm not sure how much we all really learned. If we had gotten protection for the river earlier, we could have saved the industry and the government a big, costly mistake." Not to mention Connelly and Neily, who spent $100,000 in direct expenses, time, and lost business while fighting the dam—a difficult sum to recoup from weekend rafters, given the competition and the overhead. "But it was worth it. The West Branch generates $13 million a year in recreation for this state and employs 200 people. And it's not just the whitewater—it's a fishing river, a camping river, and a great family recreation river."

The latest threat, which indomitable Sandy Neily calls an opportunity, is relicensing of existing dams. The Bowater Corporation owns and manages eighteen dams on the West Branch for power production at the paper mills. Because fifty years have elapsed since the federal government issued the original licenses to dam, divert, and generate electricity with Penobscot water, the Federal Energy Regulatory Commission must issue new licenses. Current laws apply, not old ones. In return for the corporation's right to profit from the public's water, a coalition of conservation groups wants better flows for fish, improved water quality, buffers as logging-free zones along rivers, and, most important, an agreement that the industrial landholdings—as big as some states—will not be fragmented. The threat of widespread subdivision is feared—it has already occurred on some industrial tracts in New York and New Hampshire. Here in the Penobscot basin lies one of the least-developed areas in the East, our best opportunity for management of a semiwild ecosystem.

The river begins at the Canadian border, drops through pools and falls, winds in flatwater, and flattens into reservoirs. After visiting the area in 1853, Henry David Thoreau concluded an essay by calling for "national preserves" for inspiration and recreation—one of the earliest appeals for a national park system.

Down below the whitewater reach we had rafted, the West Branch thunders over Debsconeag Falls and slackens into large lakes with dammed outlets. Doomed in a channelized flume since 1899, our river then disappears into the chain-link, brick-wall compound of the Millinocket paper mill. A canal carries the whole river to the underground bowels of the plant, where Bowater generates mechanical and electrical power. The "back channel"—the river's natural course, out in the daylight—sits nearly bone dry. While the whole Penobscot system has problems caused by the paper industry, the sacrifice of the river in Millinocket is as utterly complete as any in America.

The final two dams on the West Branch lie just below East Millinocket, with its own sprawling paper mill, followed by Mattaceunk Dam. This uppermost of five dams on the 91-mile main stem backs water up both the East and West Branches. The river then flows 26 miles to the flatwater of West Enfield Dam.

Near the mouth of the Mattawamkeag River—a low-volume tributary that flows for 110 miles with no dams—I pushed my canoe into the 500-foot-wide Penobscot and hopped aboard. Tannin-stained water riffled around bends and lapped on shores saturated in green except for the yellow of birch and the scarlet of maple spangling the autumn scene. Two bald eagles soared overhead. Above Winn, marked by the backside of some peeling-paint homes, several islands split the rock-studded riffle.

A sign posted on the gemlike islands said that they were owned by the Penobscot Indian Nation. Kingfishers rattled from branches overhanging the water. Silver maples grew eighty feet tall, with ferns, nettle, and snakeroot greening the ground. The Penobscots collect the "fiddlehead" shoots of ferns and sell them to grocery store chains in the spring.

I floated only a short reach of the main stem but thought enviously of Roger Merchant, Jerry Bryan, and Jeff Hunt, who paddled the whole Penobscot—220 miles from the West Branch headwaters. "The expedition was a vehicle for focusing on the river," Roger explained. "We wanted to create a sense of community, to try to get the towns to turn toward the river." With Jo Eaton scheduling events under the name "Penobscot Riverkeepers 2000," the paddlers beached at the towns, talked with residents, and gave presentations to school groups. "People are deathly afraid of the 'ecosystem' view," Roger said, "yet sustainability is a big concern. And consistently, from the beginning to the last paddle-blade in the water, people were drawn to the idea of a whole river."

In our own search for the whole river, Ann and I drove downstream to Lincoln, a town with the megastructure of the Lincoln Pulp and Paper Mill as the basis of economy. Roger Merchant had sampled water here; one bottle, taken from above the mill, was totally clear, and another, from just below the mill, looked like apple juice. At West Enfield, a young mother pushed an infant in a stroller on the skinny sidewalk of the bridge and told her little boy to wave at the log trucks as they roared past. A four-story industrial brick building stretched for 200 yards on the western shore, its rusty smokestack high in the sky. Then, for 24 miles downstream, the Penobscot drifted freely, its riverfront a swamp thick with red maple.

Driving out of the woods just above Old Town, I crossed a bridge to an island in the river and parked at the Penobscot Indian Nation's community center just in time for an appointment. Half a dozen Penobscots had wrapped up a meeting and were awaiting my arrival. I sat down and told them of my interest in the river.

Priscilla Attean represented the Indians in the state legislature, though tribal delegates lack voting rights. "The Penobscot River is the artery of our culture," she began. "The ways we live have changed, but we still have a longing for the old culture. The river is important to us in many ways and is still used as part of the annual 100-mile spiritual walk, when our people canoe and walk from here to the top of Mount Katahdin."

Paul Bisulca, who leads tribal efforts on hydropower relicensing, added, "Unfortunately, the tribe has had no voice in the management of the river." After the Indians' fishing rights had been spelled out by treaty in 1818, dioxin polluted the river so much that the people can't eat the fish, formerly a primary source of food. Diversions eliminated the flow. Four dams were built below the reservation and a score of others above. Yet Bangor Hydroelectric Company claimed that its dams and power plants on the main stem had no effect on the tribe. The Indians were forced to appeal to gain status as legitimate interveners in the federal process of relicensing the hydropower dams. Now the Penobscots strive to reduce losses of Atlantic salmon at the dams, to reinstate a small flow of 350 cfs at the Millinocket dryway, and to eliminate dioxin from the paper mills.

John Banks, the tribal director of natural resources, said, "We had a good seven or eight thousand years here, but then things went steadily downhill. We now want to reverse that decline. I equate the ecological health of the Penobscot River to the spiritual well-being of the tribe."

This group of Indians were not elders known for traditional views but simply community citizens and professionals working out the means to incorporate old ways and new ways at their riverfront home. They are river people, and their work is reflected in the efforts of others across the United States as people strive to take care of their homes. With hope and a finely articulated vision, Priscilla Attean said, "Once people recognize our rights to a healthy river, they will see that a healthy river also benefits the rest of the population."

Salmon once constituted a mainstay of Indian cultures in the Northeast, Pacific Northwest, and California. Now, along the Penobscot and throughout New England, the restoration of Atlantic salmon has captured the imagination of people more than has any other aspect of river conservation. The river once supported 70,000 adult salmon, and local tradition had the first catch going to the president of the United States—a tradition that ended when President Eisenhower received his lonely *Salmo salar* in 1957.

In 1967 the U.S. Fish and Wildlife Service named the Penobscot the model Atlantic salmon restoration river, and state and federal agencies did what they could in a program that continues today. Anglers revived the presidential tradition with Jimmy Carter when brood stock were reintroduced from the nearby Narraguagus River. Some of the worst pollution was stopped when the federal Clean Water Act required industries and towns to install treatment facilities. Dam owners built fish ladders, but only two of the five dams have any downstream passageways for young smolts going out to sea. Few of the dams have adequate upstream passage facilities. Even the passage at West Enfield Dam, rebuilt in 1984, doesn't work well. The anadromous Atlantic sturgeon, alewife, American shad, rainbow smelt, and blueback herring all suffer at the same barriers that halt the salmon. Like the West Branch dams, a number of these projects are scheduled for relicensing by the Federal Energy Regulatory Commission.

While public and private utilities spend millions of dollars to retrofit existing dams for fish passage, and while the public spends millions on water pollution abatement and acquisition of ocean fishing rights even from foreign fleets, an entirely *new* dam is on the planning boards and could undermine everything that everybody else is doing. The Bangor Hydroelectric Company proposed Basin Mills Dam to block the lower Penobscot at a scenic rapid in Orono. Having fought the dam for six years, Don Shields chairs the Penobscot River Coalition and works as Trout Unlimited's New England rivers coordinator. "We now have more salmon coming to the Penobscot than to all the rest of the New England rivers combined. Even in the seven remaining wild salmon rivers of the Atlantic coast, we have very few fish coming back. That makes the Penobscot run especially important." About 3,500 salmon per year have returned to the Penobscot recently (only 1,000 in 1994), but the river offers enough habitat to accommodate up to 10,000 fish if they could survive at sea and bypass the dams.

The Fish and Wildlife Service reported that even with the best fish passage facilities, the likelihood of wild salmon restoration in the Penobscot would fall from 72 percent to 39 percent if Basin Mills Dam were built. Bangor Hydroelectric persisted and received state approval for Basin Mills in 1993, but the U.S. Department of Justice and the Environmental Protection Agency urged that the decision be overturned. American Rivers in Washington, D.C., and local and national fishing and conservation groups continued to fight the dam, seeing it as an anachronism in an age when the survival and restoration of salmon outweigh a scant 38 megawatts of electricity. In 1995 the EPA hardened its opposition, stating that the dam would undermine salmon restoration, destroy wetlands, eliminate fishing sites, harm the Penobscot Nation, and fail to meet water quality standards. In the *Bangor Daily News,* a Bangor Hydroelectric spokesman blamed the project's troubles on "somebody in Boston or Washington."

Just below the Penobscot Indian Reservation, Old Town looks like an industrial burg, and though most of its production occurred in the past, the factory for Old Town canoes remains in use. Milford Dam blocks the river here. Adjoining Old Town is Orono, where the University of Maine smells of the James River Corporation's pulp mill with its Great Works Dam, just upstream. A 10-mile-long slough, which is really part of the Penobscot River, was renamed the Stillwater River—effectively undermining any claim the Indians might have made under their treaty rights that grant them the islands of the Penobscot River.

Farther down, I wanted to see the Penobscot below the lap of high tide and to paddle from river to estuary, so I launched my canoe in Bangor. The remains of a dam, built in 1870 but breached by a flood in 1978, littered the river just upstream. The outgoing tide pulled me seaward as I admired five church steeples and the city that clings to the banks of the Penobscot. Slipping beneath a set of bridges, I passed the town's marina. Oil tank farms crowded the river. At first the water was clear to the length of a paddle and blue in reflected light, but farther downstream I noticed an odd dappling on the surface. Globs of oil dotted the river and congealed in eddies. Tom Maleck of the state Department of Environmental Protection later told me that the owner of a coal gasification plant had dumped a tarlike by-product through sewer lines into the river decades ago. The tar still bubbles up when warm water and an outgoing tide coincide.

I later spotted an osprey, an immature bald eagle, and the shiny bald head of a seal staring wide-eyed at me. More industry was finally followed by green shores. A fish jumped—one of eighty-four species that remain in the basin. But between Bangor and East Hampden, the river soured from clear to rusty with a load of particulates resembling a brown snowstorm.

Ann met me with the van above Bucksport, where I looked up Don White, a town councilman who had recently fought off a coal-fired power plant proposed for the riverfront. He and other opponents had battled the corporate public relations staff, which did everything from sponsoring a Little League team to charming male council members. "We're turning this river around," White said at the end of his story. "The river was a joke when I was a kid. You didn't *begin* to think about it for swimming or fishing. It had green slime, brown slime, foamy slime, and the stink of rotten eggs. We've come a long way. A lot of problems still need to be solved, but it's important that in the meantime we don't allow new problems to overcome us."

In our van, Ann and I rolled southward to see the river's end, where the Penobscot with its nutrients and freshwater nourishes the sea but also burdens it with poisons accumulated from Millinocket to the mouth. Beyond Sandy Point—25 miles below the head of tide in Bangor—the estuary opens to 2 miles and more, and we enjoyed the big sky not found in the forests of the East.

At Lincolnville we unracked our bicycles and wheeled them onto the ferryboat bound for Islesboro Island in Penobscot Bay. There we pedaled winding roads, swam in chilly saltwater at a gravel beach, ate raspberries and blackberries as fast as we could pick them, and eventually arrived on the southern tip of the island. The sea stretched out in a glare of sunshine. The rocky shores of Maine reared up with dark spears of red spruce and balsam fir. The bay lay gentle and vast, and small waves roughened our Penobscot water as it mixed with the Atlantic.

Chapter 2

Appalachian Rivers of Green

Waters at the Cheat River in West Virginia begin to gather on Spruce Knob, a summit high enough for the climate and plant communities of northern New England. But the runoff plunges quickly down to the heart of the Appalachians. Forks named Shavers, Dry, Laurel, and Glady all aim northward in a trellised pattern of drainage between mountain ridges that parallel each other almost perfectly. Resistant sandstone creates rockfalls, tributary deltas, ledges, and waterfalls. Rhododendron and azalea conceal the banks, and the variety of tree species is outdone in few places. Small streams curve at the edges of fields still farmed by persistent old mountaineers, then drop into moss-rimmed canyons that later break out again to bigger valleys and towns built for logging and coal digging. The living river comes to an end where tributaries of Day-Glo orange deliver mine drainage that sterilizes the water with sulfuric acid. Roaring high with rapids in springtime, the lower Cheat cuts a final gorge and then ponds into a reservoir that continues in back-to-back impoundments blocking the

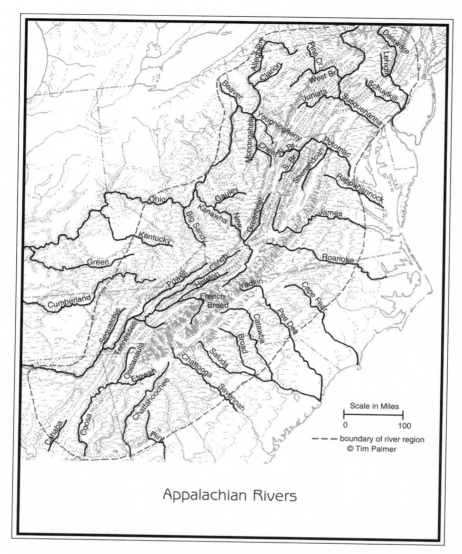

Appalachian Rivers

Monongahela and Ohio Rivers for more than a thousand miles to the Mississippi.

The Cheat describes a river of the Appalachians—typical in its fine headwaters, its rich biology of recovering mixed forests, its superb whitewater in a humid and temperate landscape, its coal-mining heritage, and its dammed-up flatwater.

Though I have lived in the West for years, I grew up in the Appalachians, and they inescapably affect me with the feeling of home. It strikes when I kick a path through ankle-deep leaves in the fall, when my boots grip soil underfoot after a winter of ice and rain and snow, when on sultry afternoons I gaze out at one ridge of mountains behind another in a backdrop stacked up like cutouts, each a lighter shade of gray out to the sky, the lightest shade of gray.

Looking at those views—thousands of them—it's easy to believe that the Appalachians are North America's third-longest mountain range and second-largest in land area. Eighty-seven percent of the range, which is scarcely broken for a 1,550-mile length from Québec to Alabama, lies in the United States. This chapter considers rivers of the Appalachian region south of the glaciated Northeast, encompassing both the mountains and their extensive foothills. Running along the range's longitudinal axis—roughly northeast-southwest—the Appalachians lie as four strips or landform provinces, each with a distinctive personality and its own brand of rivers.

Beginning in the east, the Piedmont province consists of crystalline rocks eroded down to rolling foothills, which extend 100 to 200 miles in width from the Coastal Plain to the base of the mountains. With gradient veering dramatically out of the Piedmont, the Blue Ridge province rises as a narrow belt with the highest terrain in the Appalachians and extends from eastern Pennsylvania to Georgia. This ridge is flanked by the Great Valley—an interrupted chain of end-to-end troughs, from Lake Champlain in New York to the Shenandoah River valley in Virginia and on to Birmingham, Alabama. The Ridge and Valley province, similar to the Blue Ridge, rises to the west as a network of paralleling mountains interspersed with beautiful valleys. Finally, on the western side, the Appalachian Plateau province accounts for half of the total Appalachian region and includes New York's Catskill Mountains as its highest terrain, the Allegheny Mountains rumpling half of Pennsylvania, and the Cumberland Plateau tapering down into eastern Kentucky. Streams have carved the Plateau for so long that I think of it as mostly "negative space" where water has eroded the land and carried it to the Mississippi Delta. There aren't really mountains here, just valleys.

To erode so much has taken a long time; these oldest of American mountains took shape about 300 million years ago and once looked more like the Alps. The geographic center of the range (south of New England) is the New River of West Virginia, often called the oldest river in the hemisphere and perhaps the second-oldest in the world next to the Nile, but some other Appalachian rivers may be as old. The ancestral river that geologists named the Teays ran in the present route of the New before the Appalachian uplift and was thus antecedent even to the ancient mountains.

Settlers flocked to the eastern slope of the Appalachians early in the European colonization of America, and the cultural core was as distinct as that of New England. One stereotype involves grimy towns of two-story, paint-hungry homes and a hardscrabble countryside. Those places can be found, especially in the Plateau area, but they are not dominant anymore. Rather, brick or frame ranch houses and mobile homes dot the roadsides, and commercial strips lead to most of the towns. Railroads have tracked through the larger river valleys—all of them. Roads climb and curve and dip in steeper and windier patterns than are found anywhere else in the country. Mountain farms lie beautifully upon the land, but an uncluttered sweep of countryside has become rare in many parts of the region.

New development in the Piedmont grows by leaps and bounds, and the abundance of water available in the rivers makes the influx of people possible. On this eastern side of the crest, urban escapees fix up old houses or build new ones. More growth is inevitable; one-third of the American population lives within three hours' drive of the Atlantic coast and therefore within the Piedmont or in easy reach of it. The foothills on the western side of the Appalachians describe something quite different—much of the region is a backwater of hammer-and-thongs industry producing coal, steel, chemicals, and manufactured goods, all packed tightly into narrow valleys along rivers large and small. Farms occupy thousands of square miles of hill country between the valleys, and much of the land is wooded in second-, third-, or fourth-growth timber.

To consider the rivers of the Appalachians is to consider its forests because they cover the region so completely. Deciduous hardwoods blanket 80 percent of West Virginia in scores of species. Maurice Brooks, author of *The Appalachians,* stated that these are the most extensive broad-leafed deciduous forests in the world. Riverfront mainstays are willows, sycamores, silver and red maples, birches, eastern cottonwoods, beeches, and hemlocks, but nonriparian communities of oaks, hickories, walnuts, butternuts, cherries, and dozens of other species thrive almost at the water's edge because the area's endowment of rainfall is so rich and steady.

Thirty to sixty-nine inches of rain per year and a convoluted topography spawn an enormous number and mileage of rivers—thousands of streams running for hundreds of thousands of miles. Pennsylvania alone contains 50,000 miles of waterways. Virtually everyone in the Appalachians lives within a half mile of a creek or river. Driving across the countryside one might bridge a stream every mile and a river every 10 miles, though river-sized waterways are often called creeks in this region. Even major rivers huddle close together here—the Hudson, Delaware, Susquehanna, and Potomac all lie within 225 miles of each other at their mouths. Compare this with America's West, where the entire 1,260-mile coastline between Mexico and Canada contains only four similarly large rivers.

To simplify, the wealth of rivers flows toward two watersheds—the Atlantic and the Mississippi. The Appalachian backbone, which is often found at the crest of the Plateau province, splits the flowage. The rivers typically hustle east or west as if to get out of the mountains as quickly as possible, but some of the rivers drift enchantingly, trapped between high ridges hugging the axis. The Greenbrier, for example, flows between tall green slopes enclosing its whole length. High river flows come with rain and snowmelt in the spring before the billions of deciduous trees absorb and transpire whole rivers' worth of water and lend a misty atmosphere. Low river flows typically come with dry spells in late summer and fall.

Six types of river or river reach typify the Appalachians. As in all regions, streams and creeks appear, but here, thousands of them bubble about in a lacework of small waters everywhere running off the wet, hilly ground. As a second type, the mountain-canyon rivers form a recreational and scenic highlight, with forested gorges crosshatched by resistant sandstone. These whitewater showcases include the Youghiogheny of Pennsylvania, the Gauley of West Virginia, the Nantahala of North Carolina, the Nolichucky of Tennessee, and the Chattooga of Georgia. Many of the mountain-canyon rivers lie in the Plateau province. Gentler in mien, a type I call mountain-valley rivers exude the region's pastoral charm in the Blue Ridge and Ridge and Valley provinces. These rivers quietly brush up against a hillside, curve across a limestone valley of farmland, then rub against the opposite hill and eventually pass through a gap and on to other places. Penns Creek in Pennsylvania and the Shenandoah in Virginia are two among scores of these.

With so much water here, the rivers soon grow to become high-volume giants that don't meander across flats as rivers do in the Midwest but muscle through deeply inset, often narrow valleys. On the Appalachians' western slope, with routes etched into the Plateau, the Allegheny of Pennsylvania, the Kanawha of West Virginia, and the Cumberland of Kentucky are examples. On the eastern slope, the big rivers often flow as outsized versions of the mountain-valley rivers already mentioned, then cut through "water gaps." These spectacular notches were carved at right angles to the sandstone-capped ridges when the mountains were pushed up or "rejuvenated" above their previous height. The Delaware at the Delaware Water Gap and the Susquehanna at Harrisburg exemplify these.

Finally, with lower gradients and lower hills around them, two types of foothill river maunder out from either side of the mountains. The Piedmont rivers of the east wind out of the Appalachians with low gradients through farmed and settled landscapes. The western slope rivers drift out through the diminishing Plateau. Because the western foothills consist of soft, horizontal layers of mostly shale, their streams erode easily, and without hard strata to direct the water one way or another, the streams wander in a dendritic or angular-branching pattern, seeming to go in every direction but eventually collecting in large rivers that wash off to the Midwest.

Only one river completely transects the Appalachians—the Hudson, described in chapter 1. Three east-flowing rivers, however, breach the Blue Ridge province through cleft gaps: the Potomac, James, and Roanoke. Crossing the mountains in the opposite direction, the New and the French Broad, which rise in North Carolina, nearly transect the Appalachians as they begin high in the Blue Ridge and journey many miles northwestward.

The Ohio easily tops the list of largest rivers, carrying 92,530 cfs before it leaves the Plateau. This mother of Appalachian rivers flows at 281,000 cfs at its mouth in the Midwest; most of the water originates in the Appalachians, and it includes tributaries as sizeable as the Tennessee. The Susquehanna—the largest river to flow entirely in the Appalachian area—carries 42,180 cfs at the end of its 444-mile course and is the largest river on the East Coast south of the St. Lawrence. The Tennessee runs with 37,100 cfs where it leaves the Appalachian Plateau near Chattanooga, Tennessee, and swells to 68,000 cfs as it joins the lower Ohio in the Midwest. The other giant rivers include the Allegheny, with 18,810 cfs in Pennsylvania, the Delaware, with 14,500 cfs in Pennsylvania and New Jersey, the Coosa, with 13,860 cfs in Alabama, the Kanawha, with 12,840 cfs near its confluence with the Ohio in West Virginia, and the Monongahela, which runs with 12,460 cfs before it meets the Allegheny to form the Ohio. The Cumberland carries 11,830 cfs as it leaves the Appalachian Plateau in Kentucky (it grows to 28,030 before it meets the lower Ohio in the Midwest). The Potomac flows with 11,520 cfs at tidewater. This set of rivers is one of the largest in

America, outdone only in Alaska and in the Coastal Plain and Midwest, both of which draw substantial flows from Appalachian headwaters.

Along big rivers and small, what the Indians lived with for 12,000 years and what the first European settlers found was surely an ecosystem of extraordinary abundance. In the lower Potomac River, Captain John Smith in 1608 reported fish "lying so thicke with their heads above water, [that] for want of nets, we attempted to catch them in a frying pan." Two centuries later, John James Audubon was still able to write of the Ohio River as "magnificent" and "majestic," having "almost uninhabited shores."

Much of the important biological wealth that remains resides in the limestone waters of the Appalachians. With plentiful calcium compounds in solution, these alkaline streams are superb producers of life. Invertebrates and shellfish absorb the calcium to grow their shells. They in turn provide food for fish, amphibians, reptiles, mammals, and birds. Protection of the limestone rivers is thus an important step in safeguarding the biological values of the Appalachians. The more acidic waters draining the Appalachian Plateau produce good fisheries, though they are rarely as notable as the limestone streams. With less buffering capability, the Plateau streams are easily ruined by mine drainage or acid rain. These problems further heighten the importance of the alkaline streams, whose higher pH counteracts, or buffers, the acidic waters when the two mix. Bald Eagle Creek, for example, neutralizes the acidic West Branch of the Susquehanna in Pennsylvania enough that fish can live below the confluence.

An unparalleled splendor of biological diversity results from the region's long span of ten degrees in longitude from New York to Alabama. Some eastern slope rivers, including the Delaware, still carry anadromous species such as American shad and blueback herring, which live in the Atlantic but spawn in the rivers. The Susquehanna was once among the great anadromous fisheries of the nation. Millions of shad were netted near the mouth of the river; single hauls of a net sometimes took days to empty. But hydropower dams as early as 1840 terminated the spawning runs. Arduous efforts by the state of Pennsylvania have finally resulted in restoration of a small part of the old runs; the fish are lifted or provided with ladders at the private hydroelectric dams.

In species diversity, rivers of the southern Appalachians are uniquely rich owing to their temperate climate, productive limestone chemistry, isolation by steep topography, and lack of glaciation, which repeatedly wiped out warm-water species to the north. Here the ice did not interrupt evolution; species continued to evolve and diversify. All these factors in the southern Appalachians contribute to what National Biological Survey biologist Noel Burkhead called the richest temperate upland fish fauna in the world. Tennessee, with 307 fish species, has more than any other state. The rivers of the southern Appalachians house about 350 fish species, or 44 percent of the 800 species north of Mexico. Some of these display colors as brilliant as those of fishes of tropical coral reefs. For example, the candy darter (*Etheostoma osburni*) sports orange stripes on a dazzling blue-green body in streams of the New River basin. Twenty percent of the southern Appalachian fish fauna is imperiled, however, primarily by siltation of streams caused by farms, development, roads, and now a new round of logging. Large rivers, which accumulate evidence of everything we do to the land, are more affected than small ones in what promises to be a deadly arena of extinction unless changes are made.

North, south, and in between, only a handful of Appalachian acres have been spared disturbance. Almost everyplace has been logged. In the late 1800s, 300 million board feet of timber could be held in one storage boom of logs in the West Branch Susquehanna River at Williamsport, Pennsylvania. Because of the region's early settlement, population density, efficiency of extraction, and gentle gradients of large waterways, most Appalachian rivers have been further developed.

The Ohio represents the ultimate used-up river. Twenty dams impound every mile of its length for barges. The Army Corps of Engineers and the Tennessee Valley Authority have built flood-control reservoirs on nearly all sizeable tributaries. Highways, railroads, and development usually crowd both banks. Below Pittsburgh, the Ohio's chain of bankfull reservoirs constitutes the most industrialized riverfront in the country, with old steel mills lining banks of cement or culm for miles. The Ohio fed its water to the industrial giants for a century, but the biological decline in the basin now ranks as one of the most significant losses of natural habitat and species diversity in North America. Since 1970, industries along the upper Ohio have similarly declined in a deep-seated recession of mill closings brought about by foreign competition, high labor costs, a deteriorating environment, and corporate managers who siphoned profits away for other investments rather than upgrading their existing mills and communities. The supply of water, however, is plentiful, and the rivers here will likely reinvigorate the local economy someday, a process already evident in lands of warm climate to the south.

The Appalachian rivers long ago fell victim to some of America's worst pollution. Many municipalities remain poor and still treat their sewage inadequately—a problem destined to worsen with cuts in federal funding. Mine drainage is a widespread plague on the Appalachian Plateau, responsible for 53 percent of all the polluted river miles in Pennsylvania, the most afflicted state. Acid rain worsens with fallout from air pollution produced by industries in the Midwest and the western Appalachian foothills. West Virginia suffers some of the nation's worst acid rain. A pH of 2.9—expected in test tubes but not in nature—is commonly found in rainwater of Wheeling, where it eats the features from limestone statues. In 1990, Pennsylvania and Maryland were ranked among the worst seven states for their industries' and municipalities' violations of water pollution laws. The situation had not changed greatly since maps of the U.S. Water Resources Council in the late 1970s had showed America's worst point-source pollution in the western Appalachians of Pennsylvania, West Virginia, and Kentucky, along with adjoining portions of the Midwest.

Against the nation's 200-year momentum of rapacious change, a mostly undeveloped large river such as the New in West Virginia stands out as a resource of striking rarity. Hundreds of medium-sized streams, however, still offer great biological and recreational value. Significant undammed rivers are West Virginia's 174-mile Greenbrier and the Delaware, which runs for 340 unimpounded miles, including tidewater. A 221-mile reach of the Susquehanna has no dams in New York and Pennsylvania. The Rappahannock of Virginia flows for 207 miles without dams, including 115 tidal miles on the Coastal Plain.

For all the problems in the Appalachians, remarkable potential exists for reclaiming rivers. Thanks to the region's temperate climate, trees grow quickly and forests heal well relative to drier regions. Erosion can be slowed as native ground cover regrows. Antiquated dams can be eliminated without economic loss. Twenty-nine dams, for example, once blocked the Lehigh of Pennsylvania in a section that is now one of the most popular whitewater runs. Pressures for new growth in the remote Appalachian areas have not been great. West Virginia, for example, was one of only four states whose population declined in the 1980s.

Given the innate natural wealth of the Appalachians, it seems that this region may contain the real geography of hope—a term once applied to the American West, where big spaces instilled good feelings but where the curve of destruction is still bending upward rather than downward, as it may be in the Appalachians. Future generations may find the attention now given to protection of wild ecosystems elsewhere being redirected to reinstate healthy habitat and new, sustainable economic value to this region of mild climate, plentiful rain, and abundant streams and species—a wonderland of rivers that we treated poorly for two centuries but could still coax back to life.

To look at some of the important rivers of the Appalachians, I start in the north, where chapter 1 left off. The Pocono Plateau of northeastern Pennsylvania includes the cobbled streambeds, waterfalls, and sphagnum bogs typical of the glaciated Northeast. Among many clean and lightly developed tributaries to the upper Delaware, the Lackawaxen River has the rocky New England look, and the Lehigh cuts through a water gap with sharp rapids. After its East and West branches join, the Delaware is 224 miles long to tidewater, followed by 96 miles of estuary. This river can be thought of as a bridge between regions; in its upper reaches, towns and villages reflect the architecture of New England, but the river then flows through the Appalachians to the Coastal Plain.

Like the upper Delaware, Pine Creek of north central Pennsylvania lies at the glacial edge. Its upper watershed marked the southern limit of glacial advance, where a terminal moraine once dammed a large lake. When the moraine burst, it released floods that carved out the Grand Canyon of Pennsylvania—an 800-foot-deep chasm that is a highlight of river scenery in the East and centerpiece to one of the finest canoeing streams.

Also in the North Central Highlands of Pennsylvania, the West Branch Susquehanna perfectly typifies the Appalachian Plateau. Miners have worked its headwaters, causing acid drainage that pollutes this otherwise idyllic stream and hundreds of miles of its tributaries. Along its 249-mile course it receives the scenic Moshannon, Sinnemahoning, Kettle, Pine, Lycoming, Loyalsock, and Muncy Creeks, all sizeable enough to be called rivers in any other region of the country. With a flow of 10,810 cfs, the clear water of the West Branch joins the brown main stem of the Susquehanna in central Pennsylvania.

A larger stream of 15,320 cfs above the confluence, the main stem Susquehanna wanders down from New York through farmland, around islands, over small dams, and beneath ridges thick with hardwoods. The combined West Branch and main stem flow through water gaps of the Ridge and Valley province, pass Harrisburg with a broad rockiness unequaled in the East, and spill through back-to-back hydropower reservoirs to become the principal source of water for Chesapeake Bay. The Susquehanna's vital flow has long nourished this largest of American estuaries, once thick with oysters, American shad, and other marine life but now diminished and threatened with complete exhaustion, owing in large part to the polluted farm runoff also delivered by Pennsylvania's largest river. The Juniata—the largest Susquehanna tributary next to the West Branch—flows through limestone valleys and ten separate water gaps.

The 314-mile Allegheny drains the northwestern quadrant of Pennsylvania and picks up the beautiful Clarion as a tributary, then joins the 128-mile, totally dammed Monongahela at Pittsburgh to create the Ohio River. One might regard the diminutive headwaters of the Allegheny above Coudersport, Pennsylvania, as the source of the Mississippi. Though its route is shorter, the Ohio carries a much greater volume than the Mississippi where they meet in Illinois.

The 981-mile Ohio, draining ten wet states, is the third-largest river in America. Counting the Allegheny, it ranks ninth in length. Though the river flows into the Midwest, the Appalachian Plateau extends downstream for 400 miles from Pittsburgh to Maysville, Kentucky. It is no coincidence that the Ohio's location, like that of the Missouri River, traces almost perfectly the line of southern glacial advance in the ice ages. For thousands of years the ice sheets blocked ancestral rivers from flowing north and forced streams to run near the ice's melting southern edge, which became the paths of these two great rivers. Because this route leads from the heart of the Appalachians to the West, pioneers floated flatboats down the Ohio to settle the frontier, negotiating the Falls of the Ohio. Now impounded, this rapid at Louisville, Kentucky, once dropped twenty-four feet in 3 miles.

The Ohio drains thousands of streams from the western side of the Appalachians, including much of West Virginia's extraordinary river collection. In the Cheat basin, Blackwater Falls is one of the most scenic in the East—a picture of mountain headwaters at their best. To the south, paddlers revere the Gauley, with its powerful, difficult rapids, as one of the foremost whitewater runs in the country.

With headwaters in the 100-mile, undammed South Fork, the New River eases out of North Carolina and crosses Virginia with rapids, quiet interludes, and eight dams. Below Bluestone Dam in West Virginia the river is a highly productive warm-water fishery before it plunges over Sandstone Falls and finally carves the New River Gorge. In this ultimate big-water eastern canyon, high flows create rapids rivaling some of those in the Grand Canyon. Serving as a boundary of the southern Appalachians, the 320-mile New marks the beginning of the rich diversity of life in southern streams. Not only fish but also salamanders, frogs, snakes, turtles, millipedes, and other families of creatures thrive in rich diversity here and in other healthy river basins to the south. Sections of the New also offer the best glimpse of what a big artery like the Ohio once resembled.

This glorious river's pathetic end comes with a dam at Hawk's Nest that diverts all but 100 of the New's 9,088 cfs for power at a Union Carbide metal alloy plant. The infamous tunnel for the diversion, dug during the 1930s, was reportedly the site of the worst industrial health tragedy in American history. Silicosis, caused by breathing dust in the poorly vented tunnel, caused the deaths of 764 of 1,213 laborers, most of them African Americans. Below the diversion, the Gauley and New join to form the Kanawha, dammed and lined with chemical factories all the way to its confluence with the Ohio.

In southwestern West Virginia, more rivers draining coal country rival the "Chemical Valley" of the Kanawha for ugliness. The Tug River is known as the "sewer of the billion-dollar coal field," and the Big Sandy and Guyandotte are infamous for their blackened bedloads of coal debris, bankside litter, and grimy, wrecked shorelines.

A leap across the Appalachians to the Piedmont of Maryland takes us to the Gun Powder Falls, Patapsco, and Patuxent Rivers, flowing to Chesapeake Bay with small rapids, sycamore and tulip tree forests, and reservoirs alternating with choice lengths of riverfront set aside in valley parks near suburban Baltimore. The Potomac next crosses the region, and as the first sizeable river south of it, the Rappahannock rises in the Blue Ridge Mountains. With whitewater in its upper reaches, it later drifts in long tidal bends to Chesapeake Bay.

The James River flows from the mountains, collecting its headwaters from the Cowpasture and the once-beautiful Jackson, which the Army Corps of Engineers flooded in the early 1980s in one of the final gasps of the dam-building era. As the main artery of Virginia, the James crosscuts the Blue Ridge at Glasgow in an intramountain passage 15 miles long and 2,000 feet deep—the longest of all the Appalachian water gaps. Seven dams block most of this gorge, leaving Balcony Falls as the sole survivor. Then the James flows for 143 undammed miles—the archetypal river of the Piedmont, with slow currents brushing by red-dirt farms. At Richmond, 245 miles from its beginning, the river encounters the Fall Line. This dramatic geologic feature consists of solid rock where the Piedmont drops to the Coastal Plain and where many rivers become tidal. At the Fall Line in Richmond, the James flows with 7,060 cfs and produces America's only Class IV commercial rafting run of steep, rock-studded rapids within a major city. The Fall Line produces its most pronounced rapids in the north, though they are often obscured by dams such as those on the Schuylkill near Philadelphia and the Brandywine at Wilmington, Delaware.

South of the James, the 380-mile Roanoke River is dammed ten times but retains some of the least-developed river frontage in the mid-Atlantic region. This river boasts the largest number of endemic, or native, fish species on the Atlantic slope in Virginia and marks the beginning of the rich aquatic fauna of the southeastern Appalachian rivers, much as the New marks the boundary across the central and western mountains. The Yadkin River runs southeast across the Piedmont in North Carolina before it becomes the Pee Dee of the Coastal Plain. Southward, the Linville River plunges with dazzling steepness through a 14-mile-long gorge, dropping 240 feet per mile—one of the most extreme boatable descents in the Appalachians and comparable to the Black Canyon of the Gunnison in the Rockies. Guidebook author Walter Burmeister called the 1,700-foot-deep gorge "the ultimate display of white water found in the Appalachian Mountains." It flows to the heavily dammed Catawba River, which becomes the Wateree of the Coastal Plain. The Fall Line again appears with rapids in the Saluda River at Columbia, South Carolina, and reappears as far south as Columbus, Georgia, on the Chattahoochee River, which flows to the Gulf of Mexico.

Rivers flowing off the southwestern face of the Appalachians include the Kentucky River, with dams and locks extending far upstream as it drifts across hill country to the Ohio. Southwest of it, the 360-mile Green River includes a passage through Mammoth Cave National Park, where tributaries called the Echo, Roaring, and Styx flow underground, providing habitat for blind fish. The lower Green crosses the limestone lowlands that bridge the Appalachian foothills and the Midwest. The 720-mile Cumberland River begins at strip-mine headwalls in eastern Kentucky, then spills over the seventy-foot-high Cumberland Falls—the second-highest in the East on a large-volume river. The Cumberland's Big South Fork ranks as one of the premier southern Appalachian rivers for whitewater and wild gorges. Below the sprawling Wolf Creek Reservoir, the Cumberland winds slowly westward before being dredged and dammed for 380 miles of barge route, including flatwater at Nashville.

The Tennessee's vast river basin dominates the southwestern Appalachians, though it begins in western Virginia with the pastoral and paralleling Powell, Clinch, and North Fork Holston, which have significant undammed lengths of about 170, 230, and 193 meandering miles, respectively. With their unusual free-flowing lengths in the heavily im-pounded Tennessee basin, these streams host a surviving though en-dangered diversity of fish species. They are also superior mussel-pro-ducing streams; thirty-two species occur at one site. With the world's largest concentration of mussel varieties, the southern Appalachians support 125 of 300 species found in North America—a third of the world's total. Dams, dredging, development, grazing, and poaching for illegal marketing to Japan have taken a grim toll; 30 to 60 percent of the species that remain are likely endangered. Now the zebra mussel poses the greatest threat of all. This exotic from the Black and Caspian Seas invaded America in 1988, probably by escaping with bilgewater from a European freighter coming to the Great Lakes via the St. Lawrence Seaway. The zebra mussel has proliferated at a pestilent rate and eliminates native mussels by anchoring onto their shells and pre-venting them from opening. Native mussels are the most endangered family of American fauna, and the few unspoiled streams of the south-western Appalachians are critical to their survival.

For flood control and hydropower, the Tennessee Valley Authority dammed the main stem Tennessee and the sizeable Little Tennessee River almost continuously; reservoirs flooded 600,000 acres and opened the Tennessee's 652 miles to barges. Though New England has more small dams, this part of the country, along with the southern Mid-west and Oklahoma, has a greater density of large reservoirs than any other region in the United States. The broad Tennessee had earlier pos-sessed the continent's biologically richest riverine ecosystem, most of it now lost. Remaining is a fine 24-mile section of the Obed River and Falls Creek Falls—one of the tallest in the East at 256 feet. The Se-quatchie River flows for 120 miles without dams and enters the lower Tennessee below Chattanooga.

As the Tennessee's upriver extension, the 260-mile French Broad River flows across North Carolina to its confluence with the smaller Holston River, where the Tennessee begins. Though polluted in the Asheville area, the powerful and rapids-studded French Broad is mostly undammed except for its lower reaches. A tributary, the Nolichucky, cuts through superb whitewater gorges lying 3,000 feet below sur-rounding mountains; its headwaters begin on Mount Mitchell, the high-est summit in the East at 6,684 feet. The Nolichucky later crosses farm-land and flows into reservoirs in Tennessee.

The topographical and biological highlight of the southern Ap-palachians is the Great Smoky Mountains; some reports indicate 130

Delaware River above Callicoon, PA, NY

Susquehanna at West Branch confluence, PA

Ohio, Allegheny, and Monongahela at Pittsburgh, PA

Greenbrier River below Fort Spring, WV

Dry Fork Cheat River, WV

North Fk., South Br. Potomac tributary, WV

New River, Sandstone Falls, WV

Cumberland River and Falls, KY

Cowpasture River, VA

James River in Richmond, VA

Nantahala River, NC

Chattooga River, GA, SC

Cape Fear River in the Piedmont region, NC

Potomac River below Harper's Ferry, VA, MD

Potomac below Great Falls, VA, MD

Potomac at Georgetown, Washington, D.C.

different species of trees living there. The scenic Little River runs off the Tennessee side to the west, and the Oconaluftee runs off the North Carolina side. Just to the south lie the popular rapids of the Nantahala; though small, it is one of the most-floated whitewater rivers in the country. Paddlers also seek the Ocoee of Tennessee, though it is heavily manipulated by power diversions and dams.

At the southeastern fringe of the Appalachians, the Chattooga River flows with notorious whitewater at the Georgia–South Carolina boundary and is the only major river in the southern Appalachians without significant development on its banks. Its waters leave the mountains via the Tugaloo and Savannah Rivers. The Chattahoochee flows off Georgia's mountains and past Atlanta as one of the most-used and most-natural urban rivers in America. The beautiful Etowah of northern Georgia is plagued by impoundment, siltation, and development that endanger its rich biology. With the Oostanaula, it forms the Coosa River—a heavily dammed artery of the southern Appalachians. Thoroughly unexpected, the Little River of northeastern Alabama carves a spectacular gorge 30 miles long and 500 feet deep before emptying into the dammed-up Coosa.

At the southern limit of the Appalachians, which finally ease down to the Coastal Plain southwest of industrial Birmingham, the 160-mile Cahaba hosts 131 fish species in what may be the richest fish fauna for a stream of its size in America. In one section, Cahaba lilies grow so profusely that they seem to make a river of flowers.

From the Delaware to the Cahaba, the Appalachians represent a riverscape of enormous abundance, though the region has suffered more than its share of losses. Among all the streams, the splendor, abuse, and recovery of an Appalachian river are best seen on the Potomac.

The Potomac River

High in the Appalachians near the winsome mountain town of Monterey, Virginia, the river first appears. The twelve-inch-wide trickle of the South Branch Potomac gains size through Bluegrass Valley, then speeds northward with great things and awful things to come.

Along this 140-mile branch lie pastures and farms, some kept up since the Indian days and some abandoned to goldenrod and to swallows in tumbledown barns. Below the village of Franklin, Ann and I veered left on a small road leading to a natural showcase of the east-

ern mountains with the unlikely name of Smoke Hole. The U.S. Forest
Service road hugs a canyon wall as the river spills over ledges and
sieves through boulder piles, the South Branch running big enough to
make a prized canoeing run in the springtime. Eagle Rock climbs ver-
tically from the floodplain, and sycamores congregate on valley flats.
This umbrella of the eastern riparian forest thrives on the flood regime;
new generations sprout after high waters recede. When we visited, the
black maples, tulip trees, and birches wore a flashy October yellow,
while honey locusts clung to their olive green. Dogwoods shone pink
and red, linden and ash, yellow-green, all of them dazzling under blue
skies that defined a perfect autumn. The rugged canyon continues for
18 miles before it hooks out of its mountain gap above Petersburg.

Hiking, camping, soaking up the scenery, and wishing all the eastern mountains were treated more like this national forest enclave, Ann
and I enjoyed ourselves along the river, clear as tap water. Reluctantly
leaving this little Shangri-la in Appalachia, we crossed the mountain to
the west and dropped to the North Fork of the South Branch, a river
system of 53 miles. Off the main road, mountain farms were perched
on grassy shoulders of the big mountains, tin roofs glinting in the sun,
chicken coops squatting on the slopes next to sun-bleached barns, pastures falling in dizzy steepness, dirt lanes going home through the
swales and apple orchards and over the ridges and down to the river.
In this age of the supermarket, it occurred to me that one could still
live here in these temperate, isolated mountains, growing food and getting by. These places pulled at my heartstrings, with memories of a
mountain farm and Appalachian stream I owned from 1973 to 1980, but
with more than that. Perhaps I felt the heritage that author René Dubos
referred to when he wrote, "Most of human life during the past ten
thousand years has been spent on small family farms."

To see the next Appalachian highlight of the Potomac basin, we
drove down the North Fork Valley to Seneca Rocks, one of the most
spectacular rock faces in the East and a mecca to climbers. One need
not lead a twenty-pitch ascent; a trail goes to the summit, where views
spread the North Fork Potomac out across the Appalachian washboard
below. While private land and roadside homes checker the valleys, the
Monongahela National Forest accounts for most of the area's mountain
land. The Potomac riffled by with sycamores cantilevered to shade
trout pools. But the pools didn't look quite right.

The flood of 1985 had left its mark here in a big way, depositing
house-sized piles of logs, rocks, and debris in the riverbed. The torrent
had dug out new channels and filled old ones. That is the way of rivers.

They in fact depend on traumatic rejuvenation to expand and renew riparian corridors, invigorate rapids, and gouge out pools as trout havens. None of that is a problem; in fact, these are called "disturbance" ecosystems. The problem centers on the roads and homes built in the way. In the months following the flood, the federal Soil Conservation Service, at local request, turned teams of bulldozers loose to clear miles and miles of the streambed, transforming it into the skinniest long gravel pit in America. The North Fork now slowly repairs itself as it rearranges the gravel and recruits new pools and riffles, but recovery of the river's complex ecosystem and restoration of its indigenous chain of life will take decades.

As if that weren't enough, the Soil Conservation Service (renamed the Natural Resources Conservation Service in 1995) continued to spend money for riprap, dumping stones on the banks to keep the river from accomplishing its natural migrations back and forth. Free federal aid to farmers amounted to $25 per foot of river frontage and millions altogether. West Virginia is a conservative state, but even it proposed that farmers getting the subsidy agree to a fifty-foot-wide easement where native plant life would be allowed to take root and help with its free contribution to the job of stabilizing riverbanks. The Farm Bureau argued for subsidies without controls, and its rhetoric made this issue of taxpayer-funded largesse sound like a crisis of private-land rights gouging out the heart of America. In 1994, large amounts of federal money were still being spent to riprap private land, with a token five-foot buffer zone to be left natural.

Below the North Fork–South Branch confluence lies Petersburg, a typical and pleasant Appalachian town with a J. C. Penney Catalog Store, Rose's Bargain Center, Shirley's Crafts, a Nautilus and Fitness Club, a 7-11, a hardware store, a café, and a new restaurant, which gets most of the business. In the old vinyl-and-formica café, Ann and I struck up a conversation with a man who commutes a long way to Harrisonburg, Virginia, to do plumbing. "It's hard makin' a livin' here, yet people don't want to leave. They move away to work, but they keep the land, and someday they come back."

With the idea of keeping the river as a timeless centerpiece in this land that everybody reportedly likes so much, National Wild and Scenic River status was proposed for worthy sections of the South Branch and North Fork above Petersburg. The designation would ban dams, which nobody seems to want anyway. But at the town's bookstore, proprietor Nancy Cooley said, "If you talk about conservation around here, the hair on people's backs goes up *this* high. If you talk about keeping the land the way it is, they agree. But they don't want anybody telling them what to do." The antifederal sentiment does not extend to turning down the federal subsidy for riprap or the millions in disaster relief to replace floodplain development.

One of the most active eastern river conservation groups, the West Virginia Rivers Coalition, works to protect these streams and eleven others crossing national forest land, including some of the finest of all Appalachian wild rivers. Seeking local cooperation and talking tirelessly to community groups, the Coalition's Roger Harrison, a West Virginian through and through, hopes to counteract unfounded fears that federal protection would result in people losing their land or their rights to use it as they always have. Yet confronting paranoia in a rural setting is a difficult task when people hate the government to begin with, when they are suspicious of anything new, and when they fear the unknown but readily accept the change that development brings on a piecemeal basis, especially if profits are involved.

Back on the road, Ann and I drove downstream from Petersburg. Chicken farms had replaced dairies, the warehouselike poultry barns occupying benches up above the river. While twenty tons of cattle manure can typically be applied to a field without foul runoff, only seven tons of nitrogen-rich chicken manure can be absorbed effectively; industrial-scale chicken farms are a growing problem along rivers in this part of the Appalachians. Eight hundred new chicken houses sprang up between 1990 and 1994. Doctors and lawyers in places such as Petersburg carry beepers, not for their primary professions but to notify them when the computer-controlled temperature and feeding mechanisms in their untended chicken factories go awry. Moorefield, a small riverside town settled in 1777, proudly advertises itself as the "poultry capital of West Virginia."

At Romney, which somehow changed hands fifty-six times during the Civil War, we searched for a view of the river but couldn't find it. A man named Steve pulled up in his pickup, offered help, and said, "Follow me. You can see it from back behind the house." Quiet and wooded, the South Branch lay in a steep draw. "As a kid," Steve recalled, "I was always in the river, but I don't think I've been down there since the flood. People these days pretty much take the river for granted."

Ann and I left the South Branch with feelings of attachment to this magnetic, pleasant place but also a sense of social isolation and a feeling of pessimism about how well local people will care for their river. We drove uphill and westward toward the North Branch Potomac, in the Appalachian Plateau province, locally called the Allegheny Mountains. The farm country we had just left seemed like a benign mountain culture as we headed into the backwaters of Appalachia. We passed a hardscrabble trailer in the woods and a couple of sag-roofed homes. At Mount Storm, the legacy of coal mining—the hallmark of the Plateau—immediately became evident. A coal-fired power plant punctured the skyline and dirt roads were widened, blackened, and rutted with strip-mine access. Coal trucks snorted down the highway by the minute, gray dust whirling at their wheels.

Even though the South Branch is significantly longer and its North and South Forks yield longer continuous mileages, most sources consider the North Branch the headwaters of the Potomac because surveyors set the Fairfax Stone there to mark the land grant of 1736—the original ownership claimed by Europeans. Nearby, at the base of Backbone Mountain, the North Branch (the "ledgiest river you will ever encounter," according to *West Virginia Whitewater*) enters a 13-mile roadless reach below Steyer. Until recently, mine acid sterilized its water, and its pH was so low that it even killed bacteria feeding on sewage, a problem somewhat improved today.

After rolling down a free fall of a mountain road, we dropped in on Kitzmiller, where the Potomac rounds out its Appalachian images: we had seen the farm country of the South Branch, the wild country of the North Fork South Branch, and now the coal country of the North Branch. Pure Appalachia, rows of look-alike company houses climbed the hills. Acrid coal smoke curled out of chimneys on the damp October afternoon. The yellow-brown riverbed lay between levees pushed up by the Army Corps of Engineers.

The Corps' big project here was not the levee but Jennings Randolph Dam, completed in 1981 and flooding 8 miles of river below Kitzmiller. Its main purpose was to increase low flows at Washington, D.C., where a growing population threatened to drink the Potomac dry during droughts. Acid mine drainage just happened to stratify in the reservoir, and the Corps found that low-acid water could strategically be released, giving rise to an unexpected trophy trout fishery below the dam. As I put my canoe in the water there, two fly fishermen from Washington, D.C., caught and released fourteen-inch trout and wondered aloud why they drive all the way to Montana each summer to fish. Ann paddled with me for a few miles, then took advantage of the abandoned railroad bed for her daily run. She jogged back to the van, then drove over the mountain to Piedmont, the town where my one-day canoe trip would end.

My route took me through rapids foaming over boulders and ledges, all wrapped in a cloak of red and gold foliage. Birch leaves speckled like stars in front of serrated cliff faces. Limbs of sycamores were penciled in white on the charcoal background of the rainy day; heavy drops beat crimson leaves off the trees and into the water. Clouds gripped the mountains halfway up their steep slopes. Working with Maryland and West Virginia, the Conservation Fund, which buys land for preservation, had recently acquired property here, guaranteeing protection for this outstanding Appalachian gorge. In 1993 the governors of the two states had formed a task force to examine ways of improving recreation on the long-neglected but born-again river. Late in the afternoon, I beached my canoe at the mouth of the Savage River, where Ann had parked the van along that splendid stream of hardwood shores, clean water, and jet-fast rapids.

Below there, the North Branch wraps around the Westvaco Company's Luke Mill: railroad tracks by the water, sawdust piles sixty feet high, a smokestack whose top nearly disappears in fumes or water vapor, lights glaring in an orange sky at night, company houses dug into mountainsides with streets so steep that wide-angle mirrors hang at intersections. Just downriver, Westernport, Maryland, lies on the western shore, while Piedmont, West Virginia, occupies the other bank. This beat-up Appalachian mill town has buildings sided half in aluminum and half in tarry shingles. My route took me past a derelict hotel brightened only by American flag decals in the windows. Men who were not hunting wore camouflage on the streets, and the bars opened for lively business in the morning. A low-rider's bumper sticker claimed, "My kid beat up your honor student."

The scene presented a great paradox. While the mill along the Potomac made paper for publications including *National Geographic* and earned profits for its owners, its local justification was to provide jobs so people could live well. Yet it seemed that survival in mill-town squalor was the key challenge here. Were these Appalachian river towns always brimming with economic and social ills? What had this industry accomplished by polluting the Potomac, stripping the countryside of wood, and throwing people into a cycle of poverty? Of course, the mill town represents some people's entire concept of life. But would they have had better lives elsewhere?

To see the mill's direct effects on the river, I walked down to the logical place—the sewage treatment plant. Westvaco has spent a lot of money to reduce its cancer-causing dioxin discharges, which for years necessitated a ban on eating bottom-dwelling fish, not just here but for

50 miles downstream. The company reportedly cut the toxin by 90 percent and the ban was lifted, but as one government official told me, "Water quality is an ongoing problem there."

The Potomac ran dark and clear as it approached the discharge of the treatment plant, which serves both the paper mill and the towns. But then, in the middle of the stream, five pipes surfaced from cement casings. Like vents from hell, each of the six-inch-diameter conduits vomited brown water full force. In 200 yards, the whole Potomac turned a manure shade of brown. Above the Luke Mill, seventeen species of fish are found; below the mill, only three bottom feeders scrounge for organics. The undersides of river rocks smelled like rotten eggs for miles downriver.

Evacuating this place and moving 30 miles down to Cumberland—the largest city on the Potomac outside Washington's urban area—Ann and I walked through a scene of colonial and industrial heritage mixed with modern living: here a log cabin George Washington used as an office, there a Mister Donut. Industries along the river lay in ruins, their parking lots sprouting weeds. Earlier, Indians had called their village here Caiuctucus, "the joining of the waters of many fishes." Their name is a reminder of wholesale extinctions during an industrial era in which Cumberland played the role of King Coal.

The Potomac fizzed over a fifteen-foot dam and the suds frosted the water like the first rinse of a washing machine. It smelled poor, but nothing like the way it used to. "You couldn't sit here," a retired railroad engineer told me at a picnic table downstream of Cumberland. "It stunk too bad up until about 1970."

A beneficiary of George Washington's pet project—canal building—Cumberland became the terminus of the Chesapeake and Ohio Canal in 1850. But the same day construction began in Washington, D.C., a competing company broke ground for the Baltimore and Ohio Railroad, which won the race to Cumberland by eight years and captured the business. The C & O nominally survived until floods shut it down in 1924.

What was at first a nostalgic movement to protect the relic canal gained momentum, and Congress created the Chesapeake and Ohio Canal National Historical Park in 1971. Three million people visited in 1993—more than visited Grand Teton National Park. A towpath–bicycle trail touches every canal community along the river and enables one to pedal from Appalachian hinterlands to M Street in Washington. Most of the strip of land between the towpath and the river falls within the national park, forming, in effect, the left half of a river park, 185 miles long. The West Virginia shore lacks protection, but most frontage for now remains undeveloped.

The park I saw represented a compromise between wholesale development and protection. A conservation effort had arisen here after the Army Corps of Engineers in 1963 called for sixteen dams on the river and its tributaries (only Randolph Dam was built). Next, boosters promoted conversion of the canal into a highway. Instead, Secretary of the Interior Stewart Udall recommended national park status for a large corridor, and President Lyndon Johnson asked for a program to make the Potomac "a model of beauty and recreation for the entire country." While supporters backed this unprecedented call for a "national river," local people feared condemnation of private land. The Nixon administration dropped the proposal, and it never resurfaced.

Knowing the importance of bottom-up planning, the Interstate Commission on the Potomac River Basin in 1994 sponsored the Potomac River Watershed Visions Project. Commission staff worked with local communities to clarify their "visions" for this watershed, which is under growth pressure from tidewater to Cumberland. Project director Jim Cummins explained, "We're not proposing new programs. We're just getting people to work together, and it's impressive what's going on. We see growing concern for the river. There are now adults who grew up with an environmental ethic. They see that our rivers define the quality of life."

Having seen the headwaters, I wanted to round out my own vision of the Potomac. So below Cumberland I found a river with enough water to continuously float a boat and launched my canoe for a 153-mile, ten-day trip to White's Ferry, on the outskirts of Washington. Ann needed to interview people in the city for her book, so we said goodby, and I pushed off from shore at Oldtown. The earth-brown waters of the North Branch smelled faintly of distant sewage—an odd odor of organic rot. This was diluted when the North Branch joined the clean waters of the South Branch; then I floated on the main stem Potomac, wide and breezy. The Ridge and Valley profile of Gap Mountain stood tall on the horizon.

In the evening, alongside the bridge at Paw Paw, I came across Jerry Skaggs, a West Virginia fish and game agency employee who picked up barrelsful of trash along the river. He said, "You work and work, and then you get discouraged at something like this. I'm thirsty. I'm tired. I want to go home. But look at this mess. These people are pigs. If you'd pinch 'em, they'd squeal." On better days, Jerry surveys the biology of the South Branch, "a great smallmouth bass stream." Twenty-five years ago he shipped out to Vietnam, but he returned as soon as he could. "I'm a land person," he explained, and he left no doubt that there was only one land—West Virginia, where his family had settled in 1748. I couldn't resist telling him that my ancestors had settled just to the north, along the Youghiogheny River, in 1787, but with his family's seniority Jerry might have just thought I was a newcomer.

Below Paw Paw, the river snaked around twelve bow tie bends in an undeveloped valley. Mussel shells four inches long glinted on the bottom; sycamores four feet in diameter clung to the shores.

The day had been uneventful until two hunters appeared briefly on the left shore and quickly slipped into the woods. Their canvas coats and rifles reminded me of a happy childhood when I hunted daily with my grandfather, plugging rabbits and squirrels whenever I could. A minute later I heard the frightening *pszzz* sound of an airborne bullet. It splashed into the water twenty feet upstream of me, and then I heard the sharp crack of a rifle, a low-caliber model good for squirrel hunting. I was certain there were no squirrels out there. Just on the slim chance that the hunters had fired toward me by accident, I yelled, "Don't shoot this way." I paddled downstream and toward their shore so they would have to come out to the water's edge to take another potshot in my direction.

It was the first time in twenty-five years of canoeing that I had been shot at, and I was still getting used to the idea when I arrived at the recreation site of Little Orleans. Here I picked up some friendlier company—my brother. Together, he and I had often paddled the Youghiogheny at Ohiopyle, Pennsylvania, where we reveled in daylong whitewater excitement. But now we enjoyed the prospect of just drifting on a river neither of us had ever seen. We would find a gravelly campsite along a Potomac riffle.

We loaded Jim's mountain bike on top of our camping gear; he would pedal back to his truck after one day on the water. At dusk we camped on a cobble bar, and in the morning we cruised downstream, engulfed in a thick mist that nearly hid the shores. As the fog burned off, clear water marked the mouth of the Cacapon River, one of the Potomac's larger and finer tributaries, with only one small dam on its 113-mile course. This includes the 29-mile Lost River as the Cacapon's headwaters, which are separated by 2 miles of dry channel where the Lost River flows underground. "Let's paddle the Cacapon next," I suggested to Jim. Too short, my brother's trip ended at Hancock, where I dropped him off at a public ramp. He hid his camping gear in the woods and sped away up the towpath while I waved good-by.

Typical of middle Potomac towns, Hancock shows new interest in its riverfront with a canoe livery and bustling activity along the canal. I met old Kenneth Eiden, who stood around taking in the action and reflecting on seventy years of fishing and trapping snapping turtles. "Everybody here eats 'em, fusses 'bout 'em, loves 'em."

The next morning, from my camp on an island, I watched as a white disk of sun rose through the fog and mist spiraled skyward in miniature versions of a funnel-shaped dust devil. An osprey soared over shores luxuriantly green and gold, water smooth and slow, the bottom blended by gravel and sand.

Later in the morning I muscled through 6 miles of deadwater and past hundreds of cottages and trailers slotted fifty feet from each other. Then I hefted my load around Dam Number 5, built for the Chesapeake and Ohio Canal. This structure and Dam Number 4, downstream, were being restored by the National Park Service. Why not just let the twenty-foot-high dams crumble, I mused, and the river return to its free-flowing channel? An official explanation leans heavily on canal memorials, but a Park Service official leveled with me: "The landowners in the flatwater pools wanted the dams fixed, and you know the kind of political pressure that can be brought to bear." The Potomac Edison Power Company, which is not paying for the repairs, also generates small amounts of electricity there.

Downriver, I looked forward to Williamsport because of its reputation as an old riverfront town on the canal. What I found was a four-foot-high dam dominated by a monolithic power plant. Soon I entered my third reservoir, with 13 miles of deadwater lined by cottages and trailers and then more cottages and trailers. Algae matted the shores in what seemed to be a eutrophic, nitrogen-rich pool.

The next day I reached Shepherdstown, a Civil War fording site. I dragged my canoe into brushy cover and walked the streets of the most attractive town in West Virginia, also the home of Shepherd College. In the bookstore I met Cassie, who had moved from California with her children. "This looked like a good place to raise the kids," she explained, "and my parents had moved here because it's accessible to Washington."

At my camp across the river, the wind blew a blizzard of falling leaves, hinting ominously of winter. Jumping bass startled me at night, and just before dawn I awoke to the leaf-crunching steps of a fisherman. In early morning sun I passed the mouth of Antietam Creek, downstream of the Civil War battlefield where Union and Confederate troops had in one day killed or wounded 28,000 of each other's men.

After bucking a stiff headwind, I encountered the broken remains of Dam Number 3: a litter of cement and rusty reinforcement bars that had once blocked the river. The currents had reclaimed the riverbed, the natural Potomac triumphant after 150 years. I ran a set of rapids called the Needles and drifted through an enchanting maze of rocks to Harpers Ferry, perched on a hillside with walls and steeples, like a stone city of the Rhine. In this vintage Civil War town, the National Park Service has expertly restored dozens of old buildings, but my impressions of the place were swamped by souvenir shops.

Back on the water, I cinched my thigh straps and prepared for some real rapids. As the Potomac's principal tributary, the Shenandoah enters here, and the confluence coincides exactly with the river-created gap through the apex of the towering Blue Ridge. The same sandstone that caps the mountains forms an archipelago of islands. Rocks speckled the width of the Potomac, which pushed through chutes and tongues and over tiny falls.

The sun dipped low. Warm light turned the smooth slicks to golden blue and the foam to sparkling yellow. Half stripped of leaves now, the 1,000-foot Blue Ridge shone purple—the amalgamated colors of bark, twigs, buds, and moist atmosphere. I sat back and sighed in admiration, but not for long. A maze of rocks clogged the right side of the Potomac, so I scrambled a quarter mile over to the left side and soon felt a powerful current flushing me down. At Whitehorse Rapids, the largest on the whole main stem above Great Falls, I blew my opportunity for a clean run by a perverse tendency to cling too far to the right. Heart thumping, I banged into a sharp rock and spun around with a powerful hydraulic chomping on my tail and dragging me back as an alligator might. I braced, recovered, and popped into the pool below.

By map I had picked out an island to camp on, but the Canada geese beat me to it. Not wanting to disturb hundreds of birds' evening rest, I paddled on. At the brink of darkness I found a camp, cooked dinner, and relaxed under a starry night. I sniffed in the damp and earthy smells of autumn on an eastern river, and they stirred memories as only the sense of smell can do. I prized this reach as my favorite on the entire main stem Potomac. The rapids hissed above and below; the islands, in rocky clutter, divided the waters. The front of the Appalachians zoomed up from shore. Writer and agricultural reformer Edmund Ruffin had visited here in 1859 and noted in his published diary that the scene was "very grand, & the rivers beautiful." They still are. Trains rumbled up the valley every now and then, and the geese out in the black night honked, took off, landed, and honked some more.

At sunrise, I paddled back and forth across the fat Potomac, exploring the rocky channels, delighting in the sycamores that shaded the islands, and admiring the river's bottom, half paved in mussel shells. Bundles of water star grass waved in the current like an uncut prairie in the wind. Star grass is a sign of a healthy aquatic system; too many nutrients would allow algae to kill it. Whiskered channel catfish, twenty inches long, sulked in the weeds. In one of those scenes that seems to lie at the heart of Americana, a wader-clad angler cast for bass in morning's bright, steamy light.

At Brunswick, I beached and encountered a trim woman with weathered hands wearing jeans and a flannel shirt, her long blond hair in a ponytail, a sack slung over one shoulder. "You recycling cans?" I inquired.

"No. I'm collecting Sweet Annie. It's in the artemisia family. It smells strong. People use it for fancy wreaths." I recognized the plant as a lacy-leafed invader of Potomac floodplains. "That's it," she confirmed. "It spreads like wildfire. It'll take over the state of Maryland in a few years." She and her husband owned an organic farm. Adjusting her round-rimmed glasses and blue ball cap, she said, "I grew up in New York City, and when I was young in the 1960s and '70s I traveled all over. But here—this is where I belong. Don't you think that some particular place is right for us? But you see what's happening to it!" We talked about the new roads going everywhere, wider roads going there faster, housing tracts snatching up farms, commercial strips spreading like a cancer from the town centers. "Pretty soon Sam and I will have to move to West Virginia, where there are no jobs and no money, but all of it is worthwhile because there's no growth."

Back on the water, the scenic gap of Catoctin signaled the last of the Appalachian Mountains and my entry into the farmed foothills province of the Piedmont. Afternoon cirrus clouds caught my eye, followed by growing overcast, a moist eastern breeze, and a gut feeling that I was going to be hammered with weather.

At night, from the downstream point of a wild-hearted island above the Monocacy River, the lights of the megalopolis—continuous lights from Richmond to Boston—glowed eerie yellow on the horizon. Jets bound for Dulles International Airport tracked the sky. But here at home, two beavers, living as beavers have always done, smacked the water with their tails while I lounged at camp. I was happily surrounded by currents that slicked down both sides of the island and eddied at the point-bar in front of me. On this last night of my trip, I thought of the Potomac as an idyll of eastern canoeing: easy water, mostly undeveloped shores, good campsites, riparian forests, birds, wildlife, and small towns.

It rained all night and continued to rain all morning as I packed a drippy tent and paddled with gusto to keep warm. Off in the gray-streaked, blurred distance, I spotted the barge at Whites Ferry tracking back and forth, a ferry that has been in continuous use since before the Civil War. The rain blew in waved sheets and blotches, and the wind-sharpened drops stung my face. My canoe trip ended there as the radiant autumn turned cold and wet. Ann arrived with the van at noon, and I happily climbed in.

After 24 miles of mostly slow water below Whites Ferry, the half-mile-wide Potomac reaches Great Falls Dam, six feet high, and then Great Falls itself, a must-see on the tour of eastern rivers. In volume, this remarkable cataract is the second-largest in the East, though it is not a tall, clean drop like Cumberland Falls in Kentucky. Here at the urban edge of Washington, D.C., Great Falls is not considered a tourist draw in its own right, but, ironically, if it were in Yellowstone, it would be one of the major stops.

From the Virginia side, one can stand directly over the twenty-foot drop. Just above it, the Potomac churns over rapids and piles up against a hard schist that forces the water around an abrupt corner, staging it to thunder over the falls. Just below, more rapids rip gaping holes in the river through Mather Gorge, which could be the coast of Maine for all its exposed rock. Much like the situation at Niagara Falls, headward erosion has brought Great Falls upriver 9 miles from the original Fall Line at Roosevelt Island and left a trail of intervening rapids.

A few days after my earlier trip on the river, when the lustrous autumn weather returned for one more encore before winter's chill, I drove back to the Potomac below Great Falls and launched my boat again, accompanied this time by Ann in her kayak, my brother Jim in his kayak, and Chris Brown in his canoe. One of America's most seasoned river conservationists, Chris worked as the National Park Service's chief of programs helping local groups and governments protect scores of rivers nationwide. He also helped form the Potomac Conservancy, which aims to save open space along the lower river before it's gobbled up for multimillion-dollar homes. Most of our 8-mile route downstream was an urban oasis of primitive shores and leafy slopes leading up to bluffs where cities sit. Now and then an ostentatious new house with mowed chem-lawns and gross floodlights appeared over the edge of the bluff. But the main impression at eye level was of house-sized rocks, remnants of the Fall Line. At Stubblefield Falls we braced up and over big waves. The autumn twilight showed off the Potomac in Washington as the urban gem that it is; I know of no more desirable reach of undeveloped, free-flowing riverfront in any American city.

Chris knew it all well and guided us to where we had left Jim's truck as a shuttle vehicle. We splashed into an inlet for the C & O Canal where slalom gates had been set up. This training course serves America's best racers; many of them live within walking distance. Washington has evolved as the nation's whitewater racing capital, in large part because the Potomac offers year-round flows with good rapids.

Below our takeout, Little Falls Dam blocked the river as the fifth and final impoundment on the main stem. Then, as tidal water, the Potomac eased past the stone spires of Georgetown University. When I attended college there, I regularly fled upriver to escape the city, taking solace and feeling free again when I was by the water, even the polluted water of 1966.

The Potomac in Washington now represents one of the nation's great cleanup successes, a transformation from typhoid conduit to recreation hot spot. Owing to population increases, raw sewage in the 1960s had exceeded that of years when there was no treatment at all. A fountain in the capital was shut off for fear of windblown mists infecting bystanders with cholera. Requirements of the Clean Water Act finally caught up with recalcitrant industries and federal funding enabled cities to build sewage plants; governments spent $1 billion in the Washington, D.C., area during the 1970s and 1980s. Bass fishing, nonexistent before 1976, is now excellent. Walleye populate Washington, and 120 species of fish survive in the Potomac and its tidewaters. But any smug satisfaction should be reconsidered. Atlantic sturgeon and shortnose sturgeon haven't been seen since the mid-1970s and are probably extinct. The American shad, once hauled into purse seines so heavy that horses pulled them to shore, are nearly gone. The cleanup of the 1970s was mainly one of pollution from cities and industries. Efforts to clean up the beleaguered Chesapeake Bay, where oyster beds offer 1 percent of their historical bounty, still call for a 40 percent reduction of controllable nutrients. If the bay is to be a vital ecosystem and not just a plaything of sailors, efforts to cut pollution from the Potomac, the Susquehanna, and other rivers must be increased, especially regarding the silty runoff from farms. Agriculture contributes 39 percent of the river's nitrogen load. And the population of the region now booms with new growth, troublesome to everything natural in its path.

The wetlands that earlier existed on the riverfront in Washington have long since been filled, but parks line the banks where the Lincoln Memorial, Jefferson Memorial, and Washington Monument rise. In ponds at the Washington Monument, Asian carp that were introduced to America via Europe have spread to play havoc on native fishes. From the north, the sluggish Anacostia River enters; for years it has been a basket case of raw effluent and trashed shores. At this short tributary, sixty agencies have undertaken what they call "probably the most ambitious urban river restoration effort in the United States."

From the monuments and multicultural crowds of Washington, the tidal Potomac extends 121 miles to Chesapeake Bay, for a total river and estuary length of 407 miles from its North Branch source. At wave-tossed flatwater, Ann and I abandoned our boats and bicycled downstream from Roosevelt Island, the 19-mile trail an eyeful of freeway knots, jumbo jets screaming in and out of National Airport, street musicians at colonial Alexandria, forests of southern oak and holly, and big-sky frontage on the brackish estuary. Thousands of bikers, runners, walkers, and roller bladers kept us company on the way to George Washington's estate, Mount Vernon, which overlooks the Potomac in the great plantation style. Later, at its end, the tidal river widens to 7 miles at the broad expanse of the Chesapeake. The Potomac had brought us from Appalachian crest to Coastal Plain and from high country of the East to tidelands of the South.

Chapter 3

Rich Waters of the Coastal Plain and South

The river quivered with alligators, and their number gave me some idea of the richness of that watery place. On a partly sunken log near the bank, one of the reptiles slept half in the stream and half out, its head resting on the back of another alligator. Several babies hid camouflaged on the shoreline, and a large adult lurked with only its nose and eyes out, looking like three unshelled walnuts floating on the Suwannee River until I saw the smooth shine of big black eyes following my every motion. When my canoe drifted past, the river creature simply disappeared—no noise, no ripple, no wake, no blink, no bubble, just gone with amazing stealth. Where was it now?

The South is a land of lazy streams on hot, sultry days, of deep, dark sloughs that might run either way, depending on the water level in the parent stream. Here you can paddle through a forest of baldcypress—not just on a river surrounded by forest but *through* the forest itself, which pretty much makes it part of the river. Here lie brown water snakes basking on logs, and an occasional cottonmouth slips by, its black back cutting a wake in matching water. Near the sea, riverside marshes with cattails, black rushes, and cordgrass wave in the breeze

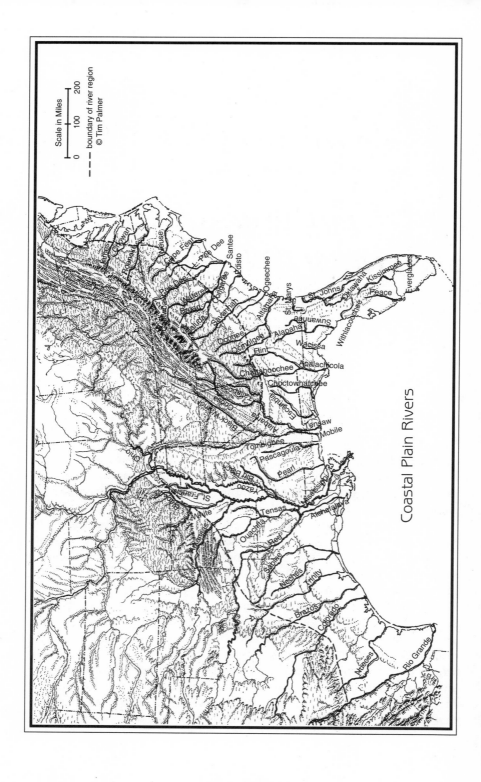

Coastal Plain Rivers

and the tides. Here is the intimate waterway through the swamp, there the monstrous flow of a big, muddy river draining the interior of America and disgorging into estuaries.

The Coastal Plain is more than America's littoral fringe from Cape Cod to Florida; another 38 percent of it runs westward across the Gulf of Mexico's shores to the Rio Grande. Most of New England lacks a coastal plain; the weight of glacial ice literally pressed the land down beneath sea level. Also deprived of a plain, the West Coast drops steeply into the ocean, a result of earthquakes occurring for millions of years. Alaska has its Arctic Plain and another coastal plain at the Yukon Delta, but Alaska is a region of its own. While a smoothly sketched line around the Coastal Plain is 2,200 miles long, its actual shoreline totals 45,500 miles because of myriad embayments, most of them the result of a river or creek entering the ocean.

Composed of soft rocks and sediment, the Coastal Plain extends inland from the Atlantic until it hits the Fall Line of the Piedmont's resistant bedrock. Rivers there typically drop over waterfalls or rapids, announcing their entry into the Plain. Along the Southeast's Atlantic shore, the Plain bulges at one point to a width of 200 miles. All of Florida, which was under the ocean until recent geologic time, is as plainlike as can be in its flatness. Along the Gulf Coast, the Plain grows wider, belted with low cuestas, or ridges that tier up to higher ground, giving rivers a bit more ability to riffle. The southern Plain runs inland—northward—until it borders the Appalachians or the Midwest. The Mississippi Delta portion of the Plain extends upriver for a surprising 550 airline miles to the Ohio River at Cairo, Illinois—once the incision of a great bay at midcontinent. More than one-third of Texas lies on the Plain, which extends to the east central portion of the state until it encounters the Great Plains at the Balcones Escarpment, Texas's equivalent to the East Coast's Fall Line.

Just offshore, flowing from Florida northward, a different kind of river can be found, the largest river of all. This is the 100-mile-wide ocean current called the Gulf Stream, carrying the equivalent of 9,000 Mississippis. Its flow from the tropics keeps the Plain warm up to Cape Hatteras, North Carolina, and somewhat warm as far as Maine. Because of this and its low latitudes, all of the province but its thin, northernmost edge has a humid, subtropical climate. Florida enjoys temperatures 40 degrees Fahrenheit higher than those of much of the Northeast in winter. Though in summer it is only 10 degrees warmer, each degree counts in human comfort, considering that humidity is in the 90 percent bracket. The Plain receives forty to eighty inches of rain per year, and that means a lot of runoff. The rivers spill into their floodplain swamps almost annually, sometimes for weeks or months at a time, and often several times a year in winter and spring. This flooding is critical to a host of plant and animal species. With a different storm season, southern and western Florida are the only places in America where runoff normally peaks in the summer and fall. The lowest flows in Coastal Plain rivers occur in late summer for most of the region. This wet, warm climate and flat, expansive geography provide for a large and distinctive set of rivers.

The vegetation along the streams evolves with fascinating variety, from the hardwoods one might see along the Potomac in suburban Washington, D.C., to the mossy oaks of Faulkner stories and to the palms associated with Caribbean islands. Along the rivers, baldcypresses and tupelos thrive in standing water for months at a time from Virginia southward. Willows occupy sandier soils. Sweet gums and red maples predominate in slightly drier areas. Pond pines and slash pines are at home with their roots in water, and loblolly pines do well in wet or drained soils. From the Pee Dee River in South Carolina southward, the rivers near the coast assume a tropical look, with Spanish moss draped from limbs, monstrous live oaks guarding high banks, each seeming to have a gnarled personality, and fan-leaved palmettos as an understory where it's easy to imagine a panther eyeing some furry meal, though only a few of the great cats survive due to habitat destruction and human occupation of all but the swampiest areas in southern Florida.

Though Cape Cod, Long Island, coastal New Jersey, and all of Delaware are included in its expanse, the bulk of the Plain is in the South. Culturally, this region begins near the mouth of the Potomac—Robert E. Lee's plantation, Strathmore Hill, is as good a starting point as any. It runs to Key West, the southernmost point in the United States except for Hawaii, though southern Florida has many cultural and physical similarities to the Caribbean. Geographer Stephen Birdsall called the South "a culture region" and included not only the Plain but much of the Piedmont and the Interior Low Plateau of Tennessee and Kentucky, along with the southern Appalachians. But regarding rivers, those are other regions. Most of Texas's portion of the Plain has a distinctive culture of farming, ranching, oil business, and new cities of glass and steel. Mexico greatly influences the coast of Texas, now experiencing explosive population growth with legal and illegal immigration and with the big families typical of the area, the Latino culture evident everywhere.

While the culture of the region is increasingly complex, with north-
erners moving south and Mexicans, other Latinos, and islanders moving north in patterns that both mesh and collide, the drainage network
here on the Coastal Plain could hardly be simpler. Rivers flow on direct routes from inland to sea, though within those routes the amount
of meandering in this low-gradient landscape is extreme. The Atlantic
and Gulf Coast watersheds are the basic divisions, with some rivers
reaching the Gulf via the Mississippi. The Texas rivers are often considered as a separate group of watersheds, but they also flow to the
Gulf.

As low as all these watersheds are, with no place on the Plain more
than a few hundred feet above sea level, the region's great extent yields
rivers of at least nine different types. First, many East Coast rivers flow
through low woodlands and then salt marshes at their mouths, a habitat type of extreme productivity owing to tidal recirculation of nutrient-
filled water. Second, New Jersey has its Pine Barrens, a small area of
dark, acidic waters draining pine forests and drifting out to saltwater.

As a third type, rivers of swamps or wooded wetlands farther inland
house the statuesque baldcypress. These black-water streams are the
most archetypal Coastal Plain rivers. Amber where shallow and black
where deep, the water is colored by a high concentration of carbon
from dissolved organic matter coupled with low amounts of sediment.
The sandy soils of these watersheds don't retain the organics leached
from vegetation, which when washed into the rivers yield the characteristic tint. Typically acidic, the blackwater streams have a pH of 4 to
6. These rivers usually rise in swamps and have beds of constantly
shifting sand and plentiful snags of dead trees along their banks. The
black water, sandy beaches exposed during low flows, and lush
swamps beyond the shorelines create a beautiful tricolored pattern of
black, white, and green found only on the Coastal Plain.

In sharp contrast, ten East Coast arteries from the Potomac southward
emanate from the Piedmont and arrive on the Plain, heady and strong
for their lowland push to the Atlantic. These tend to be silty, down
through the Cape Fear River in North Carolina. From the Pee Dee River
southward, many rivers are clear because clay gives way to sand hills
in the southern Piedmont.

A river of far southern Florida occupies a class of its own—the broad
wetland of the Everglades, with water flowing slowly southward. In
central and northern Florida, a wondrous region of springs produces
streams of luminous clarity or rich amber flows. Farther west, the arteries of the Deep South, including Alabama and Mississippi, come as

full-bodied, muddy rivers from the southern interior to the Gulf. Plentiful black-water streams similar to those near the East Coast also drain into the large rivers of the Deep South, if not directly into the Gulf. The Mississippi Delta and its Atchafalaya River and bayous form a distinct hydrologic and cultural area at the mouth of our largest river. Finally, long Texas rivers from the Great Plains cross a wide belt of the Coastal Plain and deliver sluggish, muddy waters to the Gulf.

Even though they were never gouged by ice, river valleys near sea level here in the South show the mark of glaciers. From the once alpine heights of the Appalachians, rivers eroded alluvium, which blanketed the Plain and continental shelf in silt. Then, when glaciers locked up the water, sea level dropped by 200 to 400 feet, enabling the rivers to knife new valleys into the pliable lowland soil. When the ice melted, it flooded these new valleys—evident in the snaking tidal reach of rivers such as the Roanoke—and produced the ragged inlets and bays seen most vividly at the Chesapeake. The Plain has also sunken somewhat, accentuating the effect of flooding at river mouths. Because the eastern shore otherwise consists of endless shallow bays and sandy shoals, these river-carved and then flooded inlets provide the only place for shipping ports, as found in Philadelphia, Baltimore, Charleston, Savannah, and Jacksonville. The better inlets resulted in better ports and larger cities in the north, all because of the rivers' erosion during the ice age.

Now, with sea level higher, an interesting hydrologic and biological mixing occurs unlike that in any other region: the mouths of rivers are interconnected by tidal or brackish water in a process called dismemberment—the rising ocean has flooded what were once confluences of separate streams. The Ashepoo, Combahee, and Edisto Rivers in South Carolina, for example, end in a noodle-mass of sloughs that interweave these rivers at their bottom ends. South Carolina's Waccamaw, Pee Dee, Black, and Santee do likewise, as do many coastal rivers to some degree. A fish can go down one stream and up another. In a braided pattern of low-elevation streams called anabranches, sloughs leave and then rejoin the main channel. These streams are important to a host of freshwater fish and to anadromous species, including the hickory, American, and gizzard shad of the East Coast and the Alabama and threadfin shad of the Gulf Coast. Herrings, alewives, striped bass, sea trout, smelt, and sturgeon up to six feet long also ascend the rivers to spawn. Another forty-nine marine species, regarded as ocean fish, use the sea-level rivers as well.

More than in other regions, these are culminating rivers, with many of the flows originating far inland. Being the terminus of rivers that take their water from the Appalachians, Midwest, Great Plains, Rockies, and deserts of the West, and also being in the wettest large region in the nation, Coastal Plain rivers brim with heavy flows—the third-highest flows among the river regions of America. The Mississippi, second only to the Amazon in volume on the hemisphere, averages 578,000 cubic feet per second at Vicksburg. Above Baton Rouge, some of the Mississippi's water sluices out of its main channel and into the Atchafalaya, the largest "distributary" in the country at 196,700 cfs, counting its Mississippi contribution and sizeable tributaries such as the Tensas and Red Rivers on its western side. The Mobile and Tensaw Rivers—an interconnected network above Mobile Bay—carry 67,200 cfs. Tributaries to the Mobile are the Alabama River, with 24,260 cfs, and the Tombigbee, with 23,500. The Red River, cutting across the Texas–Oklahoma border from the Great Plains, carries 30,870 cfs. The Apalachicola of Florida averages 22,400 cfs. Other big rivers are the Altamaha of Georgia, with 13,770 cfs, the Pascagoula of Mississippi, with 11,800, the Yazoo of Mississippi, with 10,900, the Suwannee in Florida, with 10,400, and the Savannah in Georgia and South Carolina, with 10,200. Some rivers of no exceptional volume have exceptional length because of slender watersheds that parallel each other but never join. The Catawba-Wateree-Santee combination in the Carolinas runs for 540 miles; the Yadkin–Pee Dee for 435 miles.

A historical pattern of changing the names of rivers tends to conceal their great lengths. More than in any other region, rivers of the South are often renamed at the confluences of large tributaries, just as streets are sometimes renamed at intersections. Some single rivers go through three or four different names between their headwaters and the sea. The Catawba becomes the Wateree and then the Santee of South Carolina. Drowning Creek becomes the Lumber River, then the Little Pee Dee. The Mobile River is only 50 miles long, but its upstream extensions are the Alabama, Coosa, and Oostanaula, for a continuous river of 800 miles.

The ample water here failed to make the rivers immune from abuse. Quite the contrary: because there was so much water, people at best took the rivers for granted and usually regarded them as a nuisance. Geographer Peirce Lewis wrote that the Coastal Plain was the "place where Americans first learned the bad habit of plundering fragile environments for immediate profit and then, when the land was exhausted, throwing it away and moving on to repeat the process." Some of the first Europeans coming to America settled here, later converting the land to cotton plantations. Farming depleted soils that were already poor because the intense southern heat enables bacteria to break down organic matter that would otherwise accumulate to make richer, blacker soils, as in the North. The land was logged, then plowed up for cotton and for rice fields in the lowest terrain, then abandoned to pines, and then logged again and again. The soil consequently washed away in the heavy southern rains, leaving iron and aluminum compounds in dirt as hard as cement when dry—a cycle not unlike the current logging, burning, and grazing in tropical rain forests. As the soils deteriorated, the rivers did too, because the rivers are where the soil went.

Today the South produces two-thirds of America's pulpwood, and the results are evident in clearcuts as big as whole cities straddling many of the region's rivers. Following the clearcuts, timber companies plant loblolly pines in rows and douse them with herbicides, creating tree farms of vacuous biology. Soybeans have also played a leading role in reducing the riparian kingdom here. The Mississippi Delta's 3.5 million acres of majestic bottomland forests, unbroken from Illinois to Louisiana, were cleared for cropping only after World War II, making the region one of the few areas in the United States that have been pioneered for cultivation since the 1940s. University of Alabama biologist Arthur Benke, who has studied Coastal Plain streams for more than fifteen years, regarded channelization and destruction of floodplain forests as the most serious cause of their degradation, especially in waters flowing to the eastern side of the Mississippi. The basin of the beautiful Sipsey River—a Tombigbee tributary—was being chainsawed down to its streambanks by timber companies in 1995.

People have drained most of the region to one degree or another for farming, logging, roads, and, now, land development of the Sun Belt boom. Though some of the original intent in drainage was to fight off malaria by eradicating mosquitoes, the "ditch culture" has had dramatic effects on rivers: runoff occurs faster, high flows drop sooner, siltation thickens, and pollution increases. As choice tracts of coastline become built out and unavailable, developers extend drainage works as they turn to the riverfronts of the interior for home sites and locations for whole new cities.

Dams flooded vast areas of lowland rivers, anyplace above the tidal zone being fair game. Canals dug for shipping heaped more ecological havoc on hundreds of streams. The Intracoastal Waterway alone crosses the mouths of thousands of streams and rivers, where dredging and shipping traffic cause incalculable losses to estuarine systems. The damage wrought by this massive canal, running thousands of miles through estuaries from New York to southern Texas, has never received much attention.

While the Intracoastal Waterway was first dredged before people thought much about ecology, we knew better by the time the Tennessee–Tombigbee Waterway was built. This ultimate pork barrel project tops the list of federally sponsored projects in which taxpayers not only allowed rivers to be needlessly destroyed but also paid for their destruction. The Army Corps of Engineers linked these two watersheds to create a shortcut for barges between the Tennessee coal fields and the Gulf of Mexico. The Tombigbee—one of the richest rivers in America for fish fauna, with 115 species—was excavated for 149 miles and shortened by 40 miles. The river bottom was dug up and dumped to fill fifty-one adjacent valleys, ruining the community of life in each. The dredging, filling, and damming spelled catastrophe for freshwater ecosystems of the fragile lowland areas, not to mention the insidious effects of opening up the interior of the country and the biologically unique waters of the Tennessee basin to exotic species. Gaining access through the canals connecting these watersheds, a transfusion of unwanted organisms can now infect sensitive communities of life. All this was done so that coal companies, with a polluting product in declining demand, could have a taxpayer-funded shortcut from their existing barge route down the Mississippi. In its first year of operation, the most costly water project in America's history received only 6 percent of the cargo projected by the Corps. This travesty of economic and ecological justice is a monument to the southern politicians who, as recently as the late 1970s, pushed the project through in spite of reasoned opposition.

Even without projects such as Tenn–Tom grafting the veins of these waterways together into Frankensteins of the riparian world, the rivers of the South are more susceptible to noxious invading species than are those of most other regions. The water hyacinth, which motorboaters say defines the word "pest," clogs southern waterways. It spread like smallpox after people from all over the South attending the 1884 King Cotton Exhibition in New Orleans were given free hyacinths to take home and plant. Hydrilla likewise displaces native vegetation and creates water quality problems.

Where wetlands remain intact they filter nutrients, retard high runoff, allow for decomposition of organic waste, and stabilize water quality. These processes maintain many of the southern rivers, but others become basket cases of pollution. Industries in New Jersey, producing the most volume of toxic waste in the nation, claim the highest noncompliance rate for Environmental Protection Agency permit requirements; 37 percent fail. Delaware has 31 percent noncompliance, and Louisiana, 26 percent. The *Green Index* ranked Louisiana, Texas, Alabama, and Arkansas among the twelve worst states for environmental conditions, with Arkansas and Alabama having some of the worst environmental policies. The chemical and paper industries, with their by-products of acrid air and wastewater, are powerful forces in all these states. Along the lower Mississippi, 136 major industries, mostly chemical and petroleum processors, occupy 150 miles of the river, once known as the Father of Waters but now called Cancer Alley.

The aquatic species of Alabama, which is about two-thirds Coastal Plain and one-third Appalachians, illustrate the wealth and jeopardy of southern waters. This incredibly diverse fauna includes members of 38 percent of native U.S. fish species, 60 percent of mussel species, and 52 percent of turtle species. But 10 percent, 65 percent, and 43 percent of these respective groups are imperiled or already extinct in the state.

Yet the situation isn't all bad. Even with their history of abuse, the Coastal Plain rivers survive in a wetlands regime exceeded only in Alaska, at the other end of the climatic spectrum. Because the shorelines of Coastal Plain streams are usually swamps or marshes, sometimes extending for miles on either side, many waterfronts remain undeveloped. Rivers and wetlands, indeed, are almost synonymous here; the Fish and Wildlife Service's map titled "Wetland Resources of the United States," shows fat, green wetland tentacles along almost every stream. Along the Ogeechee, the floodplain swamp is forty times the width of the river channel. Large blotches of wetlands appear in Florida, and interconnected strings of green bulge like veins along the Mississippi. These stand out as the blankest spots on the map; to find wild country in the East one must look to the swampy lowlands abutting southeastern rivers. The wetlands are a critical source of bacteria and organic matter for the rivers, as described by zoologist Judy Meyer of the University of Georgia. The wetlands are integral to the rivers, and to protect one, the other must be protected also.

Though the Army Corps of Engineers has systematically run snagging operations to dredge submerged wood from the rivers and their banks, many snags remain. The woody debris in a river such as the Ogeechee of Georgia is vital habitat to more than 100 species, mostly invertebrates. Fish feed on these. Food produced on the snags accounts for 60 percent of the stomach contents of half the major fish species in the Satilla River of Georgia. Leaving the snags in place is essential to the biological well-being of these rivers.

Thanks to the health maintained by many rivers of the South, fishing might be considered the regional pastime. The redbreast sunfish of brilliant yellow and orange thrives in small rivers along the entire East Coast to mid-Florida and is a favorite of anglers. Largemouth bass and bluegill, common throughout the South and Midwest, are also popular game fish.

In an interesting analysis, biologist Arthur Benke found that a disproportionate share of the nation's remaining natural, free-flowing rivers are in the Southeast. These states also have less formal protection for rivers than does any other region of high-quality rivers in the country. Map research done for *Currents of the Continent* found more long, undammed sections of river here than in any other region but Alaska (see appendix 2). The lowland geography of the region has saved the rivers; storage dams are far less feasible here because the rivers are simply long corridors at sea level and lack both gradient and adjacent hillsides amenable to dam construction.

Charles Fryling, a professor of landscape architecture at Louisiana State University who has worked for twenty years to protect the Atchafalaya River, has considered the past damage to rivers of the region and their future prospects. "Back when we did all the development of these rivers, we must have had a very strong image of ourselves—the feeling that we could do anything. Now, we see that we need the functioning natural system that we worked so hard to eliminate. We now have to piece together whatever we can with what we have left."

Looking at some of the individual rivers of the Coastal Plain, I notice that small streams drain the northern reaches. The Mullica River flows from the Pine Barrens of southern New Jersey. The Pocomoke of Maryland runs for 73 miles—a long river for the east side of Chesapeake Bay. Some of the northernmost baldcypresses grow along this river, which ends in salt marshes.

Though they come from the Appalachians, the Delaware, Susquehanna, and Potomac debouch onto the northern Plain. Near the mouth of the James River in Virginia, English colonists established their first New World settlement at Jamestown in 1607, but high water and mosquitoes, so common at the mouths of Coastal Plain rivers, plagued the colonists. South of the James, the Nottoway and Blackwater Rivers join to become the Chowan of North Carolina, a long network of mostly undammed and undeveloped mileage.

In North Carolina, the 380-mile Roanoke River emerges from the Piedmont in Virginia and flows to the wetlands empire of Albemarle Sound. People call it the Staunton in its middle reaches and, once again, the Roanoke as it nears North Carolina. Carrying 8,085 cfs, the lower river houses what The Nature Conservancy calls the largest relatively undisturbed bottomland forest in the mid-Atlantic region. Unfortunately, Kerr Dam stopped floods needed to sustain the wetland ecosystem along the river, and without high water, trees such as red maple invade the cypress-tupelo forest. Revised management of the dam, allowing occasional floods, is needed.

Though dammed above Raleigh, the Neuse River flows for 223 unimpounded miles to Pamlico Sound. Formed by the confluence of the Haw and Deep Rivers of the Piedmont, the muddy Cape Fear River drains much of southern North Carolina and carries 3,300 cfs through three navigation dams to a wide estuary. Joining the Cape Fear River near the ocean, the Black River supports cypress trees 2,000 years old—some of the oldest in the East—now protected in a Nature Conservancy preserve. The next big river to the south is the Pee Dee, with 9,850 cfs draining North and South Carolina. Entering the Pee Dee from the northeast, the Little Pee Dee ranks as one of the best lowland canoeing rivers. Drowning Creek and the Lumber River are the upriver extensions of the Little Pee Dee—a combination that flows for 290 undammed miles to the Atlantic. The Waccamaw is an unusual river that parallels the coast for 164 miles in South Carolina and passes swamps, marshes, and old plantations before reaching the Pee Dee near the Atlantic.

The Saluda and Broad Rivers of the Piedmont join to form the Congaree just below the rapids-studded Fall Line at Columbia, South Carolina. Flood flows of this river nourish Congaree Swamp National Monument, where one of the finest bald cypress forests reigns as a remnant of the primeval Southeast. The 9,425-cfs Congaree, dredged four feet deep as a shipping canal, joins the Wateree River, then enters one of the lowest-elevation reservoir complexes in the country. Fifty miles later the water emerges as the Cooper and Santee Rivers interconnected near sea level. Far enough south for palm trees to appear along its lower shores, the Edisto (2,711 cfs), with its South Fork, runs 223 miles with no dams.

As the East's largest state, Georgia has 71,000 miles of rivers and streams. At the boundary with South Carolina the Savannah drifts for 314 miles, but since the Army Corps of Engineers filled Russell Dam in the late 1970s, reservoirs have trapped most of the nontidal river. The Fall Line appears 170 miles above the ocean at Augusta, making the Suwanee one of the longer tidal rivers in America. Just to the south the Ogeechee runs 290 miles, with no dams, to the Atlantic. Draining all of central Georgia, the Altamaha is the state's largest river, running 416

Withlacoochee River, FL

Withlacoochee at the Gulf, FL

Lower Suwannee River, FL

Atchafalaya River Swamp, LA

Mobile River above Mobile, AL

Apalachicola River at Hwy. 20, FL

Suwannee River near Luraville, FL

Suwannee River at Gulf of Mexico, FL

miles when combined with its tributary, the Ocmulgee. In southern Georgia the Satilla is an exceptionally beautiful river of black water, white sand, and verdant shores.

From the Roanoke to the Altamaha, these rivers of the eastern Coastal Plain flow in remarkably parallel lines, a rare pattern world-wide. The land's gentle slope toward the ocean and homogeneous, soft strata allow rivers to erode in an almost uniform fashion.

A wealth of rivers in Florida begins with the black water of the St. Marys rising on the eastern side of the Okefenokee Swamp and then forming the border with Georgia. To the south, the St. Johns is the longest tidal river in America, with an alignment unlike any other. It begins only 7 miles from the Atlantic and isn't even separated by a hill, yet it flows northward and parallel to the coast for a remarkable 325 serpentine miles. Sluggish meanders and tidewater channels thread together a necklace of lakes in this ultimate river of wetlands. Along the way, clear springs illuminated by shafts of light serve as a winter refuge for the endangered manatee. In 1563, Jean Ribaut wrote of oysters in the St. Johns River producing pearls "in so mervelous aboundaunce." In the 1770s, William Bartram traveled on the St. Johns and wrote, "The river from shore to shore, and perhaps near half a mile above and below me, appeared to be one solid bank of fish, of various kinds." The river remains biologically rich but is affected by channelization, infestation by exotic weeds, and land development. A St. Johns tributary, the Oklawaha, meanders in a mile-wide riparian corridor of once-fabulous biological wealth and terminates in the weed-infested Rodman Reservoir, built for the aborted Cross Florida Barge Canal and now sitting useless. The dam will be dismantled if political difficulties can be overcome. The Silver River flows into the Oklawaha with transparent water where needle-nosed five-foot-long alligator gar swim among schools of oval-shaped sunfish. A canoe cruise here offered one of the most revealing windows to underwater life I have ever experienced. Hundreds of springs across central and northern Florida similarly issue from the Ocala Dome, a limestone formation holding one of the largest groundwater sources in the country.

The Kissimmee River, draining broad wetlands and now farms and ranches of south central Florida, takes its name from a mellifluous Indian word meaning "winding waters." But the Army Corps has channelized the river into straight lines in a project called Canal C-38. Excessive nutrients, once filtered out by the marshes, now go straight to Lake Okeechobee, which consequently gags on algal blooms. At a cost of hundreds of millions of dollars, some of the old meanders of the

Kissimmee may eventually be reinstated in one of the nation's most ambitious river restoration projects.

The Kissimmee's channelization, along with diversions, canals, and polluted runoff from sugar-cane fields, contributes to the tragic demise of the Everglades. This "river of grass," once the width of southern Florida, seeped as a sheet flow for 250 miles to Florida Bay. Now it doesn't seep at anywhere near the rate it used to, and pesticides foul the depleted flow while canals lead it in all the wrong directions. Though degraded, the Everglades remain one of the more critical habitats for waterbirds in the United States, and the wetland is one of only two areas outside the West where a person can be more than 10 miles from a road. Efforts to restore some of the ecosystem's quality are plagued by delay, compromise, the political clout of agribusiness, and lack of funds.

In west central Florida, the Withlacoochee's cypress swamp water winds northward, with some sections so currentless I've had to use a compass to find my way out (another Withlacoochee lies in Georgia and northern Florida). The river flows undammed for 140 miles to Rousseau Reservoir, near the Gulf of Mexico. Farther north, the Suwannee also empties into the Gulf.

The panhandle of northern Florida offers a remarkable series of spring-fed, mostly unspoiled streams flowing through baldcypress swamps and salt marshes. Coldwater Creek, Blackwater River, Shoal River, Ecofina Creek, Chipola River, and Wacissa River run with clear or tannin-colored water, many of them slicking over white sand beaches with lush shorelines. The Choctawhatchee flows for 120 undammed miles in Florida and Alabama; nearly all of its Florida frontage is now public open space—an outstanding example of a protected river.

The Apalachicola, draining Georgia and Alabama, is by far Florida's largest river. At the Gulf's Apalachicola Bay it forms one of only three significant ocean deltas in America. Granulated quartz brought from the Appalachians by this and other rivers has accumulated as glistening white sand at the Gulf shore's blue-green edge, creating some of the most beautiful beaches in America. Flat and muddy, not picturesque, neither a famous sport fishery nor a destination of boaters, the Apalachicola is simply one of the biologically richest rivers on the continent. Bridging 524 miles from northern headwaters to southern estuary, this basin supports the highest species diversity of amphibians and reptiles on the continent north of Mexico. The river winds 120 miles through undammed and uninhabited lowlands of northern Florida, where more than 1,000 species of plants grow on a 200-acre sample of ground. The river boasts the world's largest tupelo stands, habitat for ninety-five species of fish, a tidal marsh 6 miles across, and the home of a once-great Atlantic sturgeon and commercial sponge industry.

But all this is in radical decline. Woodruff Dam, at the confluence where the Flint and Chattahoochee form the Apalachicola, now blocks the sturgeon from entering their spawning grounds and stops striped bass from reaching cool upstream waters. Because of diversions and manipulations of flood flows, reductions in freshwater have stressed the estuary, which produces 90 percent of Florida's oysters. Sediment, sand, and nutrients trapped in the reservoir no longer nourish the lower river, Apalachicola Bay, and the Gulf. The Army Corps of Engineers maintains a nine-foot-deep barge channel for minimal commerce, constantly dredging silt and dumping it on the banks in smothering piles up to thirty feet deep. For protection, the Northwest Florida Water Management District has bought 35,000 acres of lower river floodplain, and in 1993 a group of Florida, Georgia, and Alabama officials began work on a plan to devise solutions to the troublesome conflicts on the Apalachicola.

Even the Apalachicola is dwarfed by the Mobile River to the west, draining the rainy state of Alabama. More than 800 miles long, this unusual river system begins with the Oostanaula River of Georgia, which becomes the Coosa. The Tallapoosa later joins to form the giant Alabama River. Near sea level, the Mobile River is formed where the Alabama meets the Tombigbee, whose watershed includes the sizeable Black Warrior River (8,041 cfs). The Mobile soon splits in two, and for 50 miles its channels are called the Mobile and Tensaw Rivers, but both have the same source and the same outlet, Mobile Bay.

The lyrically winding Escatawpa of white sand beaches and dark water crosses from Alabama into Mississippi, a state lying entirely on the Coastal Plain. Farther west, the broad Pascagoula nourishes wide hardwood swamps. With its Chickasawhay River headwaters, it flows 386 miles with no dams. Black Creek, a scenic tributary with a rich diversity of trees ranging from magnolia to American beech, is one of few Deep South rivers in the National Wild and Scenic Rivers System. Bounded by a broad, wooded floodplain, the Pearl River, over 400 miles long, drains the south central portion of Mississippi, with 7,530 muddy cfs flowing at the Louisiana border and a 303-mile undammed reach. Once living in rivers all across the Southern coast, the Gulf sturgeon still survives in the Pearl, Apalachicola, and Suwannee, but an Army Corps of Engineers dredging plan threatens the fish in the Pearl's lower 58 miles.

The bottomland Yazoo River curiously parallels the lower Mississippi before flowing into it. Other rivers, such as the Tensas on the western side of Louisiana, do likewise, and their parallel routes are entirely different from those of coastal streams in the Southeast. The pattern here owes to the Mississippi's prodigious volume of silt. When the Mississippi floods, it deposits silt most heavily where the current first slows down on the river's banks, thus building them into natural levees. With deposition also occurring in the bed of the river, the whole unit becomes elevated relative to the land around it. Eventually the elevation is so great that it keeps tributaries out and forces them along parallel courses.

John J. Audubon called the 190-mile Yazoo "a beautiful stream of transparent water, covered by thousands of geese and ducks and filled with fish." But by 1890 the watershed had been logged and replaced with cotton farms, causing rapid erosion in the rich basin.

From Mark Twain's *Life on the Mississippi* to Jonathan Raban's *Old Glory,* the Mississippi is the most written-about river in America. To call the lower river large is like calling New Orleans muggy. This river is more than half again as large as the next-largest river in America, the Niagara-scale St. Lawrence. The Mississippi's swirling flows, collecting water from the top of the Appalachians to the top of the Rockies, are among not only our most romanticized but also our most polluted.

Departing radically from its adherence to the seashore, the Coastal Plain here extends 1,000 winding river miles up the Mississippi to the mouth of the Ohio River. Separating the river from its riparian ecosystem, levees now constrain the lower Mississippi all the way through the Coastal Plain, past the tidal limit at Baton Rouge, and out to sea.

While the mouths of many East Coast rivers enter embayments that allow the sea to creep far inland, the Mississippi does the opposite; it extends out to sea by flowing through a delta that constantly aggrades with silt deposited into the Gulf. To follow the river toward its end requires a drive along leveed banks that split the 100-mile-long delta lengthwise. Bayou Lafourche runs out similarly to Grand Isle, a rare beach in marsh-edged Louisiana. The Mississippi and its related Atchafalaya River form the most extensive delta in America outside Alaska because the volume of silt here is large enough to overcome the sea's ability to wash it away.

All of the Mississippi Delta's acreage originally arrived as silt in river water, so manipulation of flows today affects not only aquatic systems but the entire landscape. The river is no longer allowed to fan out across the Delta, to spread floodwater over wetlands, to deposit silt on the floodplain, or to nourish shallow Gulf waters in a process that has built the Delta from Cairo, Illinois, to Venice, Louisiana. Instead, confined by levees, the river carries its silt far offshore to deep waters of the sea. This might imply status quo for the landmass of Louisiana except that the land is subsiding as the already deposited silt compacts and depresses the land under its weight. This subsidence is no longer offset by new silt deposits that would otherwise accumulate on top. The net effect is a sinking southern Louisiana, with as much as 50 square miles per year going under water. Shorelines erode and seawater threatens to overtake whole towns, where a dike culture challenges that of Holland. Further, the river now delivers its organically rich nutrients and its troublesome phosphates far offshore, where they throw marine ecology out of balance. And the wetlands that would otherwise be nourished are critical wintering grounds for two-thirds of the waterfowl of the Mississippi Flyway. It's one of those hopeless situations, a result of misusing rivers and land in the most fundamental ways. Short of turning the river loose again over the Delta, there seems to be no solution to this problem; levees and pumps will be fortified in populated and farmed areas as long as local people and taxpayers are willing to pay for them.

Within this Atlantis of the future, many bayous consisting of Mississippi water and local runoff weave down through the Delta, where Cajun country is the home of an American subculture. Levees, towns, farms, and homes line the bayous. Commercial fishing boats dock in long rows and harvest the richest saltwater fisheries in America, but catches have plummeted in recent years because of the distressed river system, the diminishing productivity of wetlands at the coastal edge, and overfishing.

On the western side of the Delta, the Atchafalaya serves as the outlet of the Red River and also as an oversized slough of the Mississippi. This distributary (the opposite of a tributary) diverts a third of the big river's flow and carries it along with other waters to the Gulf as a secondary outlet of America's largest river. The Atchafalaya and its overflow areas—contained by levees but still 15 miles wide—include the largest river swamp in America, primal and strange with cypress-tupelo-willow forests, a jungle of birds, a reptileland of alligators, and a diversity of fish in a southern sauce of life. Interstate 10 crosses the swamp on a bridge 17 miles long—probably the longest continuous bridge in America. With its perpetual influx of nitrogen-rich Mississippi water, the Atchafalaya is three and a half times more productive than the Everglades. Once when I was canoeing there, an eighteen-inch-long fish leaped into my boat and flopped on the floor until I lifted it out. Plagued for years by levees that squeeze the swamp into half its original size, by drainage canals, by oil drilling, and by farms, the Atchafalaya has been the subject of a long campaign for better management. Much of it is now protected, though a program of easement acquisition requiring federal funding needs to be completed.

If left alone, the Mississippi would naturally "jump" into the Atchafalaya channel, as this alternate route reaches the Gulf in 140 miles, compared with the 300-mile levee-bound course in which the Mississippi is trained to heel past New Orleans. To switch from one channel to another has in fact been the nature of the Mississippi since it began. A "control structure"—America's largest headgate—blocks the Atchafalaya's upstream inlet, where the Corps regulates the volume of water and thus maintains New Orleans as a seaport that handles more tonnage than do the docks of any other American city but New York. The Atchafalaya also diverts floodwaters away from New Orleans. The likelihood that we will succeed in telling the Mississippi what to do in the long term is doubted by some people, a problem depicted in John McPhee's *The Control of Nature*.

Moving west to the Louisiana–Texas border, I see the Sabine River with an undammed reach of 264 miles and its swamp water running to the Gulf. This is one of the westernmost rivers of abundant rain and southeastern vegetation. The Neches River comes from the biologically rich Big Thicket area of Texas. The Trinity (7,417 cfs) winds 360 miles from Dallas and Fort Worth, where it was nearly destroyed for construction of a barge canal in the 1970s, but Ned Fritz and a band of Texas conservationists worked until the project was stopped.

The Coastal Plain rivers farther west and south across Texas reflect drier country; oaks dominate on well-drained benches above the waterways. The Brazos runs for 1,280 miles but carries little water to the Gulf owing to diversions. The Colorado River of Texas runs for 860 miles but delivers a scant 2,685 cfs. The Guadalupe in its upper reaches offers some of the best whitewater canoeing in the state. Finally, the last several hundred miles of the Rio Grande cross the Coastal Plain before reaching the Gulf.

Reflecting on the vast collection of Coastal Plain rivers, Barry Beasley of South Carolina said, "These rivers are deep in the heritage of the people who live here. Your grandaddy might have taken you out to catch your first bass, and going to the rivers becomes a part of your values system. These swamps and streams are not just a natural asset but contribute to your whole identity. Fishing and trapping are what people *did* in other areas of the country, but here they never quit." Barry directs the state's scenic rivers program—the most successful one in the South. He added, "Though there has always been an interest in and love of rivers, there has not been a constituency working for them. But people with a new involvement in conservation are beginning to build a bridge to the old, traditional interests."

The Suwannee River

Many rivers of this region begin in the Appalachians or their foothills, but the Suwannee, rising quietly in a baldcypress swamp, is all Coastal Plain. Though Ann and I began our Suwannee trip in January, the air was moist and charged with springtime and felt like a tonic in our winter-weary lungs. The days seemed all the more brilliant for their shortness, and the mosquitoes and no-see-ums annoyed us only at times. We would see the Suwannee by both canoe and van.

In southern Georgia we paddled into the Okefenokee, one of the larger swamps in the country, more than 80 percent protected as a national wildlife refuge. Against the scarcely seen current, we stroked upstream toward the high point of the Suwannee River, Big Alligator Creek, 285 miles from the Gulf but only 120 feet above it. The trunks of second-growth cypress—one and two feet in diameter—fluted out in buttresses to wide bases in the waterlogged ground. Our route slipped between trees and into groves having a cathedral-hush.

After a few hours of exploring upstream, we returned and continued downriver. A bristly-whiskered otter surfaced, stared at us, hissed, and swam on, rolling up for air like a dolphin. A raccoon trotted along the shore through a tangle of brush. Turtles sunned themselves on logs and plopped into the water when the raccoon came near. The entire river supports sixty-five species of freshwater fish, not an especially large number; the diversity that is common just to the north diminishes to a more limited fauna indicative of peninsular Florida's young geologic age.

From the branch of a tupelo, a squirrel belly-smacked into the water, swam to the next tree, and ran up its trunk. Other than that, it was as quiet as a calm day in the desert, the stillness lending a reverence to the place while the glassy water reflected mirror images of black-trunked baldcypress backed by deep blue.

Near the bottom end of the refuge, a three-foot-high dam, or "sill," blocked the Suwannee. This unusual structure was built following forest fires in 1955 to raise the water level in the swamp and keep it wet and unburnable. The Fish and Wildlife Service has undertaken new studies to evaluate the effects of the sill on the swamp's ecosystem with the possibility of removing the dam, an action that would make the Suwannee one of the longest completely undammed rivers in the East.

We portaged our gear around the sill, then navigated through a dense tupelo forest lacking any clear channel, our canoe clunking on logs. The river soon consolidated, and we wound downstream on a serpentine route while pileated woodpeckers hammered on dead trunks and the wings of wood ducks whistled when the birds were flushed.

Where palmettos and pines indicated a drier bank, we pulled up to camp, halfway through a 22-mile reach with no development. The moon rose through the mossy limbs of cypresses and we sat quietly, listening to the hooting of three barred owls, the whistle of a screech owl, the slap of a beaver's tail, a curious "kluk-kluk kluk," a mysterious "lu lu lu lu," all of it tuned to a concertlike pitch of swamp life.

The next day it rained steadily, and we paddled steadily to keep warm. Chain saws whined in the distance now that we were beyond the national wildlife refuge. In clearcuts behind timbered setbacks, trees on thousands of acres were being sawed and the slash bulldozed into piles for burning. The lunar look of the logging operations was exceeded only by phosphate strip mines farther downriver, also set back from the water.

After hundreds of tight bends we arrived in Fargo, the first town along the Suwannee. Half a mile from the river, a railroad crossing was followed by a water tower on stilts, modest houses peppered about, a restaurant with trophy heads and fish on the walls, and friendly residents with deep drawls. The river access area looked as if a garbage truck had crashed there. A whiskered man arrived in a rusty red pickup and warned me, "Plenty a' gaters. Gaters eat dawgs. Boys'll go huntin' with the dawgs and the gaters'll git 'em."

Some miles later, the White Springs Shoals rumbled up ahead, one of few rapids in Florida. Here the Suwannee rushed over a ledge that created a steep wave spanning the river. We scouted, slipped through a slot on the left, and farther downstream approached the town of White Springs, perched on the northern bank. If you enter the town by road, your eye catches signs near the bridge that announce "Approaching Suwannee River," the words set with notes on a musical staff. Here and in other towns, people seem to have capitalized on the river's name more thoroughly than at any other river in America. At Live Oak one can find Suwannee Travel, Spirit of the Suwannee Campground, Suwannee Blueberry Farm, Suwannee River Log Homes, and Suwannee River Auto Parts, all named more for a song than for a river. Stephen Foster's "Old Folks at Home" ("Way Down upon the Swanee River") may include America's best-known river name in musical lyrics, yet the composer never even saw the place. When Foster wrote the tune for a minstrel show in 1851, his first choice, the Pee Dee River, wouldn't do, so he settled on this river and spelled it "Swanee." Stephen Foster State Park's manager, Bob Boyne, said, "People come from all over the world just to say they've seen the Suwannee River, and it's all because of that song."

After pulling the canoe out at White Springs, Ann and I sat down at the Hometown Cafe for breakfast and overheard a man say, "The boys went fishin' this morning at four. Why didn't you go?"

"'Cause I'm workin' on your car, and that's the only reason."

A friendly police officer warned us against camping in town. "There's some bad people in this town. You can get robbed. There were two murders last month. It looks nice here, and it is, but we have our problems, same as anyplace else. Hey, Florida is the crime capital of America." Comparing his work in White Springs with his past experience in the tough town of New Haven, Connecticut, the officer said, "Here you have every kind of problem and no backup."

The swampland of Suwannee had given way to a stream of deep, black water bordered by limestone rocks and gray bluffs sprouting with plant life. In this karst topography, sinkholes lie behind the banks where water has dissolved the limestone and the ground has caved in. Above Suwannee River State Park, the Alapaha River enters, a sizeable stream of 205 undammed miles. Probably the largest river in America that runs plentifully on one day but disappears by natural causes the next, it slips into caverns resulting from dissolved limestone. Downstream of the state park the Suwannee becomes wider and its deep, black water turns cloudy. Flows from crystal-clear springs begin to augment the river, the limestone aquifer ultimately contributing one-fourth of the river's total flow.

Seeking out Running Springs because we had heard it was undeveloped and looked "like a Tarzan movie," we bounced along a dirt road to a thick forest of oaks. Globs of trash littered the ground. A young man worked under the hood of his pickup truck; I lent him a wrench and gave him a spare hose and clamps so he could splice his fuel line. Nearby, we found a spring of utterly clear water twenty feet across and a hundred feet long, the artesian flow boiling up at one end, the current of a small creek riffling into the broad Suwannee through a narrow opening in the riverbank. Girthy live oaks along with southern magnolias, pignut hickories, Florida maples, and American hollies shaded an understory of palmetto surrounding the spring. People with four-wheel-drive vehicles had gouged out a track almost into the spring, and heavy rains had washed silt down the tire tracks and into the water. I waded out to remove a Styrofoam cup in order to take a picture. Without the trash and tire tracks, I could imagine a "dreamlike quality," as the great Florida naturalist Archie Carr had described the Suwannee's springs.

The man working on his truck said he thought we'd have no trouble camping there but warned that it was Super Bowl Sunday and you couldn't tell what might happen, and that the police might come through because a woman had been killed at the site. We drove off a distance and slept in the locked van.

Even though I was up at dawn, I found an older man and woman already fishing near camp. "What kind of fish do you catch?" I asked.

"Perch, mostly," the man replied.

"And largemouth bass?"

"Yes, lots of bass here."

"And catfish?"

"Oh yes, catfish, lot of them too."

"And sturgeon?"

"Sometimes, but not now. They're down in the ocean now." Weighing up to 400 pounds, the Atlantic sturgeon here are one of the few reasonably functioning populations of Gulf sturgeon in the United States, the others eliminated by dams and channelization on the large rivers.

Peacock Springs, nearby, was well maintained because it's a state park. Two scuba divers strapped on tanks to explore one of the largest underwater cave systems in the country, with 28,000 feet of explored passages. "When you're under water, a hundred feet seems like a thousand," one of the men said. It's easy to get lost; a sign warned that forty-five divers had died there since 1960.

Progress has been made in cleaning up some of the springs by providing the maintenance that these natural wonders deserve. Government agencies have acquired or rehabilitated some sites by blocking vehicles from the water and building steps so that swimmers walking in and out don't crumble down the banks. But even more troubling than recreational misuse, nitrates in the springs are on the rise as dairy farmers move up north from urbanizing southern Florida.

Protecting some of the springs and many miles of riverbank, the Suwannee River Water Management District has acquired important frontage as open space. Each group of river basins in Florida has a similar district, formed under state law and having acquisition and regulatory powers. By 1994 the local district had bought more than 54,000 Suwannee acres, bringing total public acreage in the basin to 110,000. This includes 170 miles of frontage along riverbanks, mainly of the Suwannee. The program is possible because of a $.50 tax per $1,000 of value on real estate transfers. With related bond issues, Florida agencies have recently spent $325 million per year buying land, exceeding by a wide margin the money spent buying open space anywhere else in the country. California ranks second and the United States government third. Since 1970, state agencies have bought about 1.3 million acres for $1.4 billion. Significant frontage on the Apalachicola, Choctawhatchee, Escambia, Withlacoochee, Myacca, and St. Johns Rivers has been protected. The acquisition efforts, together called the Save Our Rivers program, constitute one of the great successes in river preservation in America. By the year 2000 the major bond acts will expire, and much of the funds from the real estate tax will be needed simply for management of the land. "If we don't save it now, it won't be done," said Ruark Cleary, land acquisition coordinator for the state. "We're in a race with the developers."

While much of the Suwannee has been saved, it's been a long and arduous struggle, with Florida Defenders of the Environment playing a key role. A long series of studies, committees, and task forces has spanned the terms of every governor since 1978. Each has recommended better management of the floodplain and each lacked effectiveness in getting the job done. In spite of persistent county opposition, the trend has been toward better controls on both sewage disposal and development.

Moving on, Ann and I came to Branford, which calls itself the "spring diving capital of the world." We stopped for breakfast at the Gathering Cafe, where a man walked in after us and asked, "Is that your rig? I want to go to Wyoming too. There's nothing here." He complained a lot while guzzling a cup of coffee.

Another man took a seat at the counter. "I've traveled all over the country, and right here is the place. It has the rivers and everything. I came up from the South, bought a boat hull, built onto it, and live there. You can go up and down the river. It's a good place to live."

Checking out his section of the Suwannee, I launched the canoe at Branford in a rainstorm so hard that drops smacking the water made bubbles the size blown with bubble gum. The rain seemed to float as smooth slicks on top of the river; perhaps it did float, being warmer than the river water. I bailed three gallons of rainwater after the first half hour of paddling. On gray, rising waters I passed some cabins and homes, but elsewhere oaks, pines, baldcypresses, and palmettos clothed the land. The banks were caving in; on fair days, hundreds of motorboats ply up and down, throwing constant wakes ashore. At one stand of mature timber I beached, walked beyond the bank, and spread my arms to measure a live oak's four-foot diameter. An even larger baldcypress grew in a wetland that dipped low behind the riverbank.

Downstream, the Santa Fe River entered from the left. Its 2,150-cfs span is wide enough that some people motoring upriver take the wrong turn into the Suwannee's major tributary and get lost. The Santa Fe comes from central Florida and picks up the Ichetucknee River, whose vivid carpet of aquatic grass waves in a 100-foot-wide, crystalline current.

The Suwannee grew larger and cleaner with the goodness of many springs flowing in, and below the commercial strip at Old Town, the river again carried the dark water of the swamps. Yet it lacked the clarity described by naturalist William Bartram in 1773 when he wrote of a lower Suwannee "almost as transparent as the air we breathe; there is nothing done in secret except on its green flowery verges."

Where verges were once covered with forests, tangles of slash lay in heaps amid mazes of logging roads. Bulldozers had plowed up some cutover areas as if they were a field of soybeans. But farther downstream, the riverfront is in the Lower Suwannee National Wildlife Refuge. Extending to the Gulf of Mexico, it embraces an important part of the Gulf Hammock Forest, which once ran for hundreds of miles along the northwestern coast of Florida and was called "America's only jungle." Nearly all of it has been logged since the 1960s by industrial timbering operations, after the state turned down an offer to buy large tracts at bargain rates. A forest of oak and red maple yields to baldcypress in low areas and to cabbage palms scattered with a tropical flair in one of the least-developed estuaries of Florida.

Leaving the 300-yard-wide main stem, now influenced by tides, Ann and I paddled up a tributary until baldcypress knees choked the channel, which I imagined as a backwater of the Amazon. Great egrets and terns speared fish, a turtle swirled the water where it sank from sight, and hungry bass flopped at the surface.

The tide turned against us and a headwind pushed into our faces, but we saw the settlement of Suwannee not far ahead. During my last visit, in 1978, the place had had the comfortable feel of a backwater fishing community, run-down but colorful. Now it felt like swamp suburbia, with hundreds of homes and trailers. Each house had a boat, and many of them were sheltered under roofs equipped with electric winches to hoist the craft up. The whole town was latticed with canals dug into the marsh. Septic tanks for everyone were also in the marsh—cited as the suspected cause when health officials took Suwannee oysters off the market after consumers got sick. The pollution put the commercial fishermen out of business. With most of the buildings lying seven feet below the flood level of hurricane storm surges, Suwannee village received federal disaster relief to rebuild after Hurricane Elena in 1985. The money could have been used to relocate, but instead a bad situation only grew worse as the area became increasingly popular. Government funding for a $7 million sewage plant is now being debated, though much of the area could be bought for less money while eliminating the sewage problems, the flood damage, and recurring disaster-relief expense.

Fishing was the big activity there, the spotted sea trout *(Cynoscion nebulosus)* being the catch of choice. An angler showed me his creel of eighteen-inch-long, speckled fish, not really trout but drum. "These aren't so good," he apologized. "The netters get all the fish. They net illegally in the river and legally within a 3-mile limit. Texas and Louisiana restricted commercial netting, and in three years they had the best fishing ever. Not here. Since the state wouldn't take action, we've put it on the ballot to ban net fishing within 3 miles of shore." The ban passed later in 1994.

While Ann worked in the van the next day, I entered the realm of the sea trout by canoeing beyond the marshy subdivision to where the river widened and spilled among Gulf shore islands. Corkwood, more buoyant than its namesake, replaced tupelo in mangrovelike clusters. Red cedars, live oaks, and red bays grew on rises of shell middens that had been piled up by Indians as they dined on clams and oysters over a span of hundreds, if not thousands, of years. As I entered the Gulf, the shorelines supported black rush and spartina as marsh grasses, while an occasional cluster of palms waved like flags of a tropical nation. The outgoing tide made me wonder if I'd be pulled farther than was wise to go or if I'd be sucked seaward on the return trip. But the wind was breathless, and I longed to follow the Suwannee to its new life in the sea. Avoiding the dredged channel, I took a less-traveled route to the south. The last palm behind me, I passed a half acre of wet-rooted grass; beyond it lay water extending to the curvature of the earth and beyond. The Gulf of Mexico—utterly calm and unblemished—mirrored the blue-gray sky.

I drifted with the tide into broad waters. Not quite covered, the beds of oyster shells made an abrasive bar half a mile beyond any island. Birds congregated to the north: gulls, cormorants, and oystercatchers. Twenty pelicans bobbed as a shining island of white in an enormous space under the southern dome of sky. So perfect was the match and so gentle was the intersection of elements that the horizon line evaporated in merging light; the river, the sea, and the sky were all one piece.

Chapter 4

——

The Midwest:
Flowing against the Grid

The rivers in the Midwest once defined the look of the land. Riparian forests grew tall, and the waters drew the eye to their edges, to their shine, and to their movement, much as a formation of flying geese dominates a wide, open sky.

The grid has now taken over. Arrow-straight roads parallel or crosshatch each other on a checkerboard of fields. For the past hundred years settlers have shoved the streams aside and made them as straight as the roads, lined them with riprap, and filled them with silt. The rivers were bridged and almost forgotten. Viewed from an airplane, many waters in the heart of the Midwest resemble not so much rivers as flooded highways with banks of engineered precision, the whole scene resembling a schematic drawn with a ruler and protractor and crisply outlined by levees.

No other large landscape is used up more than the agricultural Midwest. Out to the horizon farmers crop every parcel, the fields of one owner abutting those of another with scarcely a dandelion in between. Furrows nip at the shoulders of the roads; corn tassels rise so close to creeks that they shade them in late afternoon. Even the East Coast

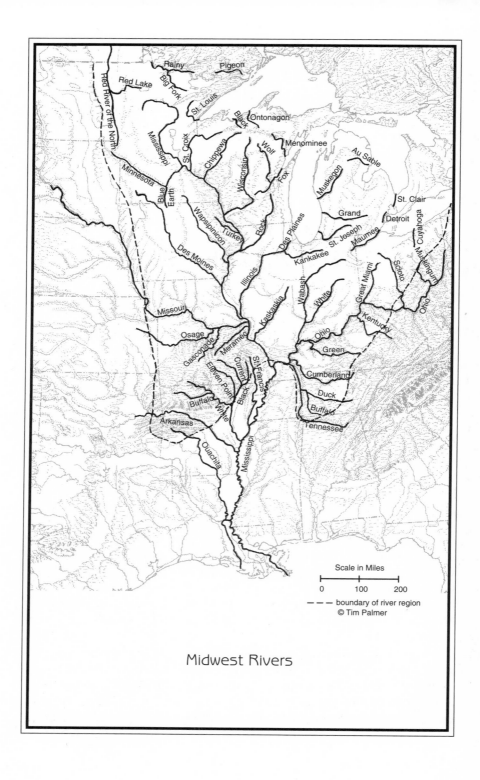

Midwest Rivers

megalopolis has more intervening swatches of woodland and native life on steep hills and along streams.

The eastern boundary of the greater Midwest lies at the base of the Appalachian foothills and extends down through Ohio, central Kentucky, and Tennessee. To the south, the Midwest meets the Coastal Plain in Missouri and Arkansas. It meets the Great Plains region of rivers at the western edges of Minnesota, Iowa, Missouri, and Arkansas; though rainfall indicates that the Midwest runs slightly farther, the long rivers of the Plains dominate to the west. To the north lies Canada, whose own Midwest extends still farther. The bulk of the American Midwest is the Central Lowland defined by the geographer N. M. Fenneman, and to the Midwest river region I add the small Superior Upland of the north, the Interior Highlands of the Ozark Plateau and Ouachita Mountains in Missouri and Arkansas, and the Interior Low Plateaus of western Kentucky and Tennessee. Without these three aberrations, the Midwest would describe a fairly monotonous region of silty rivers through gridded farmland. With them, it offers surprising diversity.

In this large region rivers span great latitudes, longitudes, and climatic zones. So distinct are the seasons here that some places see an annual fluctuation of 150 degrees Fahrenheit. High flows in the rivers typically occur in spring to the north, after the water is unlocked from ice, and in winter to the south. Low flows occur in late summer and fall.

Moving from east to west, the great emerald room of the Appalachian foothills gives way to squares of farms reflecting flatter terrain. Streams wind through the fields, and from the air their bordering greenbelts appear with sharp edges at the upper tips of their drainages, which lie in the shape of a thistle leaf. Plowed fields snip off the tips of green wherever it's dry enough to cultivate, though from the air the thistle-leaf pattern still shows as darker moist soil. To the west, the climate becomes drier and the riparian evidence diminishes, eventually becoming limited to the curved routes of major rivers, with the rest of the land under cultivation. The glinting house and barn roofs grow farther apart as the Midwest rises imperceptibly into the Great Plains.

The biological communities reflect all these changes. The large eastern deciduous forest blends into prairie, where grass once grew nearly everywhere. Trees still line wide corridors, where floods and shallow aquifers provide needed water. Not only are the floodplains more suitable for trees, but they are also less accommodating to grass because floods wash away leaves that otherwise rot into humus, and the silt becomes tightly packed. Many riverfronts here are also too wet for the colonies of ants and earthworms that elsewhere aerate the soil to the porosity needed for grasses.

Domestic crops have replaced the native grasses that once grew above the floodplains. In this heartland of American agriculture, fields of corn, soybeans, wheat, and hay run out beyond the four horizons. The corn belt, centered in the middle of Illinois, covers parts of eight large states where land is used for plowed fields, feedlots, and pig farms. This coincides with what used to be the tallgrass prairie, a splendid sea of ten-foot-high grass, virtually all of it now gone. The dairy belt takes over just north of the corn belt and extends to the north woods of Minnesota, Wisconsin, and Michigan, where longer winters rule in a heavily glaciated land of shallow, sour soils covered with connecting lakes, wetlands, and streams.

Nearly all the region is drained from north to south by the Mississippi River. Even waters of the far north used to flow southward; meltwater emptied over glacial "spillways" to the Mississippi, Minnesota, Wisconsin, Illinois, Wabash, and other rivers. After the ice receded, lower passages to the north and east allowed the northern waters to flow to the Great Lakes and the St. Lawrence basin.

The types of rivers here differ less dramatically than in most other regions, but there are definite distinctions. Many waters fit the mold of slow-moving, muddy streams through farm country composed of wind-blown soil called loess—glacial silt picked up by air and redeposited in a wind-worked flatness. Rivers of western Ohio; most of Indiana, Illinois, and Iowa; southern Michigan, Wisconsin, and Minnesota; and northern Missouri fit this bill. Streams typically begin in rivulets that have been trenched as drains in farmed fields. Many waterways are channelized, but some sections remain intact as natural rivers meandering through the flats. The streams eventually graduate to large rivers lined by levees but also with some substantial floodplain corridors.

Contrasting remarkably, the rivers of the far North are cousins to the fabulous streams of the Adirondacks and Maine—clean water turned amber with dissolved organic matter from bogs, banks dense with evergreens and hardwoods of the north, runoff tumbling over waterfalls of the Canadian Shield's exposed bedrock and into Lake Superior. Just to the south lie rivers of the glacial edge—streams of the upper Midwest and its dairy belt winding pastorally around the humpbacked glacial drumlins, cutting through the gravelly remnants of moraines, riffling to Lakes Michigan and Huron or to tributaries of the upper Mississippi. Occasional bluff-bordered rivers reflect new routes where streams were diverted when the ice blocked ancestral paths. In the southeastern portion of the Midwest, rivers of the limestone plateaus wind slowly from hill country of mixed farm and forest. To the southwest, the Ozark Plateau and Ouachita Mountains produce clear, spring-fed rivers through rolling or rugged country and across gravel bars shaded by sycamores, black willows, eastern cottonwoods, and silver maples. These hills constitute one of the choice river subregions of America and are popular for fishing and canoeing.

For giant-sized rivers, no other region but Alaska rivals the Midwest, though many of the waterways originate and mature in neighboring regions first. Here lies the mouth of the Ohio, which averages 281,000 cubic feet per second, most of it coming from the Appalachians. The Mississippi is not the largest river of the region but its second-largest, with 198,000 cfs above its confluence with the Ohio (the huge Mississippi of the Coastal Plain begins below the confluence). The Missouri, lying mostly in the Great Plains, carries 76,200 cfs to its confluence with the Mississippi. The Tennessee, principally a river of the Appalachians but joining the lower Ohio, carries 68,000. The Arkansas River flows at an average of 40,290. This river extends west to the crest of the Rockies, but most of its flow comes from rainy Arkansas. The White River of Arkansas carries 29,510 cfs; the Wabash, on the Indiana–Illinois border, flows at 27,440; the Illinois has 21,980; and the Rainy, on the border of Minnesota and Ontario, carries 12,830. The Cumberland—another Appalachian river ending in the lower Ohio—averages 11,830. Of these, the Mississippi, White, Wabash, Illinois, and Rainy are purely rivers of the Midwest, owing nothing to other regions.

Because of the rivers' size, central location, and low gradient, this network of waterways plays a prominent role in American history and culture. Many people imagine an inaccurate stereotype of Indians canoeing up and down rivers all over North America, but in the northern Midwest, that image was real. The Chippewa of the northern regions were the archetypal river people, crafting birch bark into canoes and harvesting wild rice. Since the epic trip of Marquette and Joliet down the Mississippi and up the Illinois River in 1673, rivers have served as transportation routes for white explorers and settlers through the core of the continent; Indiana and Michigan are the only states not named for a river that provided transit. The low elevations made it easy to portage from one stream to another in the glaciated North, where slopes of glacial gravel created the only barriers between basins as significant as the St. Lawrence and Mississippi. Portage trails, canals, roads, and interstate highways followed in many of the same courses earlier washed by glacial drainage channels that carried water south. Access to the Great Lakes via the St. Lawrence and later the Erie Canal was extended to the interior by a course going up the flat Chicago River to its interlocking headwaters and down the Illinois and Mississippi—a route that very nearly drains Lake Michigan to the Gulf of Mexico. Other portages included the Bois Brule–St. Croix, linking Lake Superior to the Mississippi. A route up the Fox River from Lake Michigan led to the Wisconsin River and the Mississippi. Explorers, trappers, and settlers also floated down the Ohio and then traveled up the Mississippi 140 miles to the Missouri, which they ascended to the Rocky Mountains. The Mississippi later served as an unequaled navigation corridor up and down the core of the country, and stern-wheelers plied the Ohio, Missouri, and other tributaries. After the Army Corps of Engineers channelized, dredged, and locked thousands of miles of waterways, towboats pushed barges on the largest rivers and on the Arkansas, Wabash, Cumberland, and other arteries.

With the waters of the Midwest being used so much for travel and settlement, a literature of American rivers was born here; Mark Twain's *Life on the Mississippi* is the seminal piece. That literature leans heavily on writings about navigation and has colored people's attitudes and expectations about rivers far beyond the Midwest. Nationwide, a modern awareness is tied to the adventure of traveling the waters in canoes, kayaks, and rafts. More important, a new river literature based on the life and ecological importance of the waters is just beginning to form and to supplement the 100-year-old tales of smoky midwestern steamboats and feisty westbound settlers.

Even in Mark Twain's time, wild rice—a staple in the Indians' diet— grew plentifully along rivers in the northern Midwest. Not much of this food can be gathered today because it requires clean water and healthy flows. Streams in the heart of the Midwest now rank as our most universally polluted. Runoff from fields and feedlots bears nitrates, phosphates, pesticides, herbicides, fertilizer, animal waste, and sediment. Agricultural runoff constitutes nearly two-thirds of all water pollution in America, ruining groundwater and drinking supplies in some sections of the Midwest. Pesticides are the leading cause of fish kills nationwide. Sedimentation of streams is driving some species to extinction. The eastern sand darter, for example, burrows in sand, leaving only its eyes visible, then rushes out to catch invertebrate prey. With the sand being glued over by mud, the fish has disappeared from much of its range, which once included all of Ohio.

Eroded soil is the source of the polluted runoff and also represents a critical loss for farms. Sediment in streams is worst in the desert and

Great Plains regions, followed by the Midwest. The Department of Agriculture considers one in every four acres of cropland nationwide as "highly erodible," and the Worldwatch Institute reported that each one-inch loss of topsoil in the corn belt causes a 6 percent reduction in yield. The Food Security Act of 1985 called for erosion control plans on highly erodible soils by 1995. If farmers fail to comply, they are to lose federal price supports and other benefits that now play a large part in the economics of farming, but enforcement of the provisions is another problem. The Natural Resources Conservation Service (formerly the Soil Conservation Service) and state agencies promote water quality improvements including better management of crop residue, contour plowing, buffer strips, windbreaks, gullies planted with grass, and water diverted around feedlots, but agriculture has escaped mandatory requirements. Unfortunately, the Conservation Service also continues to promote channelization, aggravating erosion.

The region contributes more than its share of point-source pollution as well. Ohio was the second-worst state lacking compliance with water quality standards for industries and sewage plants in 1991. The *Green Index* reported Ohio, Indiana, and Illinois among the worst twelve states for environmental conditions, and the rivers of these states reflect everything we do to the land. Agricultural development in the Midwest has also resulted in the draining of millions of acres of wetlands—the greatest wetland losses in America. In many areas a majority of the streams are channelized, eliminating riparian corridors. State officials report that 30 percent of Illinois's total mileage is channelized, which may be a conservative estimate. This causes aggravated riverbed and bank erosion and thus worsens siltation problems, dramatically seen in areas such as the Lake Erie plain of Ohio, Indiana, and Illinois. Huge reservoirs have flooded natural rivers; flatwater behind Bagnell Dam on the Osage River in Missouri, for example, is 129 miles long. Many of the arterial rivers, including the Mississippi above Alton, are no longer rivers but back-to-back chains of reservoirs. Even small streams of the northern Midwest are dammed at frequent intervals for hydropower. As a counterpoint to the rest of the Midwest, Michigan, Wisconsin, and Minnesota are ranked by the *Green Index* among the twelve best states for environmental policies.

To look at some of the individual rivers, I begin in the east, where the Appalachian foothills of Ohio flatten out to a tabletop and low-gradient rivers drain the loess-covered farmland of the Lake Erie plain. Amid the flatness, the Grand River cuts through a gorge east of Cleveland. In that city, the Cuyahoga in 1969 gained infamy by burning out of control where oil and debris covered its surface, but on the same

river, a national recreation area in a cleft valley between Akron and
Cleveland now attracts millions of people. The Vermilion and Black
Rivers of north central Ohio cut through unexpected limestone bluffs
to Lake Erie. The Maumee, beginning in Indiana but accumulating a
flow of 4,926 cfs across northwestern Ohio, is the largest river draining
into Lake Erie entirely from the United States. Seeing headwaters that
link revealingly close to those of the Wabash River, I can easily imagine the Maumee running the other way, as it did when it drained the
glacier-bound Lake Erie southwestward to the Wabash and Mississippi.
Other than the Ohio River at the southern border with Kentucky, the
Muskingum is the state's largest river (7,596 cfs). While the main stem
has been locked and dammed far upstream from its Ohio River confluence, the Muskingum basin includes the Mohican as one of the most
popular canoeing rivers in the central Midwest. A historic canoe route
linked Lake Erie and the Ohio River by ascending the Cuyahoga and
descending the Tuscarawas–Muskingum with only a 3-mile portage.
The Scioto River (4,579 cfs) drains the center of the state, and the Great
Miami and scenic Little Miami lie in the west.

Almost all of Indiana's water finds its way to the Ohio River at the
state's southern border. The 529-mile Wabash system is the primary
artery, joining the Ohio as its largest tributary from the north. Sugar
Creek, a Wabash tributary, is one of the more scenic streams in the
state. In the northwestern sector, the Kankakee once supported Indiana's largest wetland, which spans 4.4 million acres, most of it now
drained. The river flows westward as the main source of the Illinois
River.

In Illinois, the 420-mile Illinois–Kankakee river system is the state's
centerpiece. After an 1887 typhoid, diphtheria, and cholera epidemic
that killed 80,000 people in Chicago, the city diverted its sewage southward to the Illinois's headwaters—a wetland 6 miles from Lake Michigan and feeding the short Des Plaines River. In 1910 the Illinois still provided 10 percent of the United States's freshwater commercial fishery,
second only to the salmon-rich Columbia. But agriculture and urban development took further tolls on the Illinois, along with dams and levees, and no commercial fishery has existed for some time. The Army
Corps of Engineers maintains a dredged channel for barges. The Sangamon joins the Illinois from the east after flowing through channelized
and gridded farmland but also through bluff- and tree-lined refuges
such as Allerton Park. The lower Illinois parallels the Mississippi, separated for 25 miles by a neck of land only about 5 miles wide. The Rock
River (6,020 cfs) begins in Wisconsin and then flows through northern

Illinois to the Mississippi. The Big Muddy River is one of the state's finest canoeing streams, entering the Mississippi after winding through bottomlands of Shawnee National Forest.

West of Illinois and sandwiched between the Mississippi to the east and the Missouri River to the west, farm-covered Iowa produces slow, often muddy rivers that flow southeastward in tree-lined corridors through low hills to meet the Mississippi. The Des Moines River (7,860 cfs) is the centerpiece here, beginning in southern Minnesota and cutting diagonally across Iowa, even bisecting the state capital. From north to south, other major rivers running in parallel courses are the Wapsipinicon, or "Wapsi" (1,537 cfs), with two long undammed reaches, followed by the Cedar (3,414 cfs), Iowa (8,650 cfs), and Skunk (2,407 cfs). The Turkey River, with only one small dam at its headwaters, has one of the region's longest free-flowing reaches—161 miles. The upper Iowa, with clear, swift water, remains one of the finest rivers in the Midwest's central core, with a gorge 70 miles long and 450 feet deep in places. Headwaters of some streams, such as the Wapsipinicon and Cedar, remain unusually clear and support channel catfish, walleye, northern pike, shortnose or longnose gar, shovelnose sturgeon, and lots of turtles.

To the north, a rich rivers estate survives in Michigan. An unusual artery flowing at the boundary with Ontario, the 37-mile St. Clair River connects Lake Huron with Lake St. Clair, the sixth lake in the Great Lakes chain. The 30-mile Detroit River then links Lake St. Clair with Lake Erie. Both of these reaches are upward extensions of the St. Lawrence River. A mile across in places, its pale blue water carries constant traffic of ore boats and ocean freighters past banks occupied by industries, groomed lawns, waterfront parks in quiet midwestern towns, and inner-city Detroit.

The state's two largest nonborder rivers drain agricultural southern Michigan. The St. Joseph dips into Indiana for a while, then carries 3,260 cfs to Lake Michigan. The 256-mile Grand River, central and large enough to be considered Michigan's primary river, winds westward across the state with a flow of 3,570 cfs to Lake Michigan. The Grand River of the ice ages was enormous, picking up water from the southern glacial edge and moving it westward to the Mississippi basin. To the north, a more attractive riverland appears, with the Muskegon, Pere Marquette, and Manistee draining west to Lake Michigan; the Pine and Au Sable head east to Lake Huron. Cool water and gravel-bottomed beds here make for excellent trout streams. Many of the rivers also offer fine, easy canoeing; the Pine draws more than 2,000 paddlers on a weekend in a scene that more resembles pandemonium than river peace. Hydropower developers have built dams on most of Michigan's rivers, degrading even some favorite fishing streams, such as the Au Sable.

Lying north of Lake Michigan, the upper peninsula of the state ranks among the nation's exceptional regions of small rivers; dozens of streams tumble north to Lake Superior or wind south to Lake Michigan. Scenic waterfalls, north woods of black spruce and paper birch, healthy trout fisheries, challenging whitewater, and wetland bogs abound here. Congress added twenty of these streams, mostly on national forest land, to the National Wild and Scenic Rivers System in 1992—the greatest concentration of national rivers apart from the Pacific states. The Black River plunges 1,000 feet in 30 miles over some of the oldest granitic bedrock on earth. The Ontonagon flows through a mix of northern hardwoods, hemlock, and spruce with a flow of 1,440 cfs, making it the largest river of the upper peninsula. While jetties have been built and harbors dredged at the mouths of most rivers entering the Great Lakes, some smaller streams remain natural as they spill into these inland seas.

To the west, Wisconsin offers an abundance of rivers and lakes. The Wisconsin runs 430 miles through that state from north to south; twenty-six hydroelectric dams shackle the upper three-fourths of the river even to its lake-studded headwaters. At Wisconsin Dells, glacial ice forced the river into a new course over bedrock now evident in dramatic bluffs. Finally free of dams, the Wisconsin's lower 92 miles flow to the Mississippi with 8,662 cfs. In 1989 the state's legislature created the Lower Wisconsin State Riverway Board to manage the popular recreation corridor and protect the waterfront.

The Chippewa River roughly parallels the Wisconsin to its northwest and delivers 5,134 cfs to the Mississippi. Farther north, the Namekagon flows 98 miles southwestward and joins the St. Croix River, which forms the boundary of Minnesota and Wisconsin and enters the Mississippi with a flow of more than 4,235 cfs. Though several small dams intrude, 200 miles of the Namekagon and St. Croix combine to form the longest designated National Wild and Scenic River reach outside Alaska. Thirty species of native mussels are found here, making the St. Croix one of the Midwest's richest rivers biologically. I've enjoyed the Namekagon and St. Croix with their clean water and forested shores more than any other extended river journey in the upper Midwest. Just a short drive from Minnesota's twin cities, these rivers form one of the great river recreation corridors of the region.

Scores of other Wisconsin rivers offer good trout fishing, flatwater boating, and wildlife refuges. Whitewater paddlers know the Flambeau,

Kettle River at Banning State Park, MN

Black River, Sandstone Falls, MI

Sangamon River at Allerton Park, IL

Big Spring, a Current River tributary, MO

Cuyahoga River at Highway 82, OH

Little Minnesota River at Brown's Valley, MN

Minnesota River, farmed flood land, MN

Minnesota River at St. Peter, MN

which flows to the Chippewa in north central Wisconsin; the Wolf, which runs to the Fox River; and the Peshtigo, which empties into Lake Michigan. Sections of the Brule River run wild at the state's northeast border before meeting the northwoods' Menominee and then Lake Michigan. Another river, the Bois Brule, flows as an alluring, almost magical small stream through an aquifer of sand that yields a steady flow. Bouldered rapids and rustic lodges lie in a protected corridor of giant white pines leading to Lake Superior.

Minnesota, the Land of 10,000 Lakes, is really a land of 15,292 lakes and is also home to 25,000 miles of rivers and streams. American Rivers's *Outstanding Rivers List* devotes thirteen pages to rivers in Minnesota—by far the best-represented state in the report. In the northeast lie the Boundary Waters Canoe Area and the Voyageurs National Park— mazes of lakes linked by short rivers or no rivers. I once portaged twenty times in three days of paddling there. This lake country is one of only two places outside the West where one can be 10 miles or more from any road.

The Mississippi begins in northern Minnesota at Lake Itasca, where the stream can almost be stepped across. Long reaches of flatwater pass through glaciated farmland, woodland, and wetland and over ten dams on the 525-mile journey to Minneapolis. Much of the headwaters' frontage is now under the protection of the Mississippi Headwaters Board, the largest multicounty effort in America to care for a river.

The far northern, little-known Rainy River is an undammed giant of 12,830 cfs, flowing over two minor rapids called Manitou and Long Sault at the border of Minnesota and Ontario. From a chain of lakes, it extends 86 miles to Lake of the Woods, which has been raised nine feet by a dam in Canada. As Rainy River tributaries, the Big Fork and Little Fork offer two of the longer undammed reaches in the Midwest (see appendix 2) and include scenic waterfalls. In the far Northeast, the Pigeon River drops over waterfalls along the historic Grand Portage canoe route linking Lake Superior with the Rainy River and inland lakes of Canada.

One of the largest U.S. rivers flowing into Canada, the Red River of the North (2,558 cfs) flows along the western boundary of Minnesota for 400 miles to Manitoba, followed by a stretch of 200 miles to Lake Winnipeg. A tributary, the Red Lake River, runs 200 miles through lowlands once flooded by the ice-age Lake Agassiz.

Minnesota rivers with surviving wild sections include the Big Fork and Little Fork; the 100-mile Cloquet, with only one dam; and the 160-

mile St. Louis. Ending at Lake Superior, this stream once endured 100 small dams on its main stem and tributaries; only a few exist today. The Kettle is a swift, mostly undeveloped river that joins the St. Croix at the Wisconsin border. The upper Midwest is a vital region for waterfowl, common throughout the prairie pothole wetlands and on lazy rivers but especially plentiful on the upper Mississippi and the Minnesota River near Lac qui Parle. While catfish dominate farther south in the region, walleye do well in the northern rivers and attract anglers.

At the southeastern fringe of the Midwest, many small rivers roll off the Lowland Plateau province of western Kentucky and Tennessee. Many also slip underground in this karst topography of limestone; for example, hundreds of streams disappear into sinkholes northeast of Bowling Green, Kentucky. The lower Ohio, Cumberland, and Tennessee—entirely dammed or channelized—end their Appalachian journeys in this corner of the Midwest. Flowing into the lower Tennessee River, the 320-mile Duck River bridges the Appalachians and the Midwest with one of the region's longest free-flowing reaches. Its tributary, the Buffalo River, has no major dams for its entire 147 miles in western Tennessee.

On the western fringe of the Midwest, the lower Missouri River below Omaha, Nebraska, flows through 654 miles that are undammed but channelized for barges. Most of this extends across northern Missouri, where the Osage River (9,900 cfs) joins the river after flowing 500 miles from the center of the state. The Missouri then meets the Mississippi just north of St. Louis, a location that made that city strategic to frontier development.

The gently rolling farm country of Missouri rises to the Ozark Plateau, producing many fine rivers. With plentiful groundwater, this area rivals Florida as a land of springs. The Gasconade (2,500 cfs) flows northward for 336 undammed miles, and the Meramec (3,100 cfs) ends at St. Louis. The sycamore-lined Eleven Point is one of the most beautiful Ozark streams, with clear, quick currents, and the St. Francis has exciting whitewater. The endearing Jacks Fork, with its crystal-clear water, high-bluffed shores, and gaping caves, joins the Current River as it cuts southward to the Arkansas boundary. Congress designated these two streams for protection as the Ozark National Scenic Riverways in 1964—one of the prototypal actions taken for river protection. Among the most-canoed rivers in the nation, the Current and its Jacks Fork are used by more than 300,000 people a year. These three nationally protected Ozark rivers—the Eleven Point, Jacks Fork, and Current—may be threatened by lead mining in the Mark Twain National Forest. Other Black River tributaries have already been polluted by the toxic metal. In the southern Ozarks the Buffalo River, flowing for 148 miles through northern Arkansas to the White River, is one of the finest full-length protected corridors in America, most of it designated as a national river.

Sizeable rivers in Arkansas include the 425-mile St. Francis, coming from Missouri and entering the Mississippi with a flow of 5,274 cfs on the Coastal Plain. The Black River carries 8,410 cfs after it picks up the Current River. It then flows into the White, a 720-mile artery delivering 29,510 cfs to the Mississippi.

The Arkansas River scribes the southern boundary of the Ozark Mountains after a complete traverse of the Great Plains. Not much remains in the way of a natural river; the Army Corps of Engineers dammed, dredged, and channelized hundreds of miles from the Mississippi up to Tulsa, Oklahoma, in a seventeen-lock navigation system. South of the river lie the Ouachita Mountains of west central Arkansas, similar to the Ozarks in its quality streams separated by steep ridges. Here, the Little Missouri is one of the finer attractions for anglers and whitewater paddlers before it winds down to the Ouachita. This 605-mile artery (7,490 cfs) in southwestern Arkansas flows to the Tensas River on the Coastal Plain of Louisiana.

This brings us once again to the Mississippi, which drains not only the Midwest but also 40 percent of the nation outside Alaska. Its "headwaters" reach of 550 miles lies above Minneapolis. Twenty-nine dams built for barge traffic then block the river in back-to-back navigation pools from Minneapolis to below Alton, Illinois, near St. Louis, America's second-largest inland port of commerce. A nine-foot-deep channel is dredged for 1,790 miles from Minnesota to the Gulf of Mexico. The Upper Mississippi River Wildlife and Fish Refuge stretches for 280 miles from Wabasha, Minnesota, to Rock Island, Illinois—unusual because it was established in part for fisheries. Paddling there, I've had the distinct impression of being on an inland sea, half a continent away from salt water. This 790-mile "upper" Mississippi ends at the mouth of the Ohio, followed by the 1,000-mile "lower" Mississippi of the Coastal Plain. The river once served a biological system of extraordinary abundance with wetlands extending back from the banks for miles, and it makes possible the Mississippi Flyway, which accommodates 40 percent of North America's waterfowl and wading birds. Père Marquette traveled down the Mississippi in 1673 and in *Travels and Discoveries in North America* wrote of "monstrous fish, which struck so violently against our canoes, that at first we took them to be large trees, which threatened to upset us." These were likely blue catfish or lake sturgeon, each growing to 300 pounds. The basin still supports 300 species of native fish—about 38 percent of all species north of Mexico.

About this centerpiece of the Midwest, geographer Peirce Lewis wrote, "The Mississippi is not merely a useful river; it also serves as a potent geographical symbol." He pointed out that this waterway is the traditional dividing line in America between East and West. The river became the central conduit for transportation to the heartland in the nineteenth century. For diesel-powered towboats, the river is now dammed or dredged from the Gulf of Mexico to Minneapolis.

Agricultural development and towns close to the river gave rise to flood-control levees along its entire length below Minneapolis and to dams on almost all major tributaries. Like a curse against all attempts to tame the giant waterway, unrelenting rains in the summer of 1993 resulted in the largest flood since 1844 and the most damage ever; 1,100 of 1,576 levees failed. Entire towns went under, damages totaled $15 billion, and Congress approved a $6 billion flood-relief bill. All this happened in spite of $25 billion that the government had spent on flood control in the basin since 1927; unfortunately, that money was spent in efforts to control the river rather than to control the development that is vulnerable to floods. Eight other floods since 1883 produced nearly as much water but far lower flood crests because the river was not so confined by levees. The 1993 flood would otherwise have spread out on lower floodplains but instead climbed to unexpected heights. Some levees were undermined and others were overtopped. High water nearly surmounted the "impregnable" fifty-two-foot-high flood wall of St. Louis. The flood was aggravated not only by the strait-jacket of levees but also by the drainage of 19 million acres of wetlands in the basin above St. Louis. The potholes and marshes had earlier contained excess water; without them, runoff flows downstream faster.

Increased damage during major floods has not been the only result of the dams and levees intended to stop high water. Native fish of the Mississippi evolved in the muddy-water, flood-recurrent, free-flowing regime, and now fish species such as the skipjack herring, buffalo, paddlefish, and blue catfish are rare. Through the work of American Rivers and others, $600 million of the 1993 disaster-relief funds were used to relocate homes and restore wetlands. But driven by local politics, most government money went to rebuilding on the floodplain, ensuring that disasters will happen again. Meanwhile, the Corps is conducting a $44 million study on expansion of the lock and dam system so that barges have less waiting time. Scientists fear a collapse of the already stressed aquatic ecosystem if the $4–$6 billion expansion is built.

While the Mississippi is the central river of the Midwest, and while the northern woodlands and Ozark-Ouachita Mountains show the riverine highlights of this region, the Minnesota River offers a more typical view, and in July 1993 I set out to see this important waterway.

The Minnesota River

The river begins near the continental divide. No Rocky Mountain crest, it is a rolling prairie of farmland only 1,000 feet above sea level yet 2,000 miles away from it. Water on the northern side of a rise flows to Hudson Bay; on the southern side it flows to the Gulf of Mexico. Here the Minnesota River's course to the Mississippi embodies the essence of a midwestern riverscape. The basin is 92 percent farmland and exhibits the character, the problems, and the possibilities for improvement found elsewhere across agricultural America, and the fate of this 355-mile stream may serve as a barometer for dozens of other rivers.

From the Hudson Bay–Mississippi divide, the Little Minnesota River flows down to Brown's Valley, population 804. In this frozen moment of the old Midwest, cows grazed in a barnyard on one side of the river while the white clapboard of tidy homes occupied the other side. Elderly people tended lawns edged by flowers and vegetable gardens. Friendly feelings of the Midwest surfaced immediately at a free village campground. With Ann leading Outward Bound classes in Alaska for two months, I set off alone to see the Minnesota by first strolling through the diminutive downtown of Brown's Valley, where the hardware and liquor stores were the active enterprises.

On the bridge, five-and-a-half-foot Merlin Johnson told me about the local view of the river. "People don't do much with it here except a little illegal fishing when the walleye are spawning," he chuckled. "Like other small towns, this one's getting smaller. Old people die off and the young ones go to college or get a good job somewhere." Merlin said he wouldn't mind showing up in my book: "Just say you had a conversation with a little Norwegian," he said, then turned to head homeward after his daily visit to the bridge.

This upper basin was once flooded by the largest lake in North America—larger than all of today's Great Lakes combined. After 1,000 years, the ancient Warren River cut a channel through an ice-age moraine and released the stored water to the south, carving the broad lowlands of today's Minnesota River Valley. A remnant of the emptied Lake Agassiz remains as Big Stone Lake, a 26-mile-long glacial depression with 200-foot bluffs. The shoreline lacks the less-attractive subdivisions of lakes seen elsewhere. But later, I spotted Big Stone from a transcontinental flight and was struck at how intensively its watershed was farmed, right to the brinks of bluffs looming over the lakeshore.

Wandering down near the outlet where the Minnesota River begins, I noticed what appeared from a distance to be piles of lawn clippings dumped on the lakeshore. Mounded two feet deep, these filamentous blue-green algae had been washed in by waves. Peering into the water, I saw that algae everywhere filled the shallows with suspended thread-like strands half an inch long. Thin deposits on shoreline rocks could have been iridescent green paint, a disgusting scene. Green slime marred an otherwise idyllic setting for the small town of Ortonville.

Loaded with farm waste from 100 feedlots and with eroded soil and fertilizer, this lake's watershed has been the deserving subject of cleanup efforts since 1979. Much of the work has paid off with greater water clarity and a revitalized fishery, but the heavy rains of 1993 flushed in agricultural waste, causing the suffocating algal blooms.

An eight-foot-high dam blocked the Minnesota River's outlet, followed by Big Stone Lake National Wildlife Refuge, a wetland and tall-grass prairie managed for ground-nesting waterfowl—blue-winged teal, gadwall, shoveler, and other ducks. Below lay another dam at Marsh Lake.

The Pomme de Terre River flowed in from the north, first spilling over a low dam at Appleton, where aeration of the water produced a meringuelike topping of suds covering half the stream. Chunks of foam the size of bread loaves blew off in the wind, and a dead carp stared goggle-eyed at me from the shore. Another dam lay downstream on the Minnesota at the state's Lac qui Parle Wildlife Management Area, followed by a free-flowing river bounded by cropland and forest for 33 miles past the town of Montevideo.

The farm wastes of the Pomme de Terre and upper Minnesota are magnified as the river grows. That the water fails to meet federal and state swimming and fishing standards doesn't quite describe the problem. Resembling chocolate milk, the slurry of suspended soil carries the equivalent of one dump-truck-load of dirt every five minutes down the river. Because of toxins, the Department of Health warned people not to eat some species of fish more than once a week, though many towns drink heavily treated water from the river. Algae proliferate as a natural way of using up excess phosphorus from farm runoff, but brown algae thicken so much that sunlight cannot reach the roots of beneficial aquatic plants, causing oxygen levels to plummet in a stinking anaerobic situation.

Polluted runoff from farms and waste from food processing cause the river's problems. But even worse, people destroyed nature's process for accommodating such waste. They drained and filled the basin's wetlands, which had been a natural system of reservoirs and treatment plants provided at no cost whatever. Ninety-five percent of the basin's extensive wetlands are now drained by channelization, by ditches dug in fields, and by tile drains buried underground to sluice the water from where it would naturally be. Farmers dried up landlocked ponds and marshes by tunneling outlets through low hills or riverbanks, thereby pulling the plug in thousands of prairie potholes. The map of ditches drawn by the Minnesota Pollution Control Agency shows about as much ink as white space in the watershed. The tile drainage systems not only speeded runoff but became conduits of dirt going straight into streams. At Big Stone Lake National Wildlife Refuge, manager Jim Heinecke said, "Twenty-five years ago it took three weeks for runoff to get to the Mississippi. Now it takes three days." Farming in the river's flood zone caused similar problems, not to mention crop losses when the floods inevitably came. During the high water that occurred while I visited in 1993 Heinecke reminded me, "That's not flooded farmland; it's farmed floodland."

Through the 1960s, even the federal government helped farmers to drain their lands, though the crops produced were in chronic surplus. The motivation for such work can be credited more to philosophical warfare against wetlands than to any practical considerations for feeding people. When it was all done, the taxpayers had paid for part of the drainage systems that increased crop acreage and aggravated floods. Then they paid farmers not to grow the crops produced on the drained land. Then they paid the farmers for the loss of the same kinds of crops when a farmed floodplain was inundated. Then, through disaster relief, they paid to restore the farmland so that the process could be repeated. Thanks to the political clout of farm-region politicians, this type of economics contributed not only to a federal deficit bankrupting the national economy but also to the sickening sea of chemically laden silt in the Minnesota River and to bankrupt ecosystems and soils.

The government has cut most of its subsidies for new drainage and instead sponsors programs to buy easements for wetland protection, but what's being restored is a drop in the bucket, and other land continues to be drained. Heinecke, who works daily with the difficulties, said, "In many areas, drainage is still like apple pie and motherhood. The attitude is that if a piece of land is not being farmed, it's wasted. But a lot of farm groups now realize they have to do something different, and for the first time in this state's history, the political power of agriculture is being challenged."

One reason that a new era awaits for the Minnesota River is Del Wehrspann. An unlikely agent of change, this fifty-four-year-old rural resident near Montevideo buys cattle for a living. Appearing at noisy auctions in the Midwest, he eyeballs cows and bids on them for his agribusiness employer. About his childhood home on a farm near the Des Moines River in Iowa, he said, "I had seen that river deteriorate to the point that you couldn't eat the fish you caught. Then, in 1968, my wife, Shirley, and I moved here to this old farm. We thought we'd found the Garden of Eden. I caught forty walleyes in a week; threw most of them back. It's a beautiful river—have you seen it? Here, let me show you. Grab your jacket."

Del led me down through a field whining with mosquitoes to where his boat was tethered. He fired up the engine and we cruised upriver in the evening light. The emerald shores of silver maple and black ash above slow-moving water looked more like a midwestern jungle than an agricultural drain field in the corn belt, but I was seeing only the edge of things.

Over the hum of the engine, Del told stories. "A friend of mine sold bait, and when he got too old, I took over the business. When you sell bait, you talk to fishermen. It was then that I really began to realize what was happening to the river." About that time, the county finalized plans to extend a new drain that would dump its wastewater slurry onto the Wehrspanns' Garden of Eden. "I began piecing these parts together," Del recalled.

As a gutsy first initiative, he sued the county to stop the drain. "People asked me, 'What's more important? Ducks or feeding the kids of the world?' But the issue is not just ducks. It's drinking water, soil, and flood control. And the issue isn't feeding kids when we're paying farmers to not produce. The drains just push the water somewhere else. Farmland downstream gets flooded worse. It's not farmer versus the environment; it's farmer versus farmer. Do you see what I mean?" Some years after being forced to pay the Wehrspanns for drainage damages, the county did a turnaround and honored Del as conservationist of the year.

We rounded another half dozen bends, and the shoreline's fragile beauty lay unbroken. But—beauty compared with what? The life system of the river is badly broken. Del said, "You look at the writings of

George Featherstonhaugh in 1835 and you get an idea of what was here." In *A Canoe Voyage up the Minnay Sotor,* Featherstonhaugh wrote of mussels "stuck in countless numbers in the pure white sand, so that I could, by baring my arm, select them as we went along. . . . We moved along very agreeably amidst extensive areas of wild rice and clouds of wild ducks until we came to more rapids." Today a slimy armor of deep mud coats the bottom where Featherstonhaugh once plucked his mussels. Del said, "People call this floodplain a wasteland, but in nature's scheme of things, it's essential. A forested floodplain absorbs the silt and the waste of the farms.

"We'll never again see the river Featherstonhaugh described," Del admitted, "but we can have a working natural system. We can bring it back; I know we can. And it's happening. This is a big snowball, and it's rolling downhill." The snowball is a grassroots movement. Del and others organized CURE—Clean Up Our River Environment. "I grew up fishing, hunting, and trapping, and one of the problems now is that so many people have gotten away from that. Some people have an appreciation of nature for its own sake. But when most people get away from being involved by fishing or hunting or really living here, they lose touch, and when that happens, we've really lost it."

While citizen activism caught on in the middle and upper basin, Minneapolis suburbs found they couldn't meet water quality standards no matter how well they treated their sewage because the river itself was too polluted. "That really set the stage for action," Del explained. "Scott Sparlin and I got a chance to talk to Governor Arne Carlson. We're very impassioned about this, as you can tell. We want to make this river a model for the nation. And we can do it. Right here, we can show that a midwestern river can be fixed.

"First we need to restore flood lands and to leave them as floodplain. Then we need to return other wetlands to their natural function. That alone will fix a lot of the water quality problems because wetlands filter out the sediment. We're fortunate here because the wetlands are a tool available to us that many areas don't have. Then we need to re-examine the agricultural practices that spew out all the pollution ruining the land and water.

"I grew up with agriculture. I earn my living off agriculture. So I used my background to try to make an honest appraisal. Agriculture has been the sacred cow for too long. They hold this over your head: 'We've got to feed you.' But look at what's happening. We're selling off the future. The farmers worry, 'What will happen to our livelihoods if we change the way we do things?' And everybody else—we're all like people who buy stolen merchandise from the fence; we're stealing from nature, and society has condoned it. We say, so long as we have cheap food we won't look at what's happening. *But it's not cheap!* That dump-truck-load of soil going downriver every five minutes is our farmland. By shutting up, the public is a partner in this crime. Feather-stonhaugh asked, 'With the buffalo gone, can the Indians' extinction be far behind?' Now we need to ask, 'With the topsoil gone, can our rural economy be much later in passing?' We have only a small window of time to make meaningful change."

Encouraged by Wehrspann and Scott Sparlin, who had earlier organized river supporters farther downriver, pressed by the federal Clean Water Act, and serving a state where environmental quality is considered important, the governor created the Minnesota River Task Force. A basinwide study confirmed what river watchers already knew. Groups in local communities joined to support restoration. The state Reinvest in Minnesota program and the federal Wetlands Restoration Program meanwhile repaired thousands of small wetlands. Refuge manager Heinecke said, "If we were climbing the Empire State Building, we'd be on step two. But we're off the ground."

Talking to Del had piqued my curiosity about the rest of the Minnesota, so I set off downriver to see more of this place, so troubled yet ripe for reform. As I drove into the community of Granite Falls, the scene painted a graceful picture of the Midwest. Fields rolled out with pasture and crops. The steeples of the town announced its coming. I breezed down elm-lined streets. The downtown's cluster of practical shops served my needs. The grocer had stacked fresh produce in side-walk bins where customers gathered. People smiled and said hello without fear. It seemed that life here would be civil, crimeless, and co-operative. I envied those along the Minnesota River who belonged in the cozy, shuttered houses with warm yellow lights in the windows at night. I could see how people would not only escape cynicism but even escape the need to think much about a raft of complexities and difficulties of the larger society.

The rapids that Featherstonhaugh had reported portaging at Granite Falls were replaced by a hydropower dam in 1872. Today, water thunders over the fifteen-foot-tall dam bounded by strips of parkland. But to me, the incredible thing was the pelicans.

Once threatened with extinction, the birds congregated in a solid mass of feathers. Their stocky bodies impressed me as a life-support system for a beak capable of gulping a carp large enough for anyone's dinner. Stretching out in flight, the birds' wings spanned eight feet.

Starved for a glimpse of the past, for a scene of biological wealth, I found the sight of the pelicans reminiscent of the stories of western explorers. I estimated 500 birds in all. Individuals and pairs descended with extended feet, tucked-in bills, and a stern intensity in their eyes. They swooped over the wires crossing the river and skittered into the pool below.

Good fishing had brought the pelicans there. At times of high water, carp move upstream. During this two-month flood, they swam as far as they could—to the falls. There they lay free for the picking. One of the unlucky big goldfish rolled to the surface and, snap! Now it flopped only in the pouch of the pelican.

The flocking of so many pelicans was an unusual event. Hundreds of people a day came to see the birds. They made news across the country. Families came from Minneapolis and took delight in the wildlife at this little town on the Minnesota River. But the local response to the birds was anything but cordial. As I waited in line at the grocery store, a woman explained, "Those pelicans, they hit the wires at the power dam and cause the electricity to go out. Clerks at the bank hate them because all the computers go down. Everybody in town has to reset their clocks." Seeking a solution to the problem, state Department of Natural Resources staff went to work devising a string of flags to deflect the birds from the hot wires.

For a canoe expedition below Granite Falls, I met up with my sister and brother-in-law, Becky and Steve Schmitz, along with their children, Stevie and Jenny; the family was visiting Steve's mother in a nearby town. I departed with the kids aboard the van while Becky and Steve drove behind. Two miles below town, the last of six dams blocked the Minnesota River; 240 miles of unobstructed flow lay ahead. Stevie, Jenny, and I unloaded the boats and launched into the pushy brown flow. As Becky and Steve shuttled my van farther downriver, Jenny and I piloted the canoe; Stevie paddled Ann's kayak.

The flood of 1993 had crested, but water still lapped in the trees and required us to paddle through 200 feet of woods. The leather-brown river looked flat but hustled with surprising swiftness. Shores of dense undergrowth seemed entirely eastern here, with no sign of the aridity of the Great Plains that began not far to the west. Silver maples dominated, with willows, box elders, eastern cottonwoods, lindens, elms, and ashes. An occasional song sparrow trilled from the willows, a kingfisher rattled as it flew from one tree to the next, and a great blue heron flapped out ahead of us with a guttural croak. Yet the river lacked the flocks of birds I'd hoped to see. Where was all the wildlife?

Searching for clues, I landed in the trees and walked up the bank through the deceptively thin riparian woods and onto a farmed field, made half mud by receding floodwater. Several drains, each six inches in diameter, had been tunneled through the bank to shunt silty water directly into the river from low-lying land behind the natural levee of the riverbank. This year the river had flooded the drains' outlets long enough to simulate natural conditions—the field was a wetland. Under natural conditions, the vegetation would have been a riparian forest full of birds instead of mud-gummed soybeans.

The gentle drop of Patterson Rapids gave Stevie some current to play with in the kayak, but otherwise the river curled steadily, bend after bend, midwestern through and through. Rather than offer ourselves up as lunch to the mosquitoes on shore, we ate our sandwiches as we drifted in linked boats. Chatting happily through this green corridor, we might have continued floating for days.

The river winds around and around, the corn and soybean fields continue on and on, and the water quality gets worse and worse. After Stevie and Jenny returned to their family, I drove to New Ulm, with its shiny facades of the 1950s, stone-arched buildings from 1900, two-story homes reflective of New England immigrants, and blockish frame buildings typical of the unadorned north as far as Hudson Bay.

A riverfront park invited me to take an evening stroll as insect-eating nighthawks darted on silent wings. A plaque celebrated the steamboats that plied the river from 1853 to 1878, as if this were the most important thing that had ever happened there. Nothing was mentioned of the Minnesota for the 115 years that followed. Had public regard for the river ended with the grounding of the last wood-burner?

"Yes," Scott Sparlin said. "Until now." A local musician, Scott works full-time as coordinator of the Coalition for a Clean Minnesota River, aiming to change no less than the public image of the river. And he's doing it. Every day Scott hosts a radio show about rivers and fishing. He stresses traditional values—stewardship, concern for future generations, and the river as a bright image for business. His passion to take better care of his home is contagious. "It's not morally right to accept a degraded river and then pass it on to your children," he explained between song lyrics: "Oh river, river, where are you going? / Does anyone really know that you're flowing? / We've treated you obscene / It's time we make you clean."

I witnessed the obscene part firsthand at Mankato, a larger industrial town where food processing is big business. Here, the Blue Earth River roils in with its gut full of silt—the most polluted river in the state. In the mud of Sibley Park, silver maples had already sprouted and grown three inches high, and as plentiful as grass, only two weeks after the floodwater had begun to recede. This promising new forest was the legacy of high water.

Driving downriver, I arrived at St. Peter—an earlier name given to the river by the French. I sensed a friendly feeling in a park on the riverfront; in a natural foods store, where I could buy pesticide-free produce; and in a public library where I read Eric Sevareid's account of canoeing up the Minnesota in the 1930s. Water of the foamy Pomme de Terre River then ran "clear as crystal," and six-foot-long lake sturgeon swam in Big Stone Lake.

Farther downstream, most towns seemed to have filed for a divorce from the Minnesota. At Le Sueur, the railroad barricaded the town from a wide floodplain. At Belle Plaine, a four-lane highway separated them. Chaska had a town square but no recognition of its riverfront. Any recognition, however, must be from a distance; at Shakopee a sign indicated that the 1965 flood had topped at seven feet above the road.

Currents of the lower Minnesota slowed down, and the river's load of silt began to settle. The silt has accumulated over the centuries as natural levees that harbor wetlands. After vigorous citizen initiatives in the 1970s, sections of the floodplain on the lower 34-mile corridor were included in the Minnesota Valley National Wildlife Refuge, and Friends of the Minnesota Valley still works to complete open space protection at the doorsteps of 2.2 million people.

In the final 15 miles of the Minnesota's length, three interstate highways bridged the river, deeply inset between bluffs. At the southern boundary of Minneapolis, jetliners bore down on the Twin Cities' airport. Wetlands sprawled across the valley. Finally, the muddy Minnesota eased into the growing waters of the Mississippi for the next leg of its journey to the Gulf.

Chapter 5

——◅ ▻——

Sky-Filled Rivers of the Great Plains

A big sky arcs in blue from horizon to horizon, and a line of vivid green along the shores of a river is all that breaks the flatness of bleached grass. Meadowlarks trill with such clarity that they could be on my shoulder. A radio announcer warns of tornadoes and advises me to get out of my car and lie down in a ditch near trees if I see the ominous funnel cloud coming. From the Great Plains, my memory has photographed lonely ranch buildings, grain elevators piercing distant horizons, and a sky brewing thunderstorms on a hot summer eve. I have never forgotten the cover of my eighth-grade geography book, with a picture of the Plains so spacious and open that I ached to run through the scene for the sheer, exhilarating freedom of it all. But after being there, I best remember the canopies of cottonwoods above the banks of riffling streams.

Among all the regions of rivers, only the Great Plains completely spans the nation north to south. Prominent in the national imagination, the Plains once housed native people who lived off the buffalo but were no less dependent on the rivers, from which they drank in this dry land. To non-Indians, the Plains symbolized the beginning of the

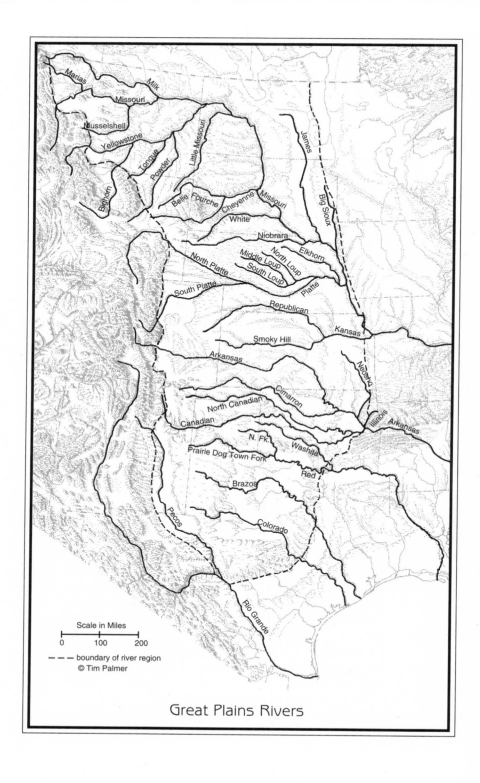

Great Plains Rivers

West. After the passing of the frontier era in the Appalachians, this region posed the next seemingly endless blockade to cross-country travel—a barrier of wind, drought, and monotony.

Even Willa Cather, the literary spokesperson for the region, complained that there was no place to hide in Nebraska. Charles Preuss, in *Exploring with Fremont,* wrote, "Fremont prefers this to every other landscape. To me, it is as if someone would prefer a book with blank pages to a good story. . . . The prairie? To the deuce with such a life; I wish I were in Washington with my old girl." Yet even Preuss yielded to the streams of the plains and noted a "rushing river with nice trees" where he camped along the Kansas. The monotony produces a sweeping elegance, especially if native grass is found rather than an overgrazed dust bowl, and especially where the rivers still nourish willows and cottonwoods in undulating strips of green.

Regardless of the great span of latitude, this region of rivers is the most homogeneous. Nearly all the waterways run from west to east, bridging the Rocky Mountains and the Midwest. These long, sparsely watered rivers lie in the rain shadow of the Rockies; storm clouds arriving here have already spent themselves by snowing or raining on the mountains as they wafted eastward from the Pacific. Most of the region lies west of the isohyetal line of twenty-inch precipitation, which runs north to south through the Dakotas, Nebraska, and Kansas, then swerves southwestward across Oklahoma and Texas, marking a semiarid climate. Only the desert region gets less moisture.

Water brought a great outwash zone of alluvium, or eroded soil, here from the Rockies. Yet the rivers—which actually get smaller because of evaporation and, now, diversions—lack the volume to wash their alluvial bedload all the way downstream. The silt of the mountains thus settles, accumulates, and causes the Great Plains to resemble a table inclined from the eastern toe of the Rockies down toward the Mississippi bottomlands. Geographer Wallace Atwood wrote, "Nowhere else in the world are there more remarkable examples of extensive alluvial fans that have blended and formed a vast alluvial plain at the base of the mountain region." With horizontal rock strata underneath, the rivers strike parallel courses of unusual regularity. In this respect, the rivers evoke those of the Coastal Plain. But the climates of America's two great plains differ so much that their rivers seem completely unrelated. And on the Coastal Plain, the river-borne sediment has accumulated owing to flood flows spilling onto the utter flatness of sea level, whereas in the Great Plains silt accumulates because low flows are unable to flush it through this region of low but steady gradient.

The dryness, alluvium, and gentle slope of the Great Plains appear almost everywhere, but variation through the region does exist. Glaciers left their gravelly, hummocky, potholed evidence in northern Montana, much of North Dakota, and South Dakota, roughly down to the Missouri River, whose route was established as a meltwater escape channel to the south. The strikingly lunar badlands between the Cheyenne and White Rivers in South Dakota are water-carved remnants of flat beds of shale and clay. The Black Hills of South Dakota—the destination that makes tourism the state's second-largest industry—are a miniature, pine-clad Rocky Mountains. The Hills forced the local drainage system to split and flow around its raised topography, resulting in an unusual ring pattern of rivers. The Upper Belle Forche River arcs northeast and then southeast to circumvent the Hills before regaining its eastward course at the Cheyenne River. Meanwhile, the upper Cheyenne mirrors that image around the southern end of the uplift. Another anomaly on the Plains, the grassy Sand Hills of northern Nebraska remain from the postglacial days of blowing dunes. They absorb and release rainfall slowly into reliably flowing rivers. Farther south, the hills of central Texas hide a rich limestone aquifer, which feeds rivers in an oak-juniper savanna supporting endangered plants and critical habitat for migratory songbirds.

A dry continental climate blankets the whole region. Uninfluenced by moderating maritime air, Great Plains temperatures vacillate to the extreme; the northern region has seen an annual difference of 180 degrees Fahrenheit, from 120 to –60. Even the southern areas experience freezing winter storms as late as March. Because of the Gulf influence, the climate moistens as the rivers move east, where many streams pick up the lion's share of their volume. Thus, a dry river such as the Arkansas, which seems to go on forever in its middle reaches without a drop of added water, finally becomes a dangerous challenge to swim across.

Responding to this climate, the western two-thirds of the Plains supports the short-grass prairie and the eastern third the tallgrass, which continues into the Midwest. Mixed-grass prairies buffer these zones. A section of interior Texas marks the Prairie Bushland province, dotted with shrubs whose roots probe deep for water. Throughout, the only place one normally sees trees is along the watercourses. Though scarce, riparian zones are vital to 75 to 85 percent of the wildlife species here and elsewhere in the West.

The tallgrass here once grew higher than a horse and the short-grass lapped up against the mountains in a sea of velvety green, but to call this area prairie today is almost nostalgic. The prairie landscape is visible, but the native grasses are mostly gone except in a few preserves. The tallgrass has been virtually all plowed under for corn, the mixedgrass obliterated for wheat. The short-grass, where 30 to 70 million buffalo once roamed, was reduced to a close-cropped pasture for cows. After a near-extinction low of roughly 500 animals, the buffalo now number between 65,000 and 140,000, all of them squared in by fences except for the lucky bison of Yellowstone National Park, a few in the Henry Mountains in Utah, and the Canadian bison of Wood Buffalo National Park, Alberta. But even the Yellowstone buffalo are shot as "trophies" when they step outside the park boundary in search of the winter range that the park so regrettably lacks.

From the Canadian border through Oklahoma, the Great Plains drain into the Mississippi River; this region comprises most of the land in the western half of that spacious watershed. Plains rivers in New Mexico and Texas drain directly into the Gulf of Mexico. Some of the region's rivers originate in the Rockies; from north to south these include the Marias, Missouri, Yellowstone, Bighorn, Platte, Arkansas, Canadian, and Pecos. Other rivers begin on the Plains without the head start of mountain snowmelt: the Little Missouri, Cheyenne, White, Niobrara, Kansas, Red, Brazos, and the Colorado of Texas.

Next to the desert region, the Great Plains has the most widely spaced rivers in America, and most are small. While large rivers decorate the Appalachians, Coastal Plain, and Midwest by the score, only thirteen in the Great Plains flow with 2,000 cubic feet or more per second. As the giant of the group, the Missouri flows with 29,360 cfs where it leaves the Plains at the Iowa border and 76,200 where it joins the Mississippi in the Midwest. The Yellowstone, with 13,080 cfs, meets the Missouri, which is a much smaller river (11,000 cfs) at the confluence. The Kansas River empties into the Missouri with 7,000 cfs. The Arkansas, once it nears the Coastal Plain at Tulsa, Oklahoma, carries 6,940 cfs, later increasing to 40,290. The Platte delivers 5,980 cfs to the Missouri. The Bighorn, a tributary to the Yellowstone, has 3,939 cfs. The North Platte carries 2,766. The Red River of the Oklahoma–Texas border flows at 2,750 cfs as it enters the Coastal Plain, then increases to 30,870. The Colorado of Texas runs at 2,685 cfs near the Gulf of Mexico, but much of its volume is attributable to the Coastal Plain climate. The Neosho, on the damper side of Kansas where it borders the Midwest, carries 2,500 cfs.

While these flows aren't much relative to those in other regions, the lengths of the rivers are. The Missouri, counting its headwaters in the

Jefferson–Beaverhead–Red Rock system, is the longest river in the United States, at 2,540 miles (without its headwaters, which go by different names, the Missouri runs for 2,341 miles—as long as the Mississippi). Waters of the Missouri run for 3,680 miles to the Gulf of Mexico, making the Missouri–Mississippi combination one of the longest waterways in the world, roughly equivalent to the Nile, Amazon, or Yangtze. The Arkansas runs for 1,460 miles, the Red for 1,290 miles, and the Brazos for 1,280 miles (all these rivers end on the Coastal Plain). The ratio of length to flow here contrasts dramatically with those of rivers in other regions. The Ohio, for example, is about the same length as the Pecos but carries 3,345 times as much water.

This was the first region white settlers encountered that appeared dramatically different from the East, and early accounts reflect opposing views. The Spaniard Coronado journeyed to today's Kansas and wrote, "The country is the best that I have ever seen for producing all of the crops of Spain . . . well watered by the rivulets of springs and rivers." But Major Stephen Long wrote in 1821 that the area was "almost wholly unfit for cultivation." Reflecting both views, we have alternately populated and depopulated the Plains, depending on the whim of water supply.

Though the region represents roughly 15 percent of the United States outside Alaska, only 3 percent of the nation's people live there, many of them now depending on the Ogallala Aquifer. This reservoir of fossil groundwater remaining from 3 to 17 million years ago is replenished so slowly that it would require 6,000 years to refill if drained dry. Farms and ranches expanded after electric pumping caught on in the 1960s, and irrigation now mines the aquifer, the largest groundwater reserve in America. Increasingly deep and costly pumping is required in Kansas, Oklahoma, and Texas, and the depleted aquifer depletes the rivers as well by causing failure of spring flows. In the face of the water problem and other hardships in the farm economy, the rural population has dwindled; Oklahoma and Texas lost 18 percent of their farmland in the 1980s to the retreating aquifer. But the cities of the Great Plains, located along major rivers, have continued to grow. The region's total population swelled by 40 percent between 1930 and 1990, a period when the United States doubled.

Unsustainable use of groundwater repeats the process that first targeted surface water. If the natural rivers meant a toehold on life for native plants and animals—and they did—then irrigators and ranchers sought to preempt that toehold for their own operations. Fickleness of runoff has not prevented people from using almost every acre for cows or crops, fence to fence and river to river. A map of irrigated acreage for the entire West shows the longest strips of watered land along the Yellowstone in Montana; the North and South Platte in Wyoming, Colorado, and Nebraska; the Arkansas in Colorado and Kansas; and the Rio Grande in New Mexico. Almost all the irrigators in these thin strips grow cattle feed in what has become a pumping, siphoning, ditch-digging assault on the natural system. The farmers have overappropriated the waterways—demand exceeds supply, and no one even considers the water needed to sustain ecosystems and a broader community of life. Only the southwestern river basins are more heavily taxed. In the Great Plains, most watersheds suffer 70 percent or more depletion in dry years. Bone dry streams in summertime result across some areas of the Plains, and wildlife and aquatic habitat are extinguished. The limitations on water, seen clearly in the western half of the Plains and even more vividly in the desert and Rocky Mountain regions, make efforts to farm and develop seem senseless relative to the logic of living and working in other, wetter regions. The Marlboro image aside, Florida, Tennessee, and Kentucky each produces more beef than do nine western states combined.

The result of the first round of exploitive settlement and cultivation here was the Dust Bowl, which left poverty in its wake. Today the result consists of scattered ranches and bankrupt local economies dependent on federal subsidies for farmers' survival and for public services. Grain products grown on the Plains ranked foremost in government subsidies in the 1990s, propping up farmers nationwide—a taxpayer-funded expense of over $10 billion per year that is more immune than Social Security to the budget-cutting axe.

As a case study of overuse, the Missouri has seen more development than any other river of the Great Plains, with 75 large dams for irrigation and flood control in its sprawling watershed and six enormous main stem dams on its midsection. Oahe Reservoir—America's longest—alone eliminated 304,000 acres of riparian land with its 230-mile length of flatwater in North and South Dakota. Researchers found that because of dams and agriculture, deciduous vegetation along the Missouri River in Nebraska and Missouri decreased by 41 percent, wetlands by 39 percent, sandbars by 97 percent, and grasslands by 12 percent in a ninety-year period, while cultivated land increased forty-three-fold. On the lower river, 85 percent of the floodplain is intensively cropped, and the fish community has declined by a remarkably similar figure of 80 percent from its 1940 level. In this formerly valuable commercial fishery, single fish once exceeded 300 pounds in weight. Of

156 fish species in the basin, 47 percent are now listed by states as rare, threatened, or endangered. As if all that were not enough, water wars ensue among Missouri River states, with users vying for still larger shares of diminishing flows.

Unfortunately, reducing the rivers reduces more than just water. Federal agencies control the flow of rivers to the degree that floods no longer deliver silt deposits. Yet a natural flow of Great Plains silt is essential for cottonwood regermination in the riparian corridor—the trees normally need the scouring of floods and deposits of silt for their seeds to germinate and for their seedlings to prosper. Without planned flood releases from the upstream reservoirs, the king of trees on the Great Plains will slowly be eliminated and, along with it, a circle of life. Researchers have documented this problem on the Milk River in Montana, but it's evident just by looking that scores of riverfronts have old and dying cottonwoods and no young trees in sight.

Even more troublesome, the Missouri River's water lacks nutrients because of sediment trapped in the reservoirs, a deficiency as upsetting to the riparian system as scurvy was to old-time sailors. Researchers Larry Hesse, Carl Wolfe, and Nancy Cole report that carbon losses have become a serious problem in the river and on its floodplain. With agriculture depleting organic matter by 25 percent over a forty-three-year period and with dams trapping carbon-rich sediment, a 65 percent loss in this vital substance has occurred. So essential is the life-building element to flora and fauna that the carbon cycle has been called "the cycle of life"—a badly crippled cycle on this great river system. New flow regimes from the reservoirs and the return of decent flows to the riverbeds must occur if these and other rivers of the Plains are to sustain some threshold of value beyond their use as irrigation conduits for surplus crops and sewers for the cities.

Because of the scarcity of water, long stretches of Great Plains rivers have no dams. In fact, the longest unimpounded reaches in the country are here—status that is unfortunately compromised by wholesale diversions. The Loup-Platte-Missouri combination runs for 996 miles without dams, including 609 miles of the channelized Missouri below the Platte in the Midwest. The Elkhorn and middle Platte of Nebraska likewise combine with the Missouri for long free-flowing mileage. The White of South Dakota, the Cimarron of Kansas and Oklahoma, and two dozen rivers in all flow many miles without dams (see appendix 2).

Looking at some of the more interesting rivers of the Great Plains from north to south, I begin with the Milk River, at the eastern boundary of Glacier National Park. It crosses into Alberta for 100 miles, then traverses northern Montana. The 625-mile stream joins the Missouri with a flow of 710 cfs, having lost much of its flow to diversions, but nearly half its length below Fresno Dam offers continuous canoeing in undeveloped country. The 210-mile Marias River flows down to the Missouri in a cottonwood-bottom landscape of rich prairie beauty, similar to the grasslands and gray bluffs of the bullish Missouri but in charming miniature. The sweetest springtime canoe trip I ever took on the Plains followed the twisting shine of this prairie stream, rich with birds and beavers through cottonwood forests that have not yet succumbed to old age but that may someday be only a sad memory below Tiber Dam. Also winding many miles across Montana, the Musselshell River joins the Missouri from the south.

A mature Missouri arrives on the Great Plains from the Rockies and curves below Fort Benton through a 149-mile section scarcely affected by civilization except for heavy cattle grazing and a resultant loss of young cottonwoods. Then the river encounters immense reservoirs. Only one-third of the main stem's length survives free-flowing and unchannelized. One-third pools into large reservoirs, and the final third of the river, below Sioux City, Iowa, is dredged and riprapped as a barge channel. That 730-mile section was dug nine feet deep and 300 feet wide and maintained to carry a scant 2 million tons of freight per year. The Mississippi, in comparison, carries 26 million tons above St. Louis. Two fine sections of the middle Missouri remain undammed and unchannelized: 39 miles below Fort Randall Dam and 59 miles below Gavins Point Dam, both on the border of Nebraska. These offer some hint of what the original Missouri had to offer—the great waterway of Lewis and Clark, trappers, and settlers.

The Yellowstone's 700-mile route begins in the Rockies, flows into the Plains near Billings, then runs for another 350 miles. Three low dams cross the river below Billings at Huntley, Forsyth, and Intake; this river would otherwise be the longest completely undammed river in forty-nine states. For its riparian corridor, fisheries, length, and volume, the Yellowstone is the preeminent river of the Great Plains and the only large river remaining with much of its original nature intact.

Joining the Yellowstone are the Bighorn River of trout-fishing fame and the Tongue, with a 100-mile reach of free-flowing water below the Wyoming state line. The Powder has rolling prairie views and a 385-mile reach without dams.

In Montana, South Dakota, and North Dakota, the Little Missouri snakes its way for 560 miles but never amounts to much in terms of volume. It runs through Theodore Roosevelt National Park and the Little Missouri National Grassland—one of few remnants of native short-grass prairie. On a backpacking trip there, I found prairie-river solitude and bison wading in the water and rolling in dusty silt. Farther south, the White River cuts through eroded bluffs of badlands in South Dakota. As a north-to-south centerline of the prairie potholes region of wetlands in the Dakotas, the 429-mile James River has erroneously been called America's longest nonnavigable river (a number of others are longer). At the eastern edge of the Plains, the Big Sioux River flows south, and at the city of Sioux Falls it has been channelized, like other prairie streams through cities.

The 310-mile main stem Platte dominates the central core of Nebraska. Once defining the location of the Oregon Trail, the Platte's route remains a transportation corridor accommodating Interstate 80. The wide, shallow, braided river takes much of its water from Rocky Mountain tributaries—the 618-mile North Platte and the 424-mile South Platte. Just before joining, these two rivers oddly parallel each other, 10 miles apart, for 45 miles. The middle Platte is a critical resting area for migrating sandhill cranes, waterfowl, shorebirds, and endangered whooping cranes. Six dams each on the North and South Platte and many diversions have destroyed habitat, and wildlife groups in Nebraska work to improve instream flows and restore critical flood events.

A set of eastbound streams joins the Platte from the north. Popular for canoeing in the spring and fall, the Elkhorn (1,120 cfs) is the northernmost Platte tributary. The Calamus houses abundant wildlife before it joins the North Loup. Like the Elkhorn and Calamus, the Dismal River is supported by groundwater of the Sand Hills, and it flows to the Middle Loup with a steady hydrograph that depends on the sandy aquifer.

The 445-mile Republican River flows across Nebraska and Kansas and joins the 540-mile Smoky Hill of Kansas. Cottonwoods survive in some sections, while others are dammed; all are subject to diversions. The two tributaries form the Kansas River, which bisects the gently rolling Flint Hills—one section of the Plains that still resembles a native tallgrass prairie. The Kansas finally joins the Missouri in Kansas City. The little-known Neosho River flows southward for 460 miles through Kansas and Oklahoma to the Arkansas.

The Arkansas River starts with Colorado snowmelt but soon is sucked dry. This river once nourished oases of deciduous groves, wetlands semisolid with ducks, and habitat of the threatened Arkansas darter and whooping crane. But today's bedraggled Arkansas in eastern Colorado rarely conveys enough runoff to satisfy the water rights of ranchers. Once replenishing the river farther down, water from the Ogallala Aquifer is now pumped onto fields instead. From the Colorado-Kansas

Little Missouri River, ND

Niobrara River below Lions Bridge, NE

Niobrara at Horseshoe Falls, NE

Snake River near the Niobrara, NE

Marias River below Tiber Dam, MT

Powder River near mouth, MT

Niobrara River below Valentine, NE

Niobrara above Norden, NE

state line eastward for 110 miles, little remains of the Arkansas but a dusty strip of brush.

While interest grew farther north to save what little was left of the Missouri and Platte, people all but ignored the Arkansas. Its habitat was lost, making the job of restoring flows and riparian life an even more onerous task. As a cultural boundary in the Great Plains, the Arkansas divides the Protestant, Republican northern settlements of Nebraska and Kansas from the Catholic, Democratic, and Hispanic influence to the south. The river exits Kansas with a flow of only 1,800 cfs and enters Oklahoma, where it passes through Tulsa. On the lower river, a linked chain of reservoirs leads to the Coastal Plain.

In Oklahoma, the 600-mile Cimarron (1,180 cfs) flows to the Arkansas. The 906-mile Canadian River, with headwaters in the Sangre de Cristo Mountains, part of New Mexico's Rockies, likewise crosses the Plains to the Arkansas. The Illinois, in the wetter northeastern corner of Oklahoma, draws thousands of canoeists as the state's favorite recreational river at the edge of the Midwest's Ozark Mountains before its 867 cfs flows into the Arkansas.

The Red River comes from northern Texas, then forms the state's boundary with Oklahoma before emptying onto the Coastal Plain and becoming a principal supplier of Louisiana's Atchafalaya River. A tributary in northern Texas boasts one of the longest river names in America: Prairie Dog Town Fork of the Red River.

The Brazos drains an enormous watershed of north central Texas but delivers a creeklike flow of 836 cfs across the Coastal Plain to the Gulf of Mexico. Southward, the 862-mile Colorado River of Texas curves across the center of the state to join the Coastal Plain. Dammed and diverted, these rivers were once lifelines of riparian habitat that is mostly forgotten today. The Pecos, rising in the Sangre de Cristo Mountains, drops through eastern New Mexico and ends up with a flow of only 84 cfs at the Rio Grande, a 926-mile study in diversions for hardscrabble ranches, riparian zones grazed to dust, and seepage from oil rigs, all summarizing much about the southern end of America's Great Plains.

The Niobrara River

Though it is not typical of the region's collection of rivers but rather one of its finest, I chose the Niobrara of Nebraska as a place to seek out the character of river life on the Great Plains.

Hunting for the Niobrara's headwaters where the map shows a stream at Lusk, Wyoming, I found no water at all but only a low swale in a rolling range of irrigated hay fields. Farther east, at the state's boundary with Nebraska, a small wetland in an open draw marked the river's course. Redwings screeched on cattails while two men plumbed sprinkler pipe that sprayed an electric cloudburst of groundwater.

Seepages have eventually grown to become a stream curling past cottonwoods with a green mat of mixed grasses, including blue grama, little bluestem, and the showy flairs of needle-and-thread. Agate Fossil Beds National Monument straddles the upper Niobrara. On knolls over-looking the river, paleontologists unearthed fossils of mammals from 19 million years ago: horned rhinoceroses as plentiful as buffalo, seven-foot-tall pigs, and horselike creatures with claws. Just east of here the Sand Hills begin, a 20,000-square-mile expanse of dunes up to 400 feet high. This sand dune area, the largest in the hemisphere, is now knee-deep in grass—the greatest sweep of unbroken grassland on the con-tinent.

I had spent most of my years canoeing on rivers of mountain regions, but I was growing excited about seeing all I could of this prairie place. It was different, and unlike many rivers through the flatter landscapes of America, it remained undeveloped. As I packed for my eight-day, 150-mile trip, the radio announced tornado warnings for eastern Ne-braska and severe thunderstorms elsewhere. Having expected only the intense heat of the Great Plains in July, I stuffed in my best rain gear.

My shuttle driver, Bonnie Metcalf, taught home economics on the Sioux reservation nearby in South Dakota and in summer drove shut-tles for canoe outfitter Lou Christiansen. "It's a vacation from school," she said of her job toting people up and down a popular section of the Niobrara.

Hearing stories of farming, of the reservation, and of the river, I rode westward with Bonnie for two hours to a dirt road south of Gordon, where the Plains felt satisfyingly remote. While Bonnie lent a hand un-loading gear, Phil Young, an agronomist for the Soil Conservation Ser-vice, pulled up. He pitched in as well, seeming pleased to have some-one to visit on this lonely prairie. "Watch for fossils," he recommended, and as easily as finding a beer-can pop-top, he plucked up a fragment of bone that had the heft of rock. "You might also want to check out the snake den," he offered. "Forty or fifty rattlesnakes, gobs of them two feet high, no kidding, just downriver." I said that I might just stay on the water. For a couple of days.

Waving good-by, I drifted off in the animated twenty-foot-wide, sand-bottomed stream. Spring flows gurgled in constantly. As the maker of scenery here, the river has entrenched its valley 200 feet into the hills. The valley bottom is often crowded with invasive juniper since the advent of fire suppression, but it is also shaded by the elegant, large-leaved eastern cottonwood, the compound-leaved green ash, and the box elder, with foliage that looks like poison ivy. Black-eyed Susans and pink splashes of Joe-pye weed brought an eastern look to the sunny banks; jewelweed dotted the damp, shady enclaves with orange. If any plant is the opposite of the juicy, tender jewelweed, it is the desert-dwelling yucca, with its dagger-sharp leaves. It also grew there, sprouting up above the grass on south-facing slopes. North faces whistled with groves of ponderosa pine, almost black in contrast to the pale sea of grass that from hilltops seemed to roll as unbroken as an ocean. The topographical map confirmed my impressions: entire sheets of patternless hills were divided only by this wiggle of river and its lonely threadline of trees.

All this came as a relief from the burnt-out cattle country in so much of the West; Nebraska gets more moisture, so bunchgrasses grow better. Here, exotic weeds such as cheat grass, star thistle, and Russian knapweed don't have the arid advantage that allows them to invade the drier ranges once the native grasses are depleted by cows. Also, if ranchers overgraze in the Sand Hills, the results show quickly on the sandy, droughty soils; the problems take not generations but months to appear. *An Atlas of the Sand Hills* calls this area one of the "best managed large tracts of rangeland in the world." While almost all the Niobrara riverfront showed evidence of cows, little of it had been beaten to dirt. Yet the cottonwood groves of cool shade had been stomped to a mulch of bark, twigs, and manure, and I saw little regermination of trees anywhere.

In the riparian thickets I saw startlingly brilliant red-headed woodpeckers climbing cottonwood trunks. Eastern kingbirds snatched insects on the wing. Sandpipers pecked on the shores, great blue herons speared prey in shallow water, and cormorants with snakelike necks dove for fish. Both Say's and eastern phoebes lived there, marking the Niobrara as a preeminent mixing zone. Here were the blue jay from the East and the western tanager from the West. Rufous-sided towhees from the East breed with spotted towhees from the West, producing hybrids. The National Park Service reported that 160 species meet the edge of their range in the Niobrara valley. The evolutionary biologists say that here, at the limits of species' ranges, adaptation and hybridization occur the most. A place of great importance, this is where evolution happens.

Running west to east, with Wyoming at its headwaters and the Midwest near its outlet, the Niobrara is the reason that the biology of the

East and the West can mix. Lying at midcontinent, this riparian corridor also allows for mixing from north and south. In cool pockets I saw the paper birches of the north woods, and in sunny glades I saw the bur oaks of the prairie.

The human scene evolves here as well in a rare case of diminishing development. Along the left bank, an abandoned house and barn spoke of the exodus from ranches. A dusty piano remained, half its keys mute. Any attempt at music was as pathetic as the tumbledown barn, discordant in these ruins along the quiet river.

As I paddled downstream, two cowboys herding eight fat cows appeared from behind the brow of a hill. We waved. I saw no one else in four days—a solitude found on few American rivers outside Alaska.

Cattle fences posed the big hazard. Every mile or two I'd slip under one without trouble. But once, while I was taking notes, a fence caught me by surprise, the current swift, the canoe sideways, the barbed wire a foot off the water. I thrust my paddle forward handle first, striking the barbed wire with the shaft just above my grip. Then I lifted the loose wire up and over as I ducked into the bottom of the boat—a close call.

Below the Merriman bridge, the river broadened to 200 feet and the boat grated on sand. Again and again I stepped out, pushed my loaded canoe across the shoaly bottom, and jumped back in. Twenty fences crossed the river in a day. Weary of barbed wire and sandbars coupled with headwinds, I camped and considered my future: 100 miles to go, with little access in that remote wildness of Nebraska. Relative to wilderness of the West, this was a civilized alternative. Relative to the East, it was wild country—once again, a river of transition. The Niobrara resembled what so many midwestern and eastern rivers used to be—qualities lost from memory elsewhere.

The best of those qualities lay in an enchanting reach above the Cody bridge. Box elders and cottonwoods hugged the shores in an emerald thicket backed by darkened pine. Springwaters trickled out of fern-covered banks, and deer bounded away from me. I climbed to a bluff and stared, half enchanted at the sea of grass.

Bouncing along the riffles the next morning, I was taken by surprise. A sign read, "Warning, absolutely no canoeing or swimming between falls and bridge." I had expected no waterfalls in Nebraska, but hearing a rumble and spotting a cloud of mist swirling where the river disappeared, I decided to take a look.

The river incredibly narrowed from 100 feet to 20 where it plunged over a U-shaped falls. The open end of the U pointed downstream, after which the strictured Niobrara entered what can only be described as a slit in sandstone bedrock. This continued for several hundred yards, the narrowest point being *one foot* wide. The entire river pummeled through underneath in a channel obviously undercut to accommodate the flow. I portaged.

Hours later, still impressed by the falls, I took the next rapid seriously, ran the three-foot drop on the right, and camped just below. Hemmed in by slopes, the area was ungrazed, and I found cottonwood seedlings everywhere. I took care not to smash them when I pitched my tent, which was essential for mosquito protection. As on other mornings and evenings, no-see-ums also troubled me, and when I climbed into the tent to eat dinner, I found two ticks crawling up my legs.

Paddling steadily the next day, I passed carp that slopped for food at the river's edges. The backs of those beefy denizens measured four inches across. I enjoyed seeing such large fish, but these introduced exotics eat aquatic plants needed for oxygen discharge and for cover of other fish and invertebrates. They root around on the bottom and make the water turbid, blocking sunlight and preventing photosynthesis, which is beneficial to the life in the river. Like almost any exotic species, they are troublesome to native life.

Pumps now and then sucked water from the river for farms. Irrigation demands near the Niobrara have not grown much, yet there is nothing to ensure that the river won't eventually be depleted, as nearly every other river on the Plains has been. A study by the Nebraska Natural Resources Commission in the 1970s reported that the Sand Hills could lose a quarter of their flow by 2020 if regulations on pumping were not enacted. As of 1995, changes in regulations and the agricultural economy had led to some reduction in irrigation in the Hills, but Long Pine Creek remained the state's only instream reservation of minimum flows for fish and wildlife. Virtually all the other rivers are degraded, and fixing a broken stream is far more difficult than keeping it healthy in the first place. By August, an estimated 99 percent of the Niobrara's flow comes from groundwater trickling back in—a flow that could be jeopardized by pumping operations many miles away. And before the river drops, tributaries and wetlands incur damage. After the current, contentious debate over Platte River flows is resolved, perhaps Nebraska will turn some preventive attention to the Niobrara.

Passing out of farmland again, I admired bur oaks in a grassland-oak savanna where only bison were absent from the scene. I pitched my tent at a small rapid as afternoon thunderheads dampened the heat and entertained me with rumbles and lightning.

At Highway 20 near Valentine, tractor-trailer rigs banged on the expansion joints at either end of the bridge; this was the first road I had seen with any traffic at all. I paddled through a few miles of flatwater to Cornell Dam, an over-the-top impoundment with the takeout only five feet from the lip of the dam—a scary exit with a killer hydraulic below. Built for hydropower, the dam is one of only four on the Niobrara (two small dams block the upper river). Because the reservoir had filled with sand, the Nebraska Public Power Company unloaded it on the U.S. Fish and Wildlife Service for one dollar, thus escaping responsibility for retirement of the dam. Assistant refuge manager Mark Lindvall cautioned me during an interview that it would be difficult to get rid of the dam; just what will be done is a good question. The situation here is a forerunner to what will happen at thousands of sites as old dams become more white elephants than the symbols of progress they were once made out to be.

At the Cornell bridge, people embark on their one-day Niobrara trips. I walked up the boat ramp to take a look and, after encountering almost no one for days, took stock of 100 cars, six canoe trailers, and a flatbed hitched to a semi and loaded with fat black inner tubes for rent. About 35,000 floaters per year enjoy this section, making the Niobrara the most popular river in Nebraska. "Because of river recreation, the Niobrara is now the identifying feature of this whole area," said Bob Hilske, director of the Middle Niobrara Natural Resources District, part of a statewide system of local soil and water management agencies. For a mile-by-mile log of this section, I pulled out my *Niobrara River Canoeing Guide* by Duane Gudgel, who operates a bookstore in Valentine and promotes good care of the river.

Here the Niobrara passes through the Fort Niobrara National Wildlife Refuge, where a 6-mile stretch along the northern shore is designated as wilderness—rare status on the Plains. A herd of 500 buffalo and longhorn cattle lives inside fences in the refuge.

Soon I caught up to the crowd—families, children, beer guzzlers, high school couples, and even groups of elderly people. Middle-aged Brenda, Beverly, and Barbara lay on tied-together inner tubes, having a good time. The next group had strapped their eight canoes together, which didn't prevent one from tipping over in a riffle and discombobulating the others.

"This river is a part of growing up in Nebraska," Bill Tiwald told me. He chaperoned eight teenagers, including two of his own, who came from Lincoln every year. Jessica Tiwald, soon to leave for college, planned to major in biology. "It's about life," she explained. "I want to

do environmental restoration work; that would be perfect." Later I paddled along with Steve Winter and the University of Nebraska's Wildlife
Management Club, whose members also came to the river every year.
A few boaters fished for common carp, channel catfish, white crappie,
and silver chub.

Spicing up the float trip, a tributary plunged sixty feet into the valley
at Smith Falls, Nebraska's tallest waterfall. On my last trip here, in 1978,
I had seen nobody. Now I saw fifty people. Downstream, new home-
sites occasionally popped into view where trees had been cleared; subdivision of ranchland is the main threat to the river. Precluding development on 54,000 acres of the region with 30 miles of river frontage,
The Nature Conservancy created the Niobrara Valley Preserve with land
bought from ranchers in the early 1980s. Here, six ecosystems mix in
what the Conservancy calls the "biological crossroads of the nation."

Recognizing a familiar spot, I beached at Sunny Brook Camp to visit
rancher Roy Breuklander, whom I had interviewed in 1978, when Norden Dam threatened this reach. A little boy back then, Roy's son now
ran 300 head of cattle by summering them on higher ground and herding them back down in winter. "That gives the cattle better shelter in
winter, and it's a little easier on the river in summer," Roy explained. In
"retirement," Roy manages a campground and canoe livery—"a good
cash crop." Camping for the night, I was tickled by a show of lightning
bugs, twenty of them flashing at once—a whimsical eastern species not
seen in the West.

Though most people end their Niobrara trips at Rocky Ford, I
portaged the difficult rapid, then ran another sharp drop before drifting into a braided reach of sand bars. White pelicans gleamed in the
shallow water. Above the Norden bridge, I ended my canoe journey by
wading through the shallows and tugging my boat ashore. For a long
time I stood ankle deep in the river, allowing the current to speed past
my feet and wash the sand away, lowering me inch by inch into the
Niobrara. A pillar of a cloud boiled into thunderheads as the setting sun
lit a brewing sky, ready to explode over the Great Plains. Red and rose
leaked out at the cloud's base and rays of sunlight pierced it. I felt
blessed to have seen the Great Plains through the lens of the Niobrara.

Near here, the mile-wide Norden Dam would have backed up the
river for 19 miles and buried the valley in order to export water 80
miles by canal to another region. About 260 farmers would have benefited from the $230 million, taxpayer-funded project, which would
have been the only large dam on this river of more than 500 miles. Half
the land was already irrigated, another 30 percent was classified as haz-

ardous for irrigation, and local ranchers would have been put out of business. A classic case in the waning days of the big-dam culture, Norden was beat by local ranchers and a national movement. Both exposed as ludicrous the trumped-up benefits of the project. They questioned the wisdom of watering surplus crops, at a cost to taxpayers of nearly $1 million per farmer, and articulated the biological values that would be lost. The project and alternatives to it smoldered while conservationists launched a campaign to make the Niobrara a National Wild and Scenic River and to nail shut the coffin of the dam. In 1991, after a truculent struggle in which dam supporters and antigovernment zealots incited opposition to Wild and Scenic status based on fear of widespread condemnation, which had never even been considered, Congress designated sections totaling 96 miles—the most significant prairie river in the National Wild and Scenic Rivers System. Emphasizing local participation, the National Park Service drafted a management plan for the river.

For a good view of the dam site, Kerri Barnes, a granddaughter in a local ranching family and a spokeswoman for The Nature Conservancy, drove me to an overlook downstream of the Norden bridge. Hundreds of yards across and braided with shifting sand, the Niobrara drifted down through deciduous forests. Pines huddled on cooler slopes while the prairie flowed out in all directions. Some of the Conservancy's 300 bison grazed on hills to the south, though 65 percent of the preserve is occupied by 3,500 cattle. Lease payments cover the Conservancy's expenses. A wooden plaque at the overlook recognized the efforts of rancher Loring Kuhre, who with his wife, Beryl, had worked to defeat the dam.

Saying good-by to Kerri, I drove on eastward toward the lower river, and at Ainsworth I camped in the town's park and breathed in "the good life"—a state slogan I remembered from highway signs at the Nebraska border. Old people picnicked together; young men batted baseballs; families with children grilled hamburgers. Even mothers smiled and said "Hi" to me in this friendly home song of a place, so nice that I wanted to stay and play ball and picnic myself. Then I thought about the Wild and Scenic River battle that had raged here, of people's quickness to hate what is feared to be different and new. Ironically, the designation prevented what would have been *really* different and new—Norden Dam. But people readily believed the right-wing, anticonservation rhetoric. Local residents, chanting against protection of the river, stormed out of a town meeting. They brought a horse to a public discussion with Senator Jim Exon; attached to the animal was an arrow pointing to the horse's rear with the label "Senator Exon." Citizens supporting protection were afraid to go into town, much less speak out in favor of the river. But Senator Exon, Congressman Douglas Bereuter, and other supporters held tight, and the designation passed in spite of the animosity.

For 120 miles below Norden, the Niobrara flushed down in shallow braids, inaccessible except at a few bridges. This reach is important to the rare piping plover and least tern, which nest on the sandbars. At the Highway 281 bridge, the Spencer hydroelectric dam blocked the stream and a brown jet of water flumed out of the twenty-foot-high structure for the final leg of the river's journey.

Down at the mouth of the river, the Army Corps of Engineers had relocated the town of Niobrara because Gavins Point Dam on the Missouri had caused siltation, raised groundwater, and made the old town unlivable. One of the first settlements in Nebraska had been reincarnated in ranch houses and commercial buildings styled for an interstate highway off-ramp.

At the last Niobrara bridge, the current rushed and caused "sand" waves to rise and fall, a result of the corrugated bed beneath them being eroded, then quickly built up again with fast-moving sand migrating downriver. I tried to walk to the mouth, where the Niobrara's average flow of 1,581 cubic feet per second meets the Missouri, but in that rainy year, even with my knee-high rubber boots I was stopped by wetlands again and again.

Finally, I contented myself at a viewpoint on a bluff in Niobrara State Park. The mouth of the river lay down below. On the hills, a savanna of bur oaks and grass stretched out to the horizon while the floodplain lay veined in cottonwoods guarding wetland crescents. Even from that distance, I could hear the swish of the Niobrara's water and sand where they met the broad Missouri.

Chapter 6

—◄═══►—

Rocky Mountain Lifelines

Everything good about rivers seemed to be wrapped up into one. Transparent water seeped out of snowbanks to rush plentifully down a bouldered bed. Above a wetland willow thicket on the floodplain, mountains rose from both banks in terraces of wildflower meadows, then fir-clad slopes, then rocky profiles jutting skyward above timberline. The stream alternately leaped over blackened rocks, then reclined in S bends over a pebbled bed of colored stones. This happened to be Granite Creek, a tributary to the Hoback and Snake Rivers in Wyoming, but it could have been any one of a hundred waterways in this celebrated region of rivers.

From Canada to New Mexico, ridges and peaks of the Rockies stack up one beyond another for 1,000 miles, with a width of up to 450 miles (the range continues another 1,500 miles in Canada). This is the largest North American mountain range. Raking off the moisture of Pacific Ocean storms, the Rocky Mountains and their prodigious snowpack make the rivers possible.

The Rockies include the mountainous terrain of northeastern Washington, which is often forgotten as a part of this range—though it is sig-

Rocky Mountain Rivers

- - - boundary of river region

© Tim Palmer

Scale in Miles

0   100   200

nificant, containing the two largest rivers of the region. Western Montana and most of Idaho form the heart of the northern Rockies. Most of Wyoming lies in the range if the dry plains of the Wyoming Basin in the central and southern parts of the state are counted. The Rockies also claim northeastern Utah, the western half of Colorado, and a north central bite out of New Mexico. The Great Plains border the Rockies on their eastern front, which rises abruptly as a fault-block where rivers issue out of canyons. The desert regions of the Columbia Plateau, Basin, and Range, and Colorado Plateau provinces adjoin on the west in a vaguely defined border where the rivers wind out of the mountains and through foothill canyons to drier country.

The Rockies date to an upheaval event called the Laramide Revolution, which occurred intermittently for 40 million years and buckled the region like an accordion from one side to the other. The mountains appear not as one continuous range but as many, each with a personality, separated by valleys and gaps and, thus, by rivers. The greatest contiguous mass of mountains rises in Idaho, a state with eighty-one named ranges and a riverscape that many people consider the finest of all for wilderness and whitewater. The "Shining Mountains," as trappers once called the Rockies, embrace not only mountains and valleys but also "holes" of lowland crossed by rivers as well as plateaus on the western slopes. The White River and Uncompahgre Plateaus in Colorado, for example, spawn dozens of streams.

The Laramide upwelling resulted in granite batholiths—large masses of hard, gray rock that form cornerstones to the regional identity. Unlike that of the Colorado Plateau to the west, the overlying sedimentary strata in the Rockies was broken, deformed, and in many cases eroded away, exposing the granite underneath. Rivers running through these "basement" complexes of granite and other resistant metamorphic rocks create the narrowest canyons, and in some reaches the foaming rivers seem to be more air than water. In Colorado alone, canyons with rivers slicing through the basement rock include Northgate of the North Platte, Gore and Glenwood of the Colorado, Black Canyon of the Gunnison, Waterton Canyon of the South Platte, and Royal Gorge of the Arkansas.

Some of the Rocky Mountain canyons are antecedent, meaning that the rivers existed before the mountains and carved into them as they arose. The Bighorn in Wyoming is an example. Others, such as the Gunnison of the Black Canyon in Colorado, are superimposed, meaning that they established their routes while flowing through soft material once lying atop the rocks seen today; eventually the rivers penetrated the harder rocks underneath, maintaining their established routes as they cut slowly into the basement complex. Some rivers were deflected by rising mountain ranges and found routes around them; the upper Snake, for example, dodged mountain ranges left and right.

Compared with rivers of the Appalachians, Rocky Mountain rivers tend to have steeper descents, reflecting the region's massive topography. Below the stair-step plunges, the flows tend more toward big, open flushes of water than the sandstone-clogged pool-and-drop of the Appalachians' artfully honed whitewater.

One of the country's most photogenic regions, defining the word "scenery" in the minds of many Americans, the Rockies are cloaked by coniferous forests of pine, fir, and spruce intermingled with aspen groves. Cottonwoods and willows line the riparian corridors throughout: narrowleaf cottonwood at high elevations, black cottonwood or closely related balsam poplar thriving lower down, and Fremont cottonwood toward the south. Lanceleaf cottonwood is also found, as well as a whole range of hybrids. Typifying the Rockies, long ridgelines of treeless high country make spectacular views from headwater streams and upper-elevation rivers.

Severe winters rule here, followed by short, brilliantly flowered summers. Small towns, once centered on the mining and logging industries, now depend on tourism, which has become the number one industry. Dozens of old mining towns metamorphosed into winter resorts and then into year-round recreational hot spots, including Ketchum, along the Big Wood River in Idaho, and Aspen, along the Roaring Fork in Colorado.

In a much-noted article titled "The American West: Perpetual Mirage," historian Walter Prescott Webb wrote, "The heart of the West is a desert, unqualified and absolute." Yet the West just as arguably possesses a mountain heart. If the human body is the analogy, the West's life-giving circulatory system is its rivers, and the sources of the rivers are the mountains, where snowmelt yields 70 percent of the West's water supplies. The forests likewise lie in the mountains, and wildlife populations here and in the foothills realize their greatest potential. It is the mountains that draw the people; they come to see the terrain of the Tetons and the high country of Colorado more than the drylands in between. Yet the towns and the farmland reside more in the deserts, where the realities of living in a hostile environment are faced. Webb's point was that "the overriding influence that shapes the West is the desert." That may be true, but the mountains, with their water, form the heart that makes life possible.

With a climate of stormy winters and dry summers, snowfall here is far more significant than rain. The heaviest storms occur at middle and high elevations, where the water is stored in solid form as snowfields that last well into summer and cause the rivers to crest in late May or early June after nighttime temperatures quit refreezing the snowpack. In much of the Rockies, 40 percent of the runoff comes in April, May, and June. Flows on a river such as the Yampa in Colorado go from several hundred cfs to 20,000 in a wet year, peaking sharply and then dropping again. Far from being the nuisance often associated with floods, the peaks of snowmelt are essential to a host of biological cycles sustaining everything from cottonwood groves to endangered fish to the pool-and-riffle sequence that is vital to trout.

It rains far more in the north—the isohyet of forty to eighty inches circles north central Idaho. Thus Washington, Idaho, and Montana contain the greatest density of streams and the largest rivers. Other pockets of twenty to forty inches of precipitation lie in the high mountains of northwestern Wyoming and all along the Continental Divide in Colorado, but these belts are too small to result in rivers at the scale of those in the north. Flows drop sharply in midsummer, but thunderstorms augment the supply slightly. The lowest flows occur during the winter freeze, a situation often accentuated to a troublesome degree by dams that hold back winter runoff for release during the next irrigation season.

Falling off the backbone of the continent, the Rocky Mountain rivers spread like the tentacles of an octopus in nine major river basins, eventually draining toward two oceans and spanning almost two-thirds of the distance from the Atlantic to the Pacific. In the Northwest, the Columbia River, with the Snake as its principal tributary, supplies the Pacific. The Missouri, which receives the abundant volume of the Yellowstone, runs northeast and then east toward the Mississippi. The Platte flows east from the mountains of Wyoming and Colorado to the lower Missouri, and the Arkansas tracks southeast from southern Colorado. The Rio Grande drains south central Colorado to New Mexico and then to the Gulf of Mexico, and the Colorado collects the waters of southwestern Wyoming and Colorado and carries them southwest to Mexico's Gulf of California. A smaller stream, the Bear River, drains a west central corner of the Rockies to the Great Salt Lake.

These rivers all flow away from the mountains, and not a single stream transects the range—a situation existing only in the Rockies and Brooks Range among all of America's major mountain masses. The closest thing to a transmountain waterway is the phenomenon of linked headwaters. The best example is the Snake River's tributary of Pacific Creek, which interlocks with Atlantic Creek and the Yellowstone-Missouri-Mississippi system. Two Ocean Lake joins the creeks at their source and creates an all-water passage from the Pacific to the Atlantic, though its terrain is so high and rugged that no road, let alone boating route, has ever followed the same path.

The nine basins include rivers and reaches of delightfully distinct types. High-country alpine streams flow in greater abundance here than anywhere else but the Sierra Nevada. Most of these plunge down steep gradients. But some sections, such as the upper Colorado in Rocky Mountain National Park, meander through flat valleys in a pattern simulating lowland rivers with recurved loops near sea level. The winding rivers of the high country result from hard rock strata or glacial moraines "damming" the streams' escape routes, causing a buildup of silt in wet mountain meadows. A second type of river reach is one that flows through somber landscapes thick with fir, spruce, and pine in the middle elevations and brightened in places by meadows along the water. In both of these types glacial moraines, landslides, and the sheer gradient of the mountains create frequent, if not continuous, whitewater. At lower elevations tributary streams dump alluvial debris into the main channel, constricting it and creating more rapids.

As a third type of river, streams cut deep, tumultuous courses through gorges in high and middle elevations and even deeper chasms in the drier foothills country that fingers out into the desert region. Unlike the desert rivers, the rivers in these canyons often include pockets of ponderosa pine on the flats, slopes of fir on cool northern aspects, and riparian thickets of cottonwoods and willows. On the low, dry western slope of the Rockies the canyons often have steeper sides than those abutting higher-elevation rivers. Down there in dry country the rivers are the only major cause of erosion, while up above, heavier precipitation erodes the flanks of the canyons and valleys, causing them to slump and incline more gradually. As a final type of Rocky Mountain river, dozens of reaches of valley streams aligned between mountain ridges wind through ranchland and support fine cottonwood groves. Many of these flow through alluvial outwash of sand, gravel, and rock that was laid down by much higher rivers when the glaciers melted.

Being in a headwaters area, the Rocky Mountain rivers are smaller than those of most other regions, but waters from these many mountains later consolidate to yield the large rivers of the Great Plains, Midwest, desert, and Northwest. Nine of the region's ten largest waterways lie in the north. The oceanic Columbia averages 101,300 cubic feet per second at the international border, where runoff of the Canadian Rockies nears the desert region of the Columbia Plateau. Second largest is the Pend Oreille (pond-o-RAY) of Idaho and northeastern Washington, flowing from a lake of the same name. The Clark Fork of Montana is really the same river, being the inlet to Pend Oreille Lake and flowing with 20,010 cfs (not to be confused with the smaller Clark's Fork of the Yellowstone in Wyoming and Montana; the "s" distinguishes the two). Dams block the entire length of the Pend Oreille in the United States and all of the Columbia in the United States, except for 50 miles in the desert region.

The third-largest river in the Rockies is the Clearwater of Idaho, flowing with 15,500 cfs into the lower Snake River. The Kootenai of Montana and Idaho carries 11,740 cfs. Only slightly smaller, the Salmon in Idaho averages 11,420 cfs before emptying into the Snake. The Flathead of northwestern Montana flows with 9,737 cfs as the principal tributary to the Clark Fork. The upper Snake River, with its Henrys Fork, leaves the Rocky Mountains above Idaho Falls with a flow of 8,779 cfs, later swelling with other Rocky Mountain tributaries to 50,000 cfs at its mouth in the desert. The Missouri, as it enters the Great Plains, carries 7,827 cfs at Fort Benton. The Yellowstone enters the Plains near Billings, where it averages 7,074 cfs. The tenth-largest river of the Rockies but the largest in the entire southern two-thirds of the range is the Colorado, leaving the region with a flow of 6,559 cfs below its confluence with the Gunnison River at Grand Junction, Colorado.

Several combinations of rivers in the desert region have longer wild mileage than anything in the Rockies. But as a region, these mountains have more water than the desert and more public land than rivers of other regions and thus include more undeveloped stream frontage and unspoiled natural assets than are found in any other region except Alaska. The Salmon is the longest undammed and relatively undiverted river in forty-nine states; the Yellowstone is the longest with only small dams and lacking major diversions, channelization, or levees. The country's finest cottonwood ecosystems thrive along the upper Snake in Wyoming and Idaho, the Yampa in Colorado, and the North Platte in Colorado and Wyoming. Exemplars of the National Wild and Scenic Rivers lie in Idaho and Montana. The rivers of the Rockies rise in some of the largest protected wilderness areas and national parks, including Yellowstone, Grand Teton, Glacier, and Rocky Mountain. Only sixteen areas in the country outside Alaska are wild enough for a person to be 10 miles or more from any road, and half of those are in the Rockies (five lie in the Yellowstone–Beartooth–Wind River region, two in central Idaho, and one in the Bob Marshall Wilderness of Montana). Much of the finest trout fishing is in the Rockies, especially in southwestern Montana and east central Idaho. Whitewater paddlers consider the rivers of Idaho to be in a class by themselves, and thousands of smaller streams highlight the Rockies with their dazzling beauty. Fewer people live here than in any other region except Alaska.

The qualities that remain heighten an appalling sense of loss at what is gone. The pollution from mining, seen vividly in the spectacular San Juan Range of Colorado and other areas, represents a sellout of the West at a titanic scale. Under an 1872 law that western politicians defend as if their careers depend on it, miners continue to destroy land and rivers without observing adequate controls, without compensating the public, and sometimes without taking responsibility for the refuse and damage left in the wake of the mines. Logging denudes whole watersheds on private and public land. Most Forest Service timber sales in the Rockies lose money for the government and cause environmental damage from erosion, loss of floodplain forests, road construction, and habitat eradication. Dams pockmark the mountains and clog up many of the finest valleys and canyons.

Even worse, irrigation withdrawals dry up hundreds, if not thousands, of small streams and deplete even large rivers in Rocky Mountain valleys, from the Salmon to the Rio Grande. Diversions for urban use ship whole rivers to other watersheds and even other oceans. In the Colorado basin, for example, transbasin diversions diminish the Colorado, Fraser, Blue, Eagle, Roaring Fork, Fryingpan, Dolores, Navajo, and San Juan Rivers. Waters of the Colorado basin's Dolores River are sent to the San Juan, and then the San Juan is sent to the Rio Grande. To replace the water of the lower Colorado, which has been diverted to the suburbs of Los Angeles, California imports its own Feather and Trinity Rivers from 600 miles away. Many of these expensive schemes create not just ecological havoc but also a domino game of water supply problems. The entire tangled patch-kit of canals, pipes, siphons, and pumps results from compacts based on state boundaries, political muscle, and easy federal money feeding behemoth engineering works rather than good sense regarding hydrology, ecology, water efficiency, energy accountability, and sustainable economic development.

On virtually all large private tracts and on 70 to 90 percent of the public land, heavily subsidized cattle damage riparian zones. Salmon and steelhead runs have been depleted or eradicated in Rocky Mountain rivers of the Columbia basin, and bull trout and other critical species are declining rapidly. In most parts of the range whole aquatic ecosystems feel the stress of all these hazards while new threats worsen. A boom-and-bust cycle has plagued the regional economy through successive eras of grazing, mining, logging, and oil development. Now federal subsidies prop up virtually every aspect of the extractive economy, through which taxpayers of the whole nation perpetuate the abuses of land and water. Thanks to the clout of private vested interests that keep politicians in line and elect a cadre of Republicans who are uncompromisingly on their side, most of those subsidies have been immune to the budget-cutting axe affecting other federal programs since the 1970s.

But relative to other regions a valuable landscape remains, and recognizing the amenities of living in a place with relatively clean air and water, open space, recreational opportunities, and scenery, people flock to the Rockies as a new homeland. Between 1970 and 1990, the population of the region grew by 60 percent. Utah, Wyoming, Colorado, and Idaho ranked among the ten fastest-growing states on a percentage basis. While newcomers consume yet more land, pollute the air in valley towns during winter inversions, and push out the wildlife, many bring a desire to preserve what is left and reform the age-old dependence on subsidized commodity extraction. Biweekly reporting in *High Country News*—a superb environmental newspaper—documents growing interest by newcomers and natives alike in protecting remaining qualities.

Looking at some of the individual rivers from north to south, I see that the Columbia flows to the United States from farther north than any other river outside Alaska. This behemoth of the West is flooded by three enormous reservoirs in the Rocky Mountains of British Columbia. But at the Canadian headwaters, a 140-mile section remains undammed. Backed by high mountain peaks, this stunningly beautiful length of flatwater with two lakes in upper reaches is one of the most outstanding river-and-wetlands complexes on the continent. Another 45-mile section of free-flowing Columbia runs across the border to Northport, Washington, where it enters the reservoir behind Grand Coulee Dam.

Also flowing from British Columbia, the 480-mile Kootenai (spelled Kootenay in Canada) is impounded for 90 miles behind Libby Dam in Montana. Then it drifts through a forested setting and drums over one of the larger falls in the Rockies, at Kootenai Falls, west of Libby. This is the only waterfall remaining undammed on the Rocky Mountain rivers of highest volume. The Kootenai receives water from the rocky but cutover wilds of the Yaak River, which quivers with blood-red kokanee salmon in the fall, and runs on westward to Idaho. The once-great river ponds into reservoirs before reentering British Columbia, where it is fully dammed except for the final 3 miles above the Columbia.

The North Fork Flathead rises in British Columbia and then forms the western border of Glacier National Park, which has some of the most spectacular mountain scenery in America. Periodically threatened by coal mining in Canada and oil and gas drilling in Montana, the North Fork for now remains a fabulous stream of natural shorelines and views to country where wolf packs howl at night; the river and its adjacent mountains form a conduit of wilderness linking Canada and Montana. The Flathead's crystal-clear water in blue-green depths and its mosaic bed of black, white, and red metamorphic rocks is one of a kind, but it has been compromised in its lower reaches by a disgusting amount of silt rinsing off road cuts dug in the 1970s. Highway engineers were attempting to fix that problem by further grading the slide-prone areas in 1994. The Middle and South Forks of the Flathead plunge through the mountains of the Bob Marshall Wilderness and Great Bear Wilderness, with their choice habitat for grizzly bears. Hungry Horse Reservoir, on the lower South Fork, represents one of the greatest losses of a wild Rocky Mountain river to impoundment. The forks of the Flathead then join a placid but scenic main stem winding down to Flathead Lake, which has been raised by a dam. Below it, the lower river flows over the ripping drop of Buffalo Rapids and through pine and sage communities to the Clark Fork. Another Clark Fork tributary, the 100-mile Blackfoot, is a nearly undammed river of small rapids and ponderosa groves flowing through forest and ranchland.

The Clark Fork, an artery of the northern Rockies sometimes called the Clark Fork of the Columbia, flows for 200 miles across western Montana. With its continuation as the Pend Oreille River, it is even longer than the Columbia above the Pend Oreille confluence (though not nearly as large). The Clark Fork includes the nation's largest Superfund site of toxic wastes—mine debris with mercury, lead, and arsenic spread along 120 miles of riverbed in its upper reaches. In other sections between four dams, the river offers stretches of rapids suitable for daylong runs and quiet water for boating. The Clark Fork feeds Pend Oreille Lake in Idaho and emerges as the Pend Oreille River's chain of four reservoirs. These begin with Albeni Falls Dam, where a thundering waterfall existed until 1955. The lower river is likewise dammed in Canada. The Clark Fork–Pend Oreille totals 579 miles—the longest river within the Rocky Mountain region.

On the eastern side of the Rockies in Montana, the Sun River plunges beautifully off the escarpment as it leaves the mountains, though dams block it twice on its way to the Missouri River. Lying east of the main mass of the Rockies in central Montana, the Smith flows northward between the Big Belt and Little Belt Mountains. This small river animates an exquisite limestone canyon with evergreens on shaded slopes and a sea of grassland on high ridges and mountaintops—one of the most carefree multiday canoe trips I have enjoyed in the Rockies.

In southern Montana, the Madison, Gallatin, and Jefferson Rivers swirl together at Three Forks to form the legendary Missouri River. But even at its origin, this artery of the West is marred by a gravel pit alongside the three rivers' confluence. The Missouri then runs 500 miles through the foothills of the Rockies, where dams repeatedly rise in the way. The uppermost reach of the Missouri system is Red Rock Creek, flowing into Red Rock River, then into the Beaverhead River, then into the Jefferson. A Jefferson tributary, the 150-mile Big Hole River, is famous for its trout and supports one of few native Arctic grayling fisheries south of Canada. The Madison rises with the Firehole River of Yellowstone National Park—a stream draining the most extraordinary basin of geysers in the world, many of them steaming at the river's banks. Trout here in the heated water spawn in December and grow an inch a month for nine months a year. Below the Firehole's confluence with the Gibbon, the Madison River attracts fly fishing enthusiasts to its riffling route. The Jefferson, Big Hole, and Madison are a few of Montana's designated "Blue Ribbon" trout waters, which total 450 miles in all. Some support a two-pound trout for every ten feet of stream. An ominous threat here is the mysterious whirling disease, first observed in the early 1990s and apparently killing many trout in the Madison and Gallatin, with the potential to spread elsewhere. The anglers' mecca of the Madison was closed to fishing in 1995, and the disease was documented in the Big Wood River and Silver Creek in Idaho as well as in many Colorado streams.

As queen of northern Rockies rivers, the 700-mile Yellowstone begins in the Bridger-Teton Wilderness of Wyoming, flows through the raw wilds of grizzly bear country to Yellowstone Lake, then plunges over a 308-foot-high waterfall—the highest on any large-volume river in America. This is one of the longer rivers in the National Park System, with about 100 protected miles. It then riffles through the aptly named Paradise Valley of Montana ranchland, between the towering Absaroka and Gallatin Ranges, and on eastward through a transition zone of foothills to the Great Plains. Amid threats of damming and diversions for coal mining in the 1970s, the state of Montana took progressive action to reserve 60 percent of the Yellowstone's flows for instream uses and wildlife. This is the most significant case anywhere of a large river being protected from excessive diversion.

The Clark's Fork of the Yellowstone flows with 953 cfs from the Beartooth Mountains, near the northeastern corner of Yellowstone National Park. Arguably the wildest river in forty-nine states, it rages through a granite canyon called "The Box," nearly inaccessible to hikers and river runners alike. A gold-mining proposal threatened the headwaters of this extraordinary river in 1995 while American Rivers, the Greater Yellowstone Coalition, and other groups fought to keep the upper watershed intact as one of the least blemished in the West.

Idaho, whose waters flow toward the Pacific, ranks as one of the preeminent river regions of America, with dozens of fine mountain streams. In the northern part of the state, the painterly but mine-polluted Coeur d'Alene River flows to the crystalline Coeur d'Alene Lake, where Indian tribes work to reclaim water quality and stop the continuing discharge of heavy metals, a hideous legacy of nineteenth-century and current mining. Throughout America's Rockies, I've seen no other network of lakes and wetlands so integral to a sizeable river, making the tragedy of the poisoning all the worse. Also emptying into Coeur d'Alene Lake, the St. Joe River has shores lined in conifers but a watershed that is being heavily clearcut; three logging trucks per minute rolled down the valley road when I last visited, in 1994. Excellent whitewater sections flow in its upper reaches, and the mouth of the St. Joe includes cottonwood trees that house the largest osprey colony on the continent.

Farther south in Idaho, the magnificent Clearwater system includes its 120-mile North Fork, with undammed headwaters of forest and whitewater. But the lower 53 miles are flooded by Dworshak Dam, causing one of the worst losses of a natural river in the West and the elimination of a large race of steelhead. The 26-mile Middle Fork of the Clearwater takes its water from the fabulous Lochsa, which plunges over steep boulder drops along Highway 12 until it meets the incomparable Selway. Flowing almost entirely through the Selway Bitterroot Wilderness, the Selway offers one of the most desired river trips among experienced whitewater travelers. Challenging rapids, prismatic water, and old-growth shorelines drain one of the largest wilderness areas in the lower forty-eight states. Rafting here, I felt that I was flying in a

Firehole River and geyser, WY

Marsh Creek, Middle Fk. Salmon headwaters, ID

Gros Ventre River, WY

Snake River below Jackson, WY

Kootenai River and Falls, MT

Henrys Fork Snake River, Lower Mesa Falls, ID

Yellowstone River below Hwy. 212, WY

Salmon River below North Fork, ID

Green River, Squaretop Mt., WY

Gunnison River, Black Canyon, CO

Green River, Wind River Mts., WY

Arkansas River above Buena Vista, CO

Animas River below Durango, CO

transparent medium, taking a slow flight over a lot of rocks. Below the Middle Fork–South Fork confluence, the main stem Clearwater runs for 74 gentle miles to the dammed-up lower Snake River.

Also at a pinnacle in the wild rivers estate of America, the Middle Fork of the Salmon tops the list of many people's favorite river trips, including mine. Diverse wildlife, sandy beaches, whispering pines, canyon corridors, exhilarating whitewater, and soothing hot springs are all part of this river experience. Congress included the entire 104-mile Middle Fork among the first National Wild and Scenic Rivers in 1968, along with the Selway, Lochsa, and Middle Fork Clearwater.

At the southwestern slope of Idaho's Rockies lie the twin rivers of the Payette, with a flow of 3,183 cfs, and the Boise, with 2,951, both drawing from multiple forks of exquisite mountain water and both popular among paddlers and anglers. Heavily diverted through farmland, the lower reaches of both rivers flow to the Snake.

In Wyoming, the Snake has its origin at the southern border of Yellowstone National Park, flows through 40 miles scarcely changed since John Colter's day, pools into the flatwater of Jackson Reservoir, then flows through Grand Teton National Park within the most classic of all mountain-and-river landscapes in America. The broad, clear river, with its rich mosaic of cottonwoods, willows, spruces, and gravel bars, riffles past the base of the Tetons, which rise to 13,770 feet. As a portrait of a rich waterfront corridor, the upper river hosts moose, elk, beavers, ospreys, eagles, and gadwalls where feeder creeks seep from springs, all with a riparian abundance rare in today's West. The only stream outside Alaska to flow so large amid such fabulous mountain peaks, the Snake carries more floaters than any other river in the National Park System. With continuing superlatives, the Snake charges through Alpine Canyon—one of the three most-paddled sections of whitewater in the West. Palisades Dam blocks the river; then, in Idaho, it runs for 60 miles through the state's largest cottonwood forest and finest bald eagle habitat. A major tributary, the 2,088-cfs spring-fed Henrys Fork of eastern Idaho, is considered the nation's premier dry-fly trout fishing stream in its glassy upper reaches at Island Park, which are full of aquatic plants. The 110-mile fork then plunges over the little Niagaras of Upper and Lower Mesa Falls before encountering farm country. Near its confluence with the Henrys Fork the Snake River enters the southeastern edge of the Columbia Plateau province, in the desert region of rivers.

Crossing over to the eastern slope of the Rockies in Wyoming, I find the beautiful Shoshone hurrying eastward from Yellowstone National Park across drylands to the Bighorn River. The Wind River drains the colossal glacial mass of the Wind River Mountains and flows south-eastward to the Popo Agie River, then curves northward as the Bighorn—one of few streams whose name changes at a bend in the river. The Bighorn is twice dammed and is often diverted for ranchland but has pieces surviving in undeveloped canyons. Entering Montana with a flow of 2,285 cfs, the river supports one of the most productive trout fisheries in the West, with 3,000 mature fish per mile, then enters the Great Plains on its way to the Yellowstone.

In the Wyoming Basin province of south central Wyoming, several other rivers created sharply etched canyons by carving the rock as it rose in response to seismic activity. These antecedent rivers include the Sweetwater, west of Alcova; the Wind, through the Owl Creek Mountains; and the Laramie, slicing through the Laramie Range.

The North Platte River originates in northern Colorado and flows to Wyoming with rapids in a mountain-ranchland setting replete with cottonwoods, then enters the Great Plains with a flow of 2,766 cfs. Even with several diversion dams, 130 miles of the upper river can be boated from Colorado to Seminole Reservoir, north of Interstate 80.

The western side of the Wind River Range in Wyoming spawns a landmark river of the West—the Green, as it curves from Green River Lakes below the photogenic Squaretop Mountain and begins its ribbonlike route southward. Up there the Green River really is a lucid green. With excellent trout habitat, the stream enters high prairie lands of the Wyoming Basin province. A final Rocky Mountain reach below Flaming Gorge Dam is bordered by ponderosa pines in a rocky trench at the eastern flank of the Uinta Mountains; then, at Ladore Canyon, the Green becomes a river of the desert region.

In Utah, the Bear River rises in high country of the Uinta Mountains and takes the most circuitous course of any river in America. Its 500-mile downward arc traces a counterclockwise curve from eastern Utah; loops in and out of Wyoming, Utah, and Idaho; and finally returns to northern Utah, only 80 miles from where it began. With a flow of 1,510 cfs, this unusual river is the principal source of the Great Salt Lake and is reduced by diversions to a tiny percentage of its natural flow in its lower reaches.

Most of Utah lies in the Basin and Range province of the desert, but the Wasatch Mountains in the north send short streams splashing westward to a dead end in the landlocked Great Salt Lake. The Logan River has some of the region's most accessible small waters, interspersed with dams and threatened with a major highway widening project in 1996. Merging into the Wasatch as the only subrange of the Rockies aligned in an east–west direction, the Uinta Mountains spawn a dozen small streams that flow toward the Green River. All are heavily diverted for irrigation as they exit the aspen- and conifer-blanketed mountains. Additional dams and diversions are proposed on the Uinta, Whiterocks, and Yellowstone (of Utah) rivers.

Though the largest rivers lie in the northern reaches, four of the region's nine great basins have their headwaters in Colorado. A vital tributary to the Colorado River, the Yampa drains the northwestern tier of the state. Bear River headwaters (not the Bear River of Utah) drain the snowy Flat Tops Wilderness before being dammed twice. The newly formed Yampa then encounters its only large reservoir, Stagecoach Dam, built in the 1980s and scarcely serving any purpose. Downstream, the Yampa makes a superb community asset as it fizzes through the town of Steamboat Springs, with its parkland and bicycle trail at water's edge. To improve whitewater boating and trout habitat, boulders have been placed in the once-degraded stream, making Steamboat a haven for paddlers in early summer. Below there, the valley widens and nourishes one of the finer riparian forests in the West. Large groves of narrowleaf and Fremont cottonwood extend downstream for 73 miles to Maybell. An unusual community of narrowleaf cottonwood, box elder, and red osier dogwood supports a host of nesting and migrating songbirds drawn to this belt of deciduous forest in an otherwise dry region. Only about 7 percent of the Yampa's runoff is consumed by water users; in this rare case in the West, the possibility still exists to reserve healthy flows for the river and its life, which includes several species of endangered fish. Recognizing the biological significance of this river, the Colorado Nature Conservancy established the Yampa River Preserve by acquiring several tracts of land. Some serve as a preserve and some as a working ranch demonstrating economic management that respects the riparian corridor. Director Jamie Williams also works with ranchers up and down the valley to encourage private protection of riverfront zones in a model of cooperation between conservation interests and agriculture.

The Yampa picks up the Elk River, with its flush of racing water colonnaded by pines and firs, then crosses the easternmost runout of the Uinta Range with a flow of 1,573 cfs. Though the geology is still Rocky Mountain, the habitat and character of the river are thoroughly desert as the Yampa enters Cross Mountain Canyon. This forms a frightening barrier of landslide-congested rapids in a waterway that is otherwise continuously boatable without ominous hazards from Steamboat Springs to the Green River and beyond.

As a tributary to the lower Yampa, the Little Snake drains the Wyoming Basin province to the north and includes a fine cottonwood forest at its mouth. Though heavily diverted, this stream is one of the best remaining in the Colorado basin for native, warm-water fishes. Exotic species have had relatively little effect here. A state-funded dam project threatens Savery Creek—a tributary in Wyoming.

The White River is the next Green River tributary to the south. Its North and South Forks rise in lakes of the Flattop Wilderness and cut through a green riparian corridor in mountains and ranchland before entering the desert region near Meeker.

As the principal artery of the southern Rockies and the Southwest, the Colorado River begins in Rocky Mountain National Park among spruces and firs. Barely beyond National Park Service jurisdiction, it is blocked at Shadow Mountain and Granby Dams, where 90 percent of its flow sluices off through a tunnel to the farms of the eastern slope. The Colorado later picks up what remains of the Blue River after its headwaters are tunneled to Denver. Tapping several other tributaries, Denver imports 56 percent of its supply from the Colorado basin, joining the ranks of Los Angeles, Phoenix, and San Francisco, which all receive their water from faraway rivers. Even more significant, east-side irrigators divert twice as much water from the upper Colorado as Denver does.

The river drops through the extreme rapids of Gore Canyon, which would have been dammed but for the cost of relocating a railroad. Below there lies a section of easy swift water in the Colorado's most popular rafting reach. The Eagle River flows in as the upper Colorado's major tributary, flanked by roads but lacking major dams for 48 miles. Downstream from the confluence with the Eagle, Interstate 70 parallels the Colorado for its journey out of the mountains, including crammed companionship through the 15-mile-long, 1,800-foot-deep Glenwood Canyon, where the double-decked interstate's lanes are stacked along the canyon walls in a highway engineer's concession to river protection interests. The Colorado here alternately froths and suffers from a power diversion.

The Roaring Fork, coming from Aspen, joins the Colorado at Glenwood Springs after picking up the well-named Crystal River, which flows from a mountain vastness in the center of the state. Easing past Grand Junction, where uranium tailings and junkyards were cleaned up to make a riverfront park, the Colorado enters the desert region.

As the Colorado's second-largest tributary, the 2,659-cfs Gunnison begins where the East River, near Crested Butte, joins the Taylor—the sweetest of streams, with the finest of rock-studded rapids and clear water. After being dammed four times, including in the upper half of Black Canyon, the Gunnison flows through an amazingly narrow gorge at Black Canyon of the Gunnison National Monument. A drop here of 240 feet per mile is the steepest of any sizeable stream in the southern Rockies. Beyond this skinny canyon with half-mile-deep entrenchment, the 16-mile-long Gunnison Gorge offers superb trout water and boisterous rapids. The main stem finally picks up its North Fork and flows gently and undammed across overgrazed drylands and several diversion dams to meet the Colorado at Grand Junction. On the lower river, Dominguez Dam is one of few remaining large dam proposals in the Rockies.

Farther south, the San Miguel River escapes from the alpine terrain of the San Juan Mountains at Telluride and cruises westward through a strung-out cottonwood oasis in the foothills. This is one of Colorado's longest nearly unimpounded rivers, which isn't saying much in a state of heavily manipulated streams. A diversion dam and several weirs interrupt 90 miles of free flow to the Dolores River. Both the upper Dolores and the adjacent San Juan begin beneath Colorado peaks but flow mostly as desert streams.

Dropping from the heart of the San Juan Mountains—Colorado's largest subrange of the Rockies—the Animas River tumbles southward past Silverton. At an elevation of 9,230 feet, this is one of the highest boatable rivers in America. The 110-mile undammed stream disappears into one of the country's premier wilderness canyons containing Class V whitewater, with some of its mileage unrunnable. Emerging from the mile-deep trench, the Animas becomes the centerpiece of Durango, where its 819-cfs flow offers pleasant rapids accessible to local boaters and tourists at town parks. Then it winds southward, nurturing some of the finest cottonwood forests in New Mexico, and joins the San Juan River.

Crossing for a final time to the eastern slope of the Rockies, I see the 126-mile Cache la Poudre of northern Colorado crashing down the escarpment through pine-clad canyons, the only designated National Wild and Scenic River in this river-rich state. The scenic Big Thompson parallels the Poudre in Rocky Mountain National Park before being plumbed for water supplies. Farther south, the South Platte exits the mountains with a flow of 834 cfs and encounters some dams, yet survives in other reaches. Through Denver, the South Platte is a model of urban river restoration, with parks, bikeways, and a whitewater racing course at a once-derelict waterfront.

The Arkansas River, fouled with metals from mines at its Leadville headwaters, plunges for 100 miles through the Rockies; several reaches below Buena Vista rank among the most-floated whitewater in the West, with 200,000 boaters in 1992. With an average flow of 715 cfs, the river cuts through the 1,200-foot-deep Royal Gorge near Canon City in one of the tightest deep canyons anywhere before emptying onto the Great Plains. As the southernmost river of the Rockies, the Rio Grande rises in the San Juan Mountains but soon enters desert country. To learn in detail about a fine river that could show me many miles and many subranges of the Rockies, I returned north, to the Salmon of Idaho.

The Salmon River

Unlike most other rivers that wind through a few canyons and then exit the Rockies, the Salmon clings to the high country and wraps around the subranges of central Idaho. It flows not away from the backbone of the West but toward it in an erratic route whose final outcome could be anyone's guess. Running north, east, then north again, it confronts the Continental Divide a full 174 miles below the river's source and then reorients toward the Pacific and crosscuts the width of Idaho's mountainous heart. Beginning in high country, it flows through forests, then desert, then forests again, then desert again. No other stream in America displays so much mountain country, continuous for the Salmon's entire distance, and its 7,000-foot descent.

In its length of wildness, its wildlife, and its mountain scenery, the Salmon could be the exemplar of the Rocky Mountain riverscape. The 406-mile stream flows through the River of No Return Wilderness—the largest wilderness outside Alaska—and past the Gospel Hump Wilderness. For 100 miles the river nourishes a cottonwood corridor, and below it, a 79-mile reach is one of the more significant sections of roadless river in America. The lower Salmon carves the country's third-deepest canyon, exceeded only by those of the Kings in the Sierra Nevada and the Snake at Hells Canyon, where the Salmon ends.

But back up at the headwaters, the Sawtooth Mountains rise as one of the most rugged and scenic ranges in America, bristling with granite ridges and canine-toothed spires and containing a wonderland of lakes, meadows, forests, and streams. The 20- by 35-mile range forms the core of the Idaho Batholith—molten granite that rose and cooled underground and is now exposed across much of central Idaho. The National Park Service rejected a proposal for a Sawtooth National Park in the early 1900s, not because of any deficiency in the plan but because officials decided that these mountains looked too much like the Tetons—as if two Grand Teton National Parks would be excessive. Objections of ranchers along the Salmon River may have influenced the decision.

Directly across the valley from the Sawtooth escarpment, the White Cloud Mountains ascend gracefully to the east. When a mining corporation proposed an open pit there at the base of Castle Peak in the late 1960s, the conservation movement in Idaho was born. Congress responded in 1972 by designating the Sawtooth National Recreation Area, preventing construction of the mine. The legislation also appropriated money for buying land and scenic easements in the Salmon River's Sawtooth Valley, and subdivision of the spectacular basin was avoided.

Efforts to protect and restore the Salmon River—another goal of the legislation—proved more difficult; the Sawtooth case was typical of protection efforts in its attention to land and its shortcomings with aquatic issues. The upper river had once provided some of the finest salmon habitat in Idaho, but after swimming 850 miles from the ocean to spawn, the fish now flopped up onto a bone dry streambed from which every drop had been diverted for cows. In a shining success for river conservation, the Forest Service in 1992 bought some of the irrigated land and the most troublesome water rights and planned to restore flows to an upper reach of this great stream.

Below the river's source, the federal and state governments have paid millions of dollars to screen private ranchers' irrigation diversions. The costs of the screens—often complicated facilities requiring headgates, debris screens, and pipes—probably exceed the market value of the pastureland in some cases. Scores of diversions still hamper the upper Salmon River, and 278 diversions in all affect migrating salmon. Each year bulldozers build rock weirs in the riverbed to shunt water into ditches that suck young smolts aside, where they die directly or face fatal delays in their downstream journey.

Unfortunately, the runs of salmon throughout the river remain only a shadow of what was. The upriver diversions take a toll, but dams blocking the Snake River downstream have annihilated fish populations and caused their numbers to reach all-time lows in the 1990s. In addition, clearcutting, mismanaged logging, and road building have caused troublesome sedimentation of salmon spawning beds, and overgrazing by cows causes streambank erosion.

I came to know the Salmon's headwaters by working in the Sawtooth National Forest in 1969 and by returning whenever I could, but later I wanted to see the whole river—at once a showcase of the Rockies and typical of the region in important ways. So one August I launched my raft as high in the headwaters as it would float. My six-week journey from Sunbeam to Lewiston on the Snake River was 401 miles—one of the longest runs outside Alaska that can be made without encountering dams, dried-up riverbeds, or levees. A hundred rapids guaranteed excitement on a trip that promised escape, serenity, exhilaration, and a new understanding to be felt as sharply as the cool autumn mornings in the mountains. The whitewater had discouraged Lewis and Clark when expedition members looked at the first big rapid below the North Fork and called this the "River of No Return." Having it considerably easier, I rowed a sturdy raft and carried up to three weeks' worth of food. I restocked at three small towns that had one traffic light among them.

I launched my fourteen-foot-long Avon Adventurer just below the cement remains of Sunbeam Dam; the old blockage had been blown to smithereens in 1934 by Idaho citizens fed up with the useless cement plug, which had impeded sockeye salmon from reaching their spawning grounds since 1913. From the moment I pushed off from shore, an atmosphere of clear water—streaked and scratched by currents—swept me effortlessly away through a mountain-canyon corridor. The sky was crisp and puffed with clouds, the forest scented with sun-warmed resin of fir. Whitewater glittered and begged to be drank, and mountains towered over me. My spirit soared to be a part of it all and to be so entwined with the flow, bound away toward hundreds of miles of Rocky Mountain river adventure.

On my second day, I set a pattern of traveling style. I rose early, built a tiny fire, sipped a warm drink, and wrote for a few hours. I took some early morning pictures and wandered upstream and down. Then I loaded the raft, embarked, and rowed 6 to 12 miles. On some days I didn't go anywhere but just lived where I was. I traveled slowly to savor such wondrous country. Firs and lodgepoles were dying out in drylands filled with orange cliffs, golden eagles, and reverberating thunderstorms. The East Fork joined the main stem, and ranchers continued to take irrigation water from dozens of ditches. Four days from my put-in I camped near Challis and walked 2 miles to town, where I bought fresh food and ate lunch alongside the sheriff and local regulars. Six more days downriver, I stopped at the town of Salmon and bought enough food to stuff my backpack full at the grocery store.

For the first 125 miles of my trip a paved road followed the river, though it was not visible much of the time. At the North Fork of the Salmon, Highway 93 continued north but the Salmon veered west, with only a dirt road etched into the narrowing valley. Here the bigger drops began. From the pool above Pine Creek Rapid a tongue of smooth water—green and shiny as mint jelly—pointed down between rocks until foam and waves pinched the green shut and the bubbles converged to whiteout conditions. I entered right of center. My route led toward an enormous hole where the river scoured a rock, then dug out a low spot before it billowed into the next wave. I hit the hole and heavy waves crashed over the bow, but I shot through.

Built for whitewater maneuverability and abuse, my raft also made a versatile home, and every morning when I packed it full of gear something made me smile. I was charmed by its smallness—by having my life consolidated that much, all of it hitched onto a tiny floating island of Hypalon. I thrilled to the self-sufficiency and escape that the raft afforded and enjoyed the security that my air-filled craft offered. I could guide my boat anywhere on this river and stop whenever I wanted. I grew used to all of this, and the days of summer drifted by.

The gravel road dead-ended at Corn Creek, where I arrived on day nineteen, though this is where most people begin their Salmon River trips. The following roadless reach was so popular that the Forest Service required reservations, but after August the requirement was lifted. I simply beached and signed a register.

I dropped into dark, wild canyons, which had heavier rapids now that the Middle Fork had joined the main stem. The upper Salmon had shown me a satisfying beauty, alive with bird life and without another single boater, but the road had intruded. Now the highway and everything that went with it receded behind me. The River of No Return Wilderness and Selway-Bitterroot Wilderness nearly join here and are two of the four largest roadless complexes in the country outside Alaska. I was committed to float to the next road—a journey of one week for most people but two weeks for me.

Surprises lay in wait every day. I had only half pitched the tent on day twenty-two when a roar like a freight train descended into the canyon and sent a chill of fear into my bones. I didn't know what was happening. Then the tops of the trees bent over, pine sprigs flew through the air, and sand blasted everything. My newly washed clothes flew from their drying line to be plastered like soggy tissue against tree trunks. In seconds the wind bent an aluminum pole that had survived ten years of storms and flattened my tent. I threw a tarp over my gear and pinned it down with heavy rocks. It occurred to me that this might be only the beginning; trees could crash on top of me. I looked up, and the wind filled my eyes with sand. Then came stinging nuggets of hail. Only a minute after it had started, the wind faded into a drizzly breeze over the sand-coated wreckage of my camp.

I called that site Windstorm, and I named other camps Purple Light, White Sand, Otter, Ponderosa, Rattlesnake. Today when I block out the world and picture forty different neighborhoods in the paradise of my mind's eye, they are the places where I camped along the Salmon River: islands, sandbars, shady groves, and the meeting places where tributaries join. Some sites lay only two feet above the waterline, others on banks where I grunted with the effort of hauling my gear but then rested with a view of a rapid that entertained me the whole evening. Some sites nestled against cliffs, some along sloughs. Otters swam by, looking like fur-covered, whiskered dolphins, hissing when surprised, and diving for mussels. Always I had the current to listen to; at night I slept with the many sounds of a rapid churning louder, quieter, louder, quieter. The intrigue of a river is that it always changes.

One day I hiked up a tributary canyon until I was halted by a No Trespassing sign at a weathered cabin. Someone was pounding nails at the nearby barn, so I walked over. The middle-aged man was surprised at first but came down from his ladder to talk. After a while he asked, "How about some home brew?" He snatched up the rifle that he always carried, and we headed for the cabin and sat down to a jug of beer that had been seasoned in a garbage can. Twenty years ago this man had emigrated from West Virginia because he had heard that wild country could still be found in the middle of Idaho. He guided hunters but was too independent for the service industry. "When you start seeing the dudes in the scope of your rifle as they step off the plane for their holiday of shooting and booze, it's time to look for another line of work." He turned to trapping, living weeks at a time on his lines in winter, sometimes snowbound, sometimes hungry, always alone.

I thanked him for the beer and for his gift of fresh vegetables from his garden and happily returned to the river. A few more days of rowing took me to Vinegar Creek, where a dirt road probed in from civilization. Most Salmon River travelers get out there, but I had two weeks to go. At Riggins I tied off to a tree and climbed the banks into town while salivating at the thought of fresh food filling my backpack again. Vegetables, cheese, beans, bread, fruit—I had run out of everything.

Below Riggins some of the best rapids of the trip awaited me; in fact, I wouldn't have minded having another boat to spot me for safety. High waves made roller coasters while boulders jammed up other drops, all of it a joy and an adrenaline rush as I pulled on the oars. A long undeveloped reach began below White Bird and ran for 49 river-singing miles, with only a few dirt roads dead-ending at the Salmon. Rock walls crimped tight in four separate canyons, and between those sections, brown hills flanked the desert floor and soared 4,000 feet up to evergreens.

The summer passed like the miles above me, and the water grew sharp to the touch. My raft became a thermometer, its air shrinking with the cold; each morning I had to pump up the sagging tubes. Rotting leaves smelled sweet on the ground. Poison ivy and hollygrape shone red beneath the yellow, sandpapery leaves of hackberry trees. When the sky poured for a whole day, I scrambled for shelter in my tent. The next morning when I emerged, snow outlined the canyon rim.

Autumn had come to the Salmon. With it I felt a new zest, a mildly pressing urgency, as the calendar inevitably turned and the days shortened no matter how tightly I clung to them. Fall is a nostalgic time for me. I thought of other autumn trips I had taken and the friends I had taken them with. The showering leaves of October sparked me to take stock of a lifetime that, like each year, is too short.

For many miles it was wild, even wilder than it had been a hundred years ago, when gold miners worked this river; some of their cabins still stood. Surveyors then considered the Salmon's canyons as a railroad route but rejected them. The Army Corps of Engineers and Bureau of Reclamation didn't give up so easily, identifying a dozen reservoir sites. The Snake and Columbia Rivers had been dammed continuously down below, with the Salmon River next in line, and in the 1960s the Federal Power Commission nearly approved construction of Nez Perce Dam by power companies just below the river's mouth. This arguably ranks as the most destructive dam proposal in American history because it would have cut off the anadromous fish runs of the entire Salmon River and flooded the remainder of Hells Canyon on the Snake. During the same era, Secretary of the Interior Stewart Udall saw the regretful damming of the North Fork Clearwater and resolved that the nation should balance river development with protection. The National Wild and Scenic Rivers Act was the upshot in 1968, and the Salmon was recommended for inclusion. Twelve years later Congress finally designated 125 miles of the river, banning dams from the North Fork to Vinegar Creek. Other sections—including this one—lacked full protection.

Every day on the lower Salmon the rasp of jet boats echoed from canyon walls minutes before the boats arrived. Ducks and herons fled in front of the speedy craft; three-foot wakes eroded beaches. The jet boats intruded more than the road had up above.

On day thirty-seven I drifted reverently to the Salmon River's confluence with the Snake and pulled into an eddy where the two streams
converge. I gripped my way up rocks carved by these great western
waterways and saw my Salmon on the right and the Snake, with three
times the volume, on the left. Then I entered the larger flow, with only
46 miles remaining to Lewiston. This bottom end of Hells Canyon was
lazy and made me lazy, and careless.

Routinely, I landed for the night and unloaded, then pulled the raft
high onto the beach and tied it beyond the wakes of jet boats. The
Snake now posed a new threat: hydroelectric dams 100 miles upriver
flushed down water that crested far above normal flows. At my camp
along an eddy larger than a football field, I unloaded quickly. It was
late, and I was tired. I pitched the tent. Ready to take a quick bath, I
grabbed the bailing bucket, stepped toward the river, and froze. The
boat was gone! Then I saw it, far from shore, exiting the eddy and entering the powerful flow of 20,000 cubic feet per second. The raft was
doing well by itself, oars across the tubes, the empty life jacket in my
place. I had no chance of swimming to the boat from where I was—I
would never catch up once the current took hold. So I sprinted downriver over rocks and boulders, fifty yards, seventy-five yards. I looked
at the raft and tried to judge its speed, to allow myself enough lead time
to swim to it. The slackwater soon funneled into a long rapid, where
the raft could be deflected to the other side and where I could end up
in powerful undertows. I didn't want to go; I'm not a good swimmer.
Winded from running, I dived forward and splashed into the world of
the Snake.

While the current tugged at me, I thought of all that water flowing
past everything I had seen: craggy Sawtooth headwaters, the blown-
apart dam at Sunbeam, the first rapids at Pine Creek, the cottonwood
groves, the heavenly Middle Fork, the canyon's desert floor downstream of Riggins. It wasn't quite as if my life were flashing before me,
but the trip, at least, was well represented. And now I had to contend
with the larger flow of the Snake River, which came all the way from
Yellowstone. I could feel the depth and power of it. I was a tiny creature of land in a big sea of water; I was being washed out of the Rocky
Mountains and toward the sea, like a salmon smolt going out to a new
life.

Soon I knew I had swum far enough, but where was my boat? I had
gone too far downriver! The raft and I, one behind the other, now
bobbed in the current and drifted in unison toward the rapid. My only

choice was to turn and swim double-time upriver toward my boat. I finally pulled myself aboard, grabbed the oars, and rowed to shore, where I crunched onto the rocks with a sigh of relief.

At the town of Asotin, no more riffles brushed the shore and no more current pushed me along. Buzzing and droning, five motorboats were aimed my way. For six weeks I had rowed past the mountains of eight ranges, deep and spacious forests, cactus-dotted deserts, and gorges of blue-black rock, but now my river lay flat and finished. I rowed through several miles of ponded water to the marina at Lewiston. Below that city lay four Snake River reservoirs and four Columbia River reservoirs linked nonstop almost to sea level. I had come to the end of the river.

Chapter 7

Rivers of the Deserts and Drylands

While the water in rivers always comes from somewhere else—up-stream—this reality is stark and vivid with the desert rivers. Most of the flow begins on distant mountains, and the sensational contrast of frothing rivers in arid canyons stirs curiosity and delight. The desert rivers at first sight just don't seem possible.

The deserts and drylands range spaciously across the interior West's mountains, plateaus, canyons, steppes, and plains, including not one but three sizeable provinces of landscape. First and northernmost, the Columbia Plateau province covers 100,000 square miles of eastern Washington, Oregon, and southern Idaho. Creating one of the world's major areas of lava, molten minerals oozed across the land as many as twenty times and accumulated as black rock a mile or more thick. Second, the Basin and Range province (sometimes called the Great Basin) is larger than the other two desert provinces combined. This giant swath of sagebrush West is not one basin but many, with 150 mountain ranges separated by intervening valleys encompassing parts of Oregon, Nevada, Utah, California, Arizona, New Mexico, and Texas. Finally, the stunning Colorado Plateau province occupies 150,000 square

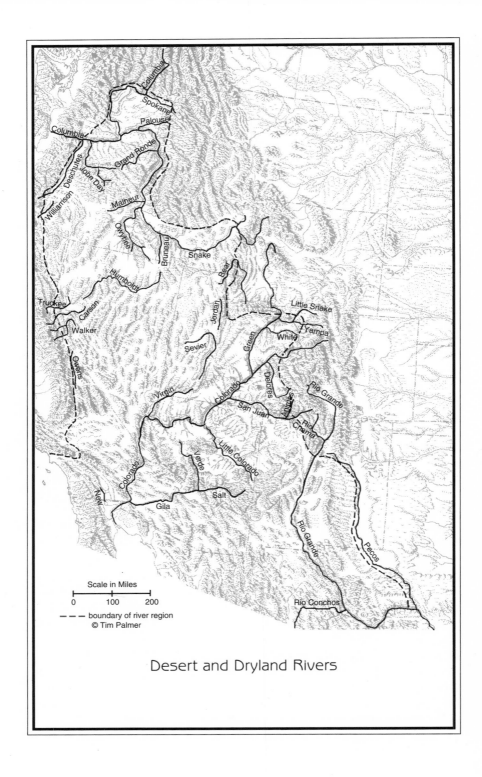

Scale in Miles

0   100   200

— — — boundary of river region
© Tim Palmer

Desert and Dryland Rivers

miles in Colorado, Utah, Arizona, and New Mexico. Referring to the Plateau's serrated rims of canyons and the watery knife cuts at their depths, geographer Wallace Atwood wrote, "In no other part of the world are there so many striking examples of the work of running water."

The three desert provinces join like pieces of a big jigsaw puzzle to form one large dryland; combined, they are much larger than all the rest of the West beyond the Great Plains, not counting Alaska. The region is bordered along its eastern and northern fronts by its principal nourisher, the Rocky Mountains, and along its western front by the Sierra Nevada of California and the Cascade Mountains of the Northwest. Being entirely in the western cordillera of combined mountain masses, the desert rivers always offer views of peaks and plateaus. Many small ranges rise within the region—for example, the Blue Mountains of Oregon, the Ruby Mountains of Nevada, the La Sal Mountains of Utah, the San Francisco Peaks of Arizona, and the Zuni Mountains of New Mexico.

The powdery, sizzling dryness of every place that is not river-nourished or spring fed owes to the rain shadow cast by the Sierra and the Cascades, which rake moisture from Pacific storms and leave little for downwind regions until the clouds encounter high country once again at the Rockies.

Deserts are not just deserts but vary as the Laurentian forest of Maine differs from the southeastern forest of Georgia. The rivers of the drylands pass through five distinct ecological zones. The Palouse grasslands lie in the far north, sandwiched between drier sagebrush to the west and wetter forests to the east. This hill country was long ago converted to wheat fields. The intermountain sagebrush blankets the largest desert area, from the Columbia River to southern Nevada. The Mojave of southeastern California, with its Joshua trees, is the most arid desert. The Sonoran desert of southern Arizona includes fan palms and saguaro cacti. Finally, the Chihuahuan desert is characterized by agaves and cacti in a section of southern New Mexico, western Texas, and northern Mexico.

The classic desert river carries golden-brown water cutting through steep-walled red-rock canyons. More than a dozen river reaches fit this canyon-corridor image perfectly—for example, the entrenched meanders of the Green River in Labyrinth Canyon, the San Juan River at its Goosenecks, the Dolores in Slick Rock Canyon, and the lower Yampa, all of them on the Colorado Plateau. But the ultimate desert-canyon river is the Colorado in the Grand Canyon.

Other river types also inhabit this far-flung region, which spans 1,500 miles north to south and up to 1,000 miles east to west. Many desert rivers coast as lazy, meandering streams in open country, such as the Humboldt of Nevada; the Green, in its sluggish phase between Split Mountain and Desolation Canyon; and the Snake, flowing across southwestern Idaho. As a third type, the narrow desert canyons have exquisite charm: the Narrows of the Virgin River in Zion National Park and the Escalante of southern Utah cut passages of remarkable depth and narrowness—just slits, really, in the sandstone armor of the earth. The greatest mileage of waterways in this region lies in intermittent streams called arroyos in the Southwest. Here water flows only during a short season of snowmelt or during flash floods, which can arrive without warning as a three-foot wall of viscous water. The mountain ranges within the desert give rise to a final type of rivers: streams like those in the Rocky Mountains. Perhaps the finest examples are the radially patterned rivers of the Wallowa Mountains in northeastern Oregon, tumbling crystal-clear from the center of a miniature Rockies but isolated by Hells Canyon to the east and by dry pinelands and desert elsewhere.

The five types of desert river take on special variations in the three landform provinces. The Columbia Plateau rivers show a texture of rough rockiness as their water erodes through dark volcanic basalt—chunky and sharp toothed when broken up at canyon walls and riverbeds. Some Columbia Plateau canyons appear as abrupt fissures, deep in an otherwise flat topography of sage-covered plains. These northern deserts are often overlooked because the forests farther west dominate the imagery of the greater Northwest, but river canyons on the Columbia Plateau are nearly as dry and sharply incised as those of the Colorado Plateau. Rivers of the Great Basin province wind in broad valleys between paralleling ridges, and water occasionally cuts through the mountains in short canyons. The few rivers here drain into wetlands that often become evaporative sinks or playas of white, calcified salt flats, except for the Rio Grande, which escapes the trap of surrounding mountains and flows in a tortuously long course to the Gulf of Mexico. Finally, the photogenic waters of the Colorado Plateau have cut deeply through nearly flat sedimentary beds of rusty sandstone, and each canyon hosts a wild world beneath the slickrock plateau.

Except for a few outsized arteries, the desert is a land of small rivers, separated by death marches of parched country. About this region author Wallace Stegner wrote, "Aridity, more than anything else, gives the western landscape its character." While the Appalachians, the Coastal Plain, and the Midwest each contains at least ten rivers averaging 10,000 cubic feet per second or more, the desert region—the largest in America—has only three. The middle Columbia flows with 188,600 cfs at The Dalles, where it leaves the region and enters the Northwest. A phenomenal sight, this river is larger than the Mississippi at St. Louis but lies in a bone dry desert. The Columbia's principal tributary, the Snake, carries a flow of 18,490 cfs through Hells Canyon and 50,000 in southeastern Washington at its mouth. The Colorado flows with an average of 17,850 cfs at Lees Ferry, just above the Grand Canyon. Though it stretches hundreds of miles from the sea, it never gets much larger; in fact, diversions reduce the Colorado to a state of terminal anemia as it enters Mexico and then to absolutely nothing before it reaches saltwater. The Spokane River flows with 6,300 cfs to the Columbia. The Green River—longer than the Colorado but carrying less water—averages 5,972 cfs (the Colorado carries 7,600 at its confluence with the Green). The Deschutes in Oregon's desert takes its 5,846-cfs flow from Cascade tributaries and groundwater. The San Juan is the Colorado's third-largest tributary, with 2,542 cfs (the Green and Gunnison are larger). The John Day averages 2,036 cfs from little-known mountain ranges in central Oregon. The Yampa flows with 1,573 to the Green. The Rio Grande in Albuquerque carries 1,068, every drop of it diverted downstream during the irrigation season. Arizona's Salt River flows at 888 cfs where it's dammed at Roosevelt; except for high snowpack years, no water escapes to the lower river, which historically flowed to the Colorado during normal high runoff. The Animas of New Mexico runs at 819 cfs on its way to the San Juan. Other desert rivers average less than 800 cfs, which means they are dry or nearly so in summer.

The length of desert rivers is another matter. Though it is nothing but a creek at the Gulf of Mexico and is smaller in volume than some single-spring discharges in Missouri or Florida, the Rio Grande is our fifth-longest river, at 1,885 miles, and drains the fourth-largest watershed. The Colorado, our seventh-longest river, flows for 1,450 miles, beginning high in the Rockies but running mostly across desert. Of the Columbia's 1,248-mile length in the United States and Canada, 460 miles cross desert. The Snake is 1,059 miles long, with four-fifths of its mileage in the desert but most of its drainage basin in the Rocky Mountains. All the desert rivers are long relative to their volume. The largest rivers all begin in the Rockies or the Cascades, but important streams lying entirely in the desert and drylands include the John Day, Owyhee,

Bruneau, Humboldt, Sevier, Virgin, Verde, Salt, and Gila, all flowing from isolated mountain ranges that are islands of snow and rain in a sea of aridity.

If any region in America remains culturally distinct, it's the Southwest, known for its adobe architecture and its style of pottery, jewelry, and weaving. The Hispanic influence is seen almost everywhere in the southern desert areas and dominates much of New Mexico, Texas, and Arizona. The Indian presence, going back 10,000 years or more, is also an integral part of the modern scene. Cultural attitudes about rivers, however, are not much different from those in the rest of the arid West. The Hispanic culture has always supported the use of rivers for irrigation without great concern for natural ecosystems, and all possible flows have been sent to farms. Traditional acequia associations in Hispanic communities take care of the ditches and ensure a supply of water for crops and cattle.

Other cultural influences include the Mormons' presence in Utah and throughout much of the desert—a force stronger than any other regionally based religious group in America. The Mormons have exercised religious zeal in making drylands green with crops and lawns and have striven to dam and irrigate to the last mile and last acre possible. Nevada has a mongrel culture of spartan ranches, casinos rife with glitter and vice, and the mining industry as an extractive enterprise. Other desert areas with widely scattered ranches exude the cowboy culture. Except for the Indians, the long-standing societies of the desert have never recognized the region's rivers as anything but an irrigation or city water supply. But today the rivers of the desert attract a new following of devotees, at first drawn to river travel and then realizing the importance of the streams to a fragile but valuable natural system.

Culturally ingrained since white settlement, diversions for irrigation are the principal ailment of desert rivers. Irrigation accounts for over 90 percent of water use in desert states. Great amounts of water are also diverted for cities, including those in southern California, which houses 17 million people and still grows. Nearly all southwestern cities depend on water imported through mind-boggling networks of dams, pipes, pumps, siphons, and canals, most of them on desert rivers. The Central Arizona Project pumps Colorado River water uphill for 190 miles to Phoenix.

Pathetically unique among all regions, desert rivers are totally dried up before reaching their historical destinations. These include the Colorado, the Rio Grande, and all rivers of the Great Basin, which flowed not into lifeless salt flats but into lakes or wetlands of biological wealth.

A reminder of these can be seen at Mono Lake, California, which is critical for many bird species. Though the lake faced a likely future of total impoverishment, a pitched battle was decisively concluded in 1994, when a hardy group of environmentalists who had fought the Goliath of Los Angeles for twenty years finally won. Even the enormous volume of the Snake River has been entirely diverted for part of the year at Milner Dam in southern Idaho. Groundwater flows later recharge the river, but a long, desiccated riverbed is left in between. The sour prophesy of explorer and U.S. Geological Survey chief John Wesley Powell has nearly come to pass: "All the waters of all the arid lands will eventually be taken from their natural channels." The John Day and Deschutes of northern Oregon are vital exceptions, carrying water all the way to their confluences with the Columbia, though the John Day is heavily tapped. With the exception of the upper Platte and upper Arkansas basins, all major watersheds in the United States that are 70 percent or more depleted in an average year lie in the desert region.

This is not just a matter of rivers being dried up at their mouths. All along the way, the diversions cut the options for life by leaving hundreds of waterways without sufficient flows for native fish and wildlife species. Thousands of miles of riparian and aquatic lifeways at hundreds of streams are ruined in a landscape whose river bottoms once offered oases of habitat for most of the wildlife. A disproportionate share of America's endangered fish species are found in the desert: as of 1986, forty-five of sixty-six federally listed fishes lived in desert waters. Eleven fishes of the southwestern desert have become extinct. The American Fisheries Society listed one-third of the fishes of the Southwest as threatened or endangered. According to the Southwest Center for Biological Diversity, 150 fish species—much of the region's native ichthyofauna—face extinction in the next fifty years unless changes are made.

Where there *is* water, it's sometimes the result of irrigators returning heavy volumes of salty and polluted waste to the rivers—a severe problem in the Colorado, whose imperfect fluid is then exported to Phoenix and Los Angeles for drinking water. Rather than compensate farmers to take the saltiest land out of farming use—which generally yields only hay and surplus crops—western congressional representatives championed a $365 million desalinization plant, paid for by American taxpayers, and it has failed to work well. In many parts of the region irrigation drains carry the deadly element selenium, which is leached from fields and mines and affects streams and wetlands along rivers as large as the Green in Jensen, Utah.

The avalanche of biological breakdown from dams and diversions in the desert takes many forms. Without the natural flood and silt regime exotic plants thrive, many of them noxious and deadly to the native flora. Tamarisk is the foremost culprit here. An alien shrub spreading like a laboratory experiment gone berserk, it has taken over nearly every riparian system in the Southwest by displacing willows and cottonwoods. Little has been done to combat the invasion of exotics.

Not much effort is expended to divert additional irrigation water; that use, in fact, is declining slightly in California. But urban water managers still seek more. In 1994 Las Vegas proposed to take water from the Colorado River, a diversion that would require an unlikely change in a multistate compact, or from the Virgin River, which would be dammed.

Rather than supporting destruction of more rivers, convincing evidence shows that efficiency improvements can stretch urban supplies far into the future. Transfer of water rights from unsuitable farmland— where irrigation now causes costly salinization, erosion, and selenium poisoning—can stretch many urban supplies indefinitely without affecting good farmland.

Until recent years, people never even considered water efficiency; they simply built more dams. The John Day and Grande Ronde in Oregon and the Animas in Colorado and New Mexico are the only sizeable rivers in the region spared by dams or reservoirs. Remarkable landscapes have disappeared under the flatwater. Glen Canyon of the Colorado is the most mourned, but its loss should not overshadow such flooded gems as the salmon highway of the Columbia at Grand Coulee; the upper Hells Canyon on the Snake, which once made that river comparable in many ways to the Grand Canyon itself; and the cottonwood bosque of the Rio Grande at Elephant Butte. The Columbia is nearly all dammed, half the length of the Snake is dammed, and the Colorado is half dammed within its desert reach. This region is the area of most intense reservoir development in America, considering storage relative to river flow. So many dams have been built that the amount of water lost to evaporation from the flatwater surface is significant; it amounts to 2 million acre-feet per year in the Colorado River basin, which yields a total of only 14 million acre-feet of runoff.

Unfortunately, flooded valleys and canyons were not the end of the dams' effects on the desert rivers. With the hardware in place, water users manipulate flows for irrigation with little concern for ecosystems. Stream flows that were once naturally warm, silty, and fluctuating with the seasonal hydrograph now run cold, clear, and controlled. Such conditions may create a sport trout fishery for a short section below the dams and sound good for a river, but in fact they are nothing of the sort. More than half the native fish in the upper Colorado basin are endangered, one reason being cold-water releases from the dams. Some flows have been reinstated below a few of the dams, and small instream flows have been reserved for streams here and there, but the gains represent only a tiny fraction of what's needed to restore desert rivers to even a semblance of health.

Curious now about the character of the individual desert and dryland rivers, I see that in the north the midsection of the Columbia crosses an arid plateau of crusty lava. The river and adjacent channels here mark the route of the Missoula Flood, which occurred during the ice ages. When the outlets of the 1,000-foot-deep Lake Missoula ruptured, unimaginably high flows roared across eastern Washington with a volume ten times the combined flow of all the rivers of the world. The Columbia flooded a width of many miles across the desert in a route now seen as bare scablands and dry waterfalls. These are especially evident at Grand Coulee, a waterless gorge up to 4 miles wide and 1,000 feet deep.

The Columbia isn't really much of a "river," since all but 50 of its 632 nontidal miles in the United States are impounded by reservoirs (68 percent of the river's Canadian mileage is also trapped behind dams). The one remaining reach flows gently across the desert from Priest Rapids Dam to Richland, Washington. Beginning with swift water representing the tail end of the old Priest Rapids, this canoeable section borders the Department of Energy's Hanford Nuclear Reservation, where security requirements prohibit people from setting foot on land for 35 miles. Radioactive waste has escaped in large quantities into the river, and strontium 90 continues to seep into the Columbia at 500 to 1,000 times the federal standard. Cleanup efforts have been stalled by the budget cuts of the 1990s.

Before it joins the Columbia in the reservoir behind Grand Coulee Dam, the Spokane River riffles though a black cottonwood–ponderosa pine belt as the only sizeable free-flowing river of eastern Washington, and even it doesn't flow for long. Water leaving Coeur d'Alene Lake runs for 29 miles to downtown Spokane, where a spectacular waterfall thunders over a basalt washboard. But the Washington Water Power Company diverts all the water from the upper half of the cascade. A scenic whitewater section follows, but five dams block the lower river.

The Columbia's largest tributary is the Snake, whose desert canyons in southern Idaho were once one of the fabulous spectacles of the West, featuring two falls higher than Niagara. Flowing across the Snake

River Plain, which constitutes the southern end of the Columbia Plateau, the river's sheer-walled basalt gorges guarded Grand Canyon–style rapids. The Thousand Springs issued a flow of 4,000 cfs through volcanic cliffs, and 600 miles of habitat nourished the country's largest freshwater fish, the white sturgeon. With its cliffs above the river, the Birds of Prey Natural Area still supports the largest concentration of raptors on the continent. Much of the Snake's original wealth has been lost to twenty-three dams on its main stem and to gluttonous diversions. A free-flowing river remains in the bottom half of Hells Canyon, where rocks piled upon rocks compose America's second-deepest canyon (next to the Sierra Nevada's Kings) and the deepest that can be boated. Below there, the Army Corps of Engineers dammed the Snake four times in eastern Washington, yet its flows remain vital to the survival of salmon and steelhead. This was once the largest salmon run in the world, but because of the dams some minor stocks are extinct, the population of brilliant sockeye is down to a handful of fish, and even the chinook population is endangered.

Remarkable desert tributaries to the Snake include the Bruneau of southern Idaho, averaging only 409 cfs but incising a phenomenal basalt canyon of wild water in one of America's most remote regions. The Owyhee—a sister stream to its west in Oregon—cuts for 300 miles through deep canyons with a flow of 456 cfs. The heavily diverted, cow-crowded Malheur River staggers across the drylands of eastern Oregon. The Wallowa Mountains of northeastern Oregon and their pine-clad foothills spawn a handful of fine small rivers, including the Imnaha, Grande Ronde, and Wenaha, with sections flowing through wilderness more akin to the Rocky Mountains than to the desert.

On the western side of the Columbia Plateau, the John Day during early summer runoff offers one of the longer river trips possible in the West. The stream flows from the conifer-shaded Blue Mountains of central Oregon and then through basalt deserts to the Columbia. Though stressed by diversions, grazing, high temperatures, and water quality problems, this is the only major river in Oregon without hatchery-planted fish, which frequently depress native fish populations. The main stem flows for 243 continuous miles with no impoundments except on the lower 12 miles, which are flooded by The Dalles Dam on the Columbia. West of the John Day, the Deschutes also runs northward for 252 miles to the Columbia. With a uniquely long and uniform flow for a desert river, the Deschutes draws much of its supply from springs that discharge Cascade Mountain water. The river supports a who's who of cold water game fish, including steelhead, chinook salmon, rainbow trout, brown trout, Dolly Varden, and kokanee, though many of those fisheries have declined in recent years.

The distinction of most arid state goes to Nevada, in the Basin and Range province, not much known for rivers. But here the Humboldt flows most of the way across the state from east to west. Its 385-cfs flow is used up for irrigation before it reaches the terminal Humboldt Sink. The Carson and Walker splash down from pristine sources in California's Sierra Nevada to be diverted at cattle ranches before reaching the once-rich Carson Sink. Except for the Colorado at Nevada's southern border, the Truckee is the state's largest river, carrying 538 cfs before terminating in Pyramid Lake, which is sacred to Paiute Indians and home of the rare, carplike cui-ui. Lake levels have plummeted seventy feet because the river is heavily tapped for the gambling mecca of Reno and for cattle, driving the Pyramid Lake cutthroat trout to extinction.

The Bear River of the Rocky Mountains enters the Great Basin and supplies 60 percent of the inflow to the Great Salt Lake. To its south, the Jordan River first drains Utah Lake, then absorbs rank discharges of sewage in Salt Lake City before its channelized entry into the Great Salt Lake.

The ranges of the Great Basin are mostly short, cigar-shaped mountains, discontinuous enough that most rivers detour around impeding topography. The Sevier River, however, slices through some of its mountains carrying snowmelt of central Utah, charting a long, counterclockwise loop. In this river where anglers were once able to catch fifty pounds of trout in a few hours, irrigators now divert all the water; what might escape in a wet year evaporates in Sevier Lake.

The 730-mile Green River, a landmark of the West for its length and central location, enters desert country below Flaming Gorge Reservoir, cuts through the red-rock canyon of Lodore, curves through Echo Park in the heart of Dinosaur National Monument, then races through Whirlpool Canyon. Most western canyons are incised in plateaus or issue from the bulky mass of a mountain range, but at the astonishing Split Mountain of the Green, the antecedent river had chopped in half a sandstone monolith, allowing river runners to journey through the excavated center of a mountain. Then the Green meanders across the desert to Desolation Canyon. One of the great wilderness reaches of river, Desolation and Gray Canyons extend through 85 miles of rapids, cliff walls, and some of the finest cottonwood groves along a big desert river. No bridges cross for 128 miles—one of the longest unbridged reaches outside Alaska. Below the town of Green River, Utah, the dreamy waters of Labyrinth Canyon curve beneath thousand-foot sandstone walls before the tranquil lower Green mixes with the Colorado in Canyonlands National Park.

The Yampa—the Green's principal tributary—comes from the Colorado Rockies but scribes one of the most picturesque of all desert canyons in its lower 46 miles to Echo Park. Sandstone cliffs stained in tiger stripes of manganese oxide are only one of its many dazzling features.

The White River—silty, overgrazed, and blistered with oil wells—is still a remarkable, free-flowing tributary to the Green and cuts a fine canyon with cliffs, buttes, and pinnacles below Rangeley. The Fremont cottonwood forest here is one of the finest, contrasting remarkably with a sizzling arid landscape just above the riparian zone. The White enters the Green above Desolation Canyon after a reach of 85 nearly roadless miles. Provided Indian and private lands are avoided, it offers excellent canoeing in a region where other waters often throw one into heavy rapids.

This lower Green River system offers some of the longest free-flowing sections of river outside Alaska (see appendix 2). The Elk River of Colorado's Rockies joins the Yampa, then the Green and Colorado for 587 continuously undammed miles to Lake Powell—America's longest reach of river outside Alaska lacking dams, debilitating diversions, and levees. (One low diversion structure lies on the Green above Green River, Utah but does not require a portage.) The Little Snake River is a Yampa tributary winding from dry ranchlands in southern Wyoming; the Little Snake–Yampa–Green–Colorado combination runs 554 miles to Lake Powell without dams. The Yampa, combined with the Green and Colorado, includes 547 damless miles, and the Williams Fork–Yampa–Green–Colorado runs 541 miles. A 388-mile section of the Yampa-Green-Colorado can be continuously boated from below dangerous rapids in Cross Mountain Canyon to Lake Powell. The Green and Colorado Rivers from Flaming Gorge Dam to Lake Powell have 407 miles of continuously boatable river, and much of their mileage lies in wilderness canyons.

The Colorado River—myth-making, life-giving, canyon-carving centerpiece of the Southwest—enters the desert region as a mature river below Grand Junction, Colorado. Here, Ruby-Horsethief Canyon provides a gentle introduction to the sublime worlds of canyon life to come and supports one of the healthiest populations of the endangered Colorado squawfish. Westwater Canyon follows with intense, boat-swamping whitewater, followed by gentler rapids to Moab, Utah, then flatwater to Cataract Canyon, a cousin to the Grand Canyon in its sandstone scenery and powerful hydraulics. The 12 miles of rapids in Cataract are cut short by the 186-mile reservoir of Lake Powell, which flooded the legendary beauty of placid Glen Canyon.

The 275-mile Grand Canyon, stretching from Glen Canyon Dam to the backwater of Lake Mead, follows, a reach deep in the lore and history of the West. Widely regarded as the ultimate river trip on big water, the Colorado's thundering rapids alternate with tranquil scenes, all within a cathedral-like chasm of rock. This reach was protected as one of our earliest national parks, then threatened with damming in a classic conservation battle of the century. It is still degraded by hydropower generation at Glen Canyon Dam, which results in silt entrapment and daily flushes of high water.

The Colorado of the 5,500-foot-deep Grand Canyon ends in the reservoir of Lake Mead, behind Hoover Dam. An icon in the development of water in America, this dam was the first multipurpose megaproject in the West. Below Hoover, several hundred miles of river flow southward. Called a "milk-and-honey wilderness" by Aldo Leopold in 1922, this reach now consists of six reservoirs, riprapped banks, and river bottoms overrun by tamarisk. The 13,590-cfs lower Colorado is diverted to central Arizona and southern California, leaving a salty creek for Mexico and nothing for the Cucapá Indians, who have historically depended on the river for fish. The lower Colorado once delivered enormous amounts of silt and built up a delta from Yuma, Arizona, to the Gulf of California. Most of the incoming sediment now accumulates behind Glen Canyon Dam and will eventually turn that symbol of water development into a purposeless mud hole, as nonrenewable as any use for a river can be. Along this workhorse river of the Southwest, ten major dams hold six times the annual flow of the river. Among the nine largest interbasin transfers in the West, five are from the Colorado.

A key Colorado tributary is the Dolores (785 cfs), running for 250 miles from the Rockies of southwestern Colorado. Its lower reach winds for 187 free-flowing miles in echoing sandstone canyons from McPhee Dam to the Colorado. The dam was completed only in 1984 when it flooded foothills country and reduced the springtime flows that had produced one of the finest river trips in the desert.

Near the four corners of Colorado, New Mexico, Arizona, and Utah, the 400-mile San Juan River still offers a premier 84-mile canoe voyage with swift water. Its unique goosenecks section meanders radically in a 1,000-foot-deep canyon. For a river illustrating archaeological sites and the Southwest's geology of folds, faults, and layers upon layers of sedimentary deposits, this is the best, down to its grim end in mudflats of Lake Powell. A San Juan tributary, the Navajo River, has lost two-thirds of its flow to diversions into the Rio Grande, devastating an Indian fishery. Joining the Colorado in the Grand Canyon, the Little Colorado flows for 289 free-flowing miles from a dam near its source but delivers a small flow of 244 cfs; much of its bed is often dry.

Joining the lower Colorado in the reservoir behind Hoover Dam, the 134-mile Virgin River highlights the desert of southwestern Utah. Many people call Zion National Park a "desert Yosemite" because of its red and white sandstone walls rising above the Virgin. The Zion Canyon Narrows make a spectacular defile, 2,000 feet deep and 50 feet wide at the bottom. This geologic curiosity is a thrill to hike and wade through at times of low water, though risky in the late summer flash flood season. With only Hoover Dam affecting its lowest reaches, the Virgin is one of the longest nearly undammed rivers on the Colorado Plateau and harbors endangered fish, but water users in southern Utah's "Dixie" have identified sixteen potential dam sites. Some of them would alter the flows in Zion.

Other than the Colorado, important streams in Arizona include the Verde, which runs south from central mountains to its confluence with the Salt River above Phoenix. Though four dams plug the Salt, a superb whitewater run remains on its upper reaches through a miniature, high-elevation Grand Canyon. The 630-mile Gila River likewise flows west; its normally dry channel traverses western Arizona to the lower Colorado at Yuma. This river was once a flowing asset with firm banks bordered by cottonwoods, but overgrazing reduced it to a quarter-mile-wide strip of sandy wasteland by the 1890s.

The San Pedro River, a Gila tributary originating in Mexico, recovered dramatically when the Bureau of Land Management in 1988 halted riparian grazing. Cottonwoods and willows flourished, and 400 bird species—one of the highest counts in the nation—have been found there. But the river is now suffering from depleted flows lost to nearby groundwater pumping for new urban development.

Incomparably stressed rivers lie at the far southwestern limits of the desert region in California. The Owens collects runoff of the eastern Sierra Nevada in America's deepest valley, 6 to 16 miles wide with 14,000-foot peaks on either side. Fifty miles of the willow-lined stream, which used to end in the landlocked Owens Lake, suffer complete diversion where aqueducts whisk it off to Los Angeles. Farther south, in the Mojave Desert, the bizarre and nauseous Alamo and New Rivers begin in Mexico and flow north as agricultural wastewater streams to the lowest river mouths in America, at the Salton Sea. This foul-water

Green River, Bowknot Bend, UT

Dolores River below Slickrock, CO

Virgin River, Zion National Park, UT

Rio Grande, Los Ebanos Ferry, TX, Mex.

Bruneau River, ID

Yampa River, Wagonwheel Point, CO

Colorado River, Grand Canyon, AZ

Elephant Butte Dam, Rio Grande, NM

Rio Grande, Juarez, Mex.

Rio Grande, Lower Canyons, TX, Mex.

sink sits 230 feet below sea level, with river mouths that lie only 46 feet higher than the elevation of Death Valley.

New Mexico, which, like Nevada, is a dry state without a lot of rivers, does have the lower Animas after it leaves Colorado. This river houses probably the finest functioning cottonwood ecosystem in the Southwest before it joins the San Juan at a big riverfront park in Farmington, which is overrun by exotic Russian olive trees. The Rio Chama, in the north, borders a pine and cedar forest through a golden-lit mountain-desert setting. This 115-mile river, the largest tributary to the Rio Grande in New Mexico, is a favorite of anglers and boaters in a canyon running 23 miles to Abiquiu Reservoir. After its designation as a Wild and Scenic River in 1988, federal agencies and others devised a plan to restore some of the river's natural values while satisfying irrigation needs. Below the Chama, the Rio Grande continues to the Mexican border and then to the Gulf of Mexico in a route of epic proportions that shows a few of the better features of desert rivers and a lot of the pressures affecting them.

The Rio Grande

Up in the fir forests and monkeyflower meadows of the San Juan Mountains, I wouldn't have guessed that the Rio Grande would become an archetypal desert river. Untainted water gurgles down from the snowbanks, but, denied a simple fate, it soon encounters Rio Grande Reservoir, built early in the 1900s by farmers in the San Luis Valley downstream. Below the reservoir, the youthful Rio Grande swishes against cliff faces through a superb whitewater canyon in a mosaic of pine and sagebrush.

After an interlude of mountain-backed ranchland, the river carves 12 miles through its second canyon at Wagonwheel Gap, picks up the South Fork, and drifts into a valley of ranches. Agriculture dominates by the time the river reaches the town of Del Norte, at once a northern advance of Hispanic culture and the beginning of the desert Rio Grande in southern Colorado's San Luis Valley. This is the only major river to rise in the Rockies and cross a broad sweep of the Basin and Range province.

The Rio Grande's status as an overtaxed river quickly becomes evident in the dust-blown San Luis Valley, where the stream is drained nearly dry. The Fish and Wildlife Service creates wetlands, once supplied by natural flows, where it channels water out of the Rio Grande and into duck ponds at the Alamosa National Wildlife Refuge, but there isn't enough water to do even that, owing to upstream diversions.

Not only flow problems but also mine drainage, spiked with a periodic chart of poisons, threaten and degrade the upper Rio Grande. Pollution from the abandoned Summitville gold mine above the Alamosa River broke through a levee in 1993, and containment of the hot stew of toxins required $40,000 per day in taxpayers' money. Long-term solutions will cost $100 million or more, while the Canadian mining company that was responsible escaped under the shelter of the 1872 Mining Law.

Below San Luis Valley, the Rio Grande veers south through remote country that drops deeper and deeper in a sharply etched canyon. Cliffs and remote range here support the second-highest density of nesting raptors in America. Congress designated 49 miles below the Colorado–New Mexico border in the original National Wild and Scenic Rivers System in 1968. Rugged walls of basalt are dotted with juniper, sage, and pockets of ponderosa pine, while bubbling springs replenish some of the river's flow.

The Rio Grande here presents an impassible waterfall of razor-backed rock in the Upper Box and then a lively whitewater section in the 800-foot-deep Taos Box. Highway 64 crosses on the second-highest bridge in the national highway system, rising a dizzying 667 feet above the shadowy canyon.

Having spent many years on the Rio Grande, Tom Mottl of the Bureau of Land Management presents the profile of a dedicated river manager on public lands, working first as a river ranger, then as author of a plan for the Wild and Scenic corridor, and finally as an advocate for reclaiming needed flows. "I regard this section as a benchmark," Tom said, "the only reach in New Mexico where we can see what the Rio Grande in a reasonably natural condition was once like. Yet the flows have been sharply reduced." Through compact obligations, about a third of the runoff from Colorado must go to New Mexico, but the farmers let nearly all the water pass in winter, when it isn't used for irrigation. Summertime flows have dropped to 26 cfs—a trickle. Ranchers fear that any change will be a bad change, and Colorado law hinders solutions by prohibiting the sale of water out of state—even for instream flows.

Though working on behalf of the Rio Grande was a lonely job when Tom began, it certainly isn't anymore. In 1988 citizens formed a group called Amigos Bravos to fight a mining proposal, and then they pushed for better care of the river in other ways. Staff member Brian Shields said, "The emphasis now is on working with local communities for better management." "Local communities" here means the most multicultural constituency of any river in the country. Indians live in a dozen pueblos or small settlements. "Their interest clearly goes beyond irrigation water," Brian explained. "The Taos Pueblo people say that the river is the blood of the earth; they look at the river as a spiritual place. For the Hispanic culture, the river has always been a source of livelihood—economic survival has meant farming. Finally, the American culture has pushed the familiar theme of development as much as possible, but now, new attitudes for conservation are growing."

Population growth is the fundamental environmental challenge along many rivers in America, but at the Rio Grande the phrase takes on a new urgency. Projections call for the population of the basin to double in the next twenty years, with the fastest growth taking place along the Mexican border. "As that environment deteriorates," Brian said, "people move up here. There's great concern to slow the immigration."

Rio Grande outfitter Steve Harris invests the assets of his rafting company, Far Flung Adventures, into the fight to restore the river. He and other outfitters founded Rio Grande Restoration to inform people, help Pueblo Indians monitor water quality, encourage acquisition of water rights for instream flows, and revegetate riparian zones. "People have a difficult time thinking of this as one watershed," the outfitter said from his modest base in the hills above Taos. "It's one of the most chopped-up rivers you can imagine. But we need to put it back together again."

As I traveled downstream, I saw what Steve meant: dried up here, dammed there, utterly forgotten and then resurrected later on, the river continued and discontinued down through New Mexico. White Rock Canyon was a fine reach with rapids until Cochiti Dam was built for flood control in the 1970s. In wet years, the reservoir backs into Bandelier National Monument, where it kills cottonwoods and floods archaeological sites.

Farther down, in Albuquerque, development nips at the floodplain, but some frontage has been reserved as parkland with a bike trail and a nature center used by school groups. In an interesting case, the Isleta Pueblo Indians successfully claimed that under the Clean Water Act they can set water quality standards just as states do. In order to continue spiritual traditions of the tribe, they set a standard for drinking water. Albuquerque scrambled to solve pollution problems or evade the Indians' requirement.

Throughout this reach a cottonwood forest, known in the Southwest as a bosque, (BOS-kay), extends with little interruption for 140 miles from Cochiti to Elephant Butte Reservoir—probably the longest cottonwood forest in America. Large trees line the belt of shade, but on closer examination it becomes clear that *only* large trees grow there; young cottonwoods fail to appear on the insides of bends, where they would naturally sprout. Floods once scoured the shorelines and deposited new silt, needed for the cottonwood seeds to germinate and thrive, but the floods have not occurred since Cochiti Dam was built. The silt also provided essential nitrogen for the native forest—something the invasive Russian olive trees do not need because they add, or "fix," atmospheric nitrogen into the soil. A team of federal and state officials has prepared the Bosque Biological Management Plan, calling for flood releases from Cochiti Dam at critical times to reestablish scouring and silt deposits on which new cottonwoods can germinate. For the plan to succeed, a difficult lineup of agreements is needed between water rights owners and management agencies, but Gerald Burton, a biologist with the Fish and Wildlife Service, has not lost hope. "The river has more value than that of a transport system for irrigation," he said. "The water users are feeling threatened, but many of them also see that the land is worth more as a functioning ecosystem."

Nothing is simple, and the lack of floods is not the river's only problem. Drains, ditches, and levees enmesh the midsections of the Rio Grande. The exotic tamarisk monopolizes the riparian zone with an impenetrable mat of roots and foliage, inhospitable to native plants and birds. And the diversion problems are as extreme as the tamarisk takeover. Just south of Albuquerque, Isleta Dam diverts water for irrigation and leaves river flows as intermittent as summertime rain showers for 53 miles to San Acacia. Fifteen miles farther down, a diversion dam completely dries up the river half the time during April through October. A "low-flow channel" sluices the river straight to Elephant Butte Reservoir, 70 miles downstream. Throughout the West, irrigation canals result in dried-up riverbeds as a by-product of overuse, but this canal was built for the explicit purpose of drying up a riverbed. The low-flow channel conducts the water out of the river and thereby avoids evaporation and seepage, which are considered a waste to the irrigation economy. As a result, the aquatic ecosystem was devastated; half the upper river's native fish species are extinct. Rio Grande cutthroat trout habitat is reduced to a token. The endangered silvery minnow, once at home from the upper river to the Gulf of Mexico, struggles to survive within 5 percent of its original range. New Mexico is the only western state without an instream flow law; water in the river has no "beneficial use."

Sorely affected by all these forces, the Bosque del Apache National Wildlife Refuge lies along the river in central New Mexico and offers a haven to migrating waterfowl. But this place of great management intensity consists of excavated ponds to replace the riparian wetlands that once graced the valley. Bulldozers and herbicides destroy the opprobrious tamarisk, and irrigation systems simulate river flooding in an all-out effort to get cottonwoods to grow.

Downstream, the 300-foot-high Elephant Butte Dam, built in 1916 as one of the first projects of the Bureau of Reclamation, remains the major storage reservoir on the Rio Grande. Once one of the largest reservoirs in the United States, a quarter of its capacity is now usually filled with silt. Below the dam, an 8-mile reach of free-flowing water leads to Caballo Dam, where operators shut the river tap for storage in winter. Summer is no better, when a series of five diversion dams direct the water into cotton fields and chili pepper farms all the way to Texas. Under a 1906 treaty only 60,000 acre-feet of silty return flows escape to Mexico.

The anemic and polluted Rio Grande worsens to a waking riverine nightmare at El Paso. More than 600,000 people lived on the American side and 800,000 on the Mexican side at Ciudad Juarez in 1995, and the numbers were rapidly increasing. South of the border, where 51 percent of the Rio Grande's total watershed lies, the river is known as Rio Bravo del Norte—the wild river of the north. But far from wild, the river corridor faces increasing commercial sprawl, shantytown "colonias," traffic jams, and air pollution. Beginning there at El Paso—the largest American city in the basin—the river separates as well as unites the two nations. The Hispanic influence, beginning at del Norte, has become so prevalent that nearly everyone Ann and I encountered from here to the Gulf spoke English to us but Spanish to each other.

I stood on a dusty hilltop to survey the scene below: southern mountains melted in the yellow pall of Juarez's air. That Mexican city drains 60 million gallons of raw sewage into canals, which leak substantial amounts into the river. As short on water as any city in America, El Paso advertises conservation on billboards and seeks more supplies from wherever possible. Pawnshops with high-posted signs are a regular feature of the downtown area, the malls, and the commercial strips. Not coincidentally, we entered here the window-bar belt of America—steel bars protect the windows and doors of everybody who can afford them.

Border Patrol officers in El Paso sat in four-wheel-drive vehicles above the riverbank day and night, waiting to apprehend crossing Mexicans. But for years, a freeway, a railroad, and, least of all, the river present only a nuisance to the millions of illegal immigrants entering the United States each year (in the mid-1990s, tighter patrol of urban areas

was begun). The Rio Grande defines 1,254 miles of the border, but little of that mileage is under guard. Immigration Service officials have estimated that 1.2 million illegal immigrants arrive per year, a figure of
dubious logic based on the fact that 1.2 million people per year are
caught and turned back. It costs our government $600 to apprehend
and return each person to Mexico, where he or she will promptly try
again, with a high likelihood of success. Other sources, including Border Patrol officers, estimate that 5 to 10 million people cross illegally
each year. The border is the escape valve for a country whose population doubled between 1960 and 1980 and whose growth curve shoots
up to the sky. Immigration is considered by many to be an alternative
to poverty in Mexico, though it will inevitably convert the southern
United States into an advancing Third World frontier with the same
problems that people in Mexico seek to escape.

Much of the growth surge along the border began in the 1960s, when
the Mexican government encouraged American companies to establish
industries called maquiladoras along the border and thereby avoid hir-
ing laborers in the United States. These companies also take advantage
of lax or completely overlooked environmental regulations in Mexico.
Well entrenched, more than 2,000 maquiladoras occupy the border in
a pattern likely to proliferate with the 1994 North American Free Trade
Agreement.

For a glimpse of the country we have joined in economic partner-
ship, I spied into Mexico with my binoculars from an El Paso freeway
overpass. Hundreds of tumbledown shacks in a slum of cinder blocks,
wood scraps, rusty tin, and cardboard covered steep hillsides in the
colonia of Felipe Angeles. Trash glittered in a ground cover of glass and
cans, while windblown plastic bags were snagged on every surviving
shrub and thistle. The riverbank looked like an excavated dump.

To take a closer look, Ann and I paid twenty-five cents each to cross
the bridge and joined a throng of Spanish-speaking pedestrians walking to Juarez. Muddy water slipped past the cities; the Rio Grande's
banks were completely finished in cement. A beautiful Mexican Indian
woman in brightly dyed clothing sat sullenly on the sidewalk of the
bridge with her three children and begged for money.

As soon as we were off the bridge, we entered a mass of people jam-
ming the streets. Men in front of shops selling low-priced clothing,
rugs, leather, tacky junk, and handsome crafts said, "Please come in."
But the cab drivers hustled the best: "I'll take you to the marketplace.
Many shops, good prices. You can sit down and have lunch with a
Mexican drink. With Mexican music. Your wife, she has never been to
Mexico before? Come, you will enjoy it." We said thanks but walked

deeper into the city. A little girl ran out of nowhere, clutched my leg, and pleaded, "One penny, please."

This brief introduction to the border called up troublesome thoughts about the area's appalling poverty, the heartbreaking dependence of its people on handouts, and the population boom. Stabilizing and then reducing the population seemed to be the only conceivable answer to the glut of ills, yet neither nation's government does anything about the issue. The river, as an early casualty, offers a clue about what to expect for all aspects of society and the environment in a future that promises to worsen.

Gus Sanchez, a cultural historian at Big Bend National Park, farther downriver, and a lifelong resident of the Rio Grande valley, reflected on the urbanization of the border. "Hispanic people on both sides have been involved with agriculture in a long-standing relationship with the river as a source of life. But now, people live in cities. They are just beginning to see again that the river is important, but it takes a long time to realize what we once knew." Even the agricultural view ignores the river as anything but an irrigation canal; below El Paso, Ann and I camped along a ditch carrying more water than the Rio Grande. The river then died to a trickle in a tamarisk wasteland.

Stopping to view the river from a bridge at Fort Hancock, we met a seasoned Border Patrol officer who used to work at John F. Kennedy International Airport in New York. While we talked, she checked the intermittent traffic of Mexicans. "People get green cards to work in the states and then collect American welfare. One woman showed up in labor. We had to call an ambulance. The child is now a U.S. citizen. His mother is entitled to all sorts of benefits, and someday he'll be able to bring the family into the country. The system encourages these abuses."

The river stretches through hundreds of miles of remote terrain where check stations are a rarity. What's to prevent people from crossing anyplace?

"Nothing. It happens all the time. If the Border Patrol doesn't find people within twenty-five miles, they're as good as safe. Who makes the beds in St. Louis motels? Who serves the fast food in Denver?" A loophole as wide as the unpatrolled border allows their employers to get off unless they "knowingly" hired the illegal immigrants. Why does this system continue? A patrolman farther downriver offered an explanation: "The politicians making the rules take their orders from the businessmen making money off the system."

Below Fort Hancock, the Rio Grande exists only as a trickle for 212 miles until the Rio Conchos joins it near the Mexican town of Ojinaga. I had heard this was the border town least affected by American culture or commerce, so Ann and I unracked our bicycles and pedaled across. From the bridge we checked out the unappetizing water that flows from the Conchos. Then we bounced over rough streets to the town square, paved and checkered with trees whose limbs were oddly amputated.

"Buenos dias," I offered to an old man who raked leaves along a back street. "Good morning," he answered. Eventually we emerged on top of a 100-foot embankment, the muddy Rio Grande down below. A man and woman from a house at the bottom of the hill raked plastic and junk in an effort to maintain some dignity at their humble river-front home that was disadvantaged by gravity; trash rolls down from streets up above. Two currish dogs came barking at our heels. We pedaled back to the United States.

The dusty town of Presidio, Texas, held walled-in ranch houses, trailers, industries, weeds on its margin, and friendly people. This spot boasts some of the highest temperatures in the United States.

Downriver at Redford, I asked around and located Enrique Madrid, an author of historical papers about the area. A lifelong resident, he is steeped in the culture of the region. We discussed border issues and the river. "At the current rate of growth, Mexico will have a population of 1.4 billion in 100 years—all those people on the other side of the river, except they won't *be* on the other side. There is no place for people to go but north. It feels isolated here, but it is not. This river has the world's problems." I asked if a society so crowded would be worth living in. "Human beings always adapt. They will still love their children. We resolve our problems.

"The concerns of most people are not ecological problems but where their food will come from next week. The river is not something that people think much about. For thousands of years people just wanted to *cross* the river. To go *down* the river meant to end up in a canyon and be lost in the desert. When I grew up here, we swam and fished like Huckleberry Finn. But in recent years, you didn't go close because you might run into a drug dealer, and if you saw the wrong thing, your life might be in danger. It's not so bad now. But still, the only people going to the river are crossing the river."

Enrique spoke of the need to work together in a world of one people. He believed that we must dissolve differences in order to govern ourselves. "When both sides become one, the river will disappear. Then it will not be regarded as a divider."

With more questions than answers, we moved on downstream. For the 309 miles from Presidio to Amistad Reservoir the river runs through one canyon after another separated by open basins. This is one of the longer free-flowing and boatable lengths of river in the United States outside Alaska, and only one bridge crosses it. Colorado Canyon runs for 21 miles. Three magnificent canyons named Santa Elena, Mariscal, and Boquillas run for 107 miles through Big Bend National Park with rapids but mostly gentle flows. Though many people boat there, the reputation of the place has been soured by gunshot incidents since the 1980s when a canoeist was killed. A few years later a two-hour gun battle ensued between floaters and a young, apparently deranged, Mexican. A man and his daughter were murdered at a remote roadside campsite in 1991. In 1994 a sniping incident occurred in Mariscal Canyon, but nobody was hit. Local river runners shrug off the problem and never complain of difficulties. Phil Koepp, chief of resources management at the park, said, "This *is* the frontier. But compared with San Antonio, with 400 homicides a year, this park seems like a safe place."

Ann and I put her kayak and my canoe in the water below Mariscal Canyon so that we could float the lower end of Big Bend National Park and continue through the Lower Canyons to Dryden Crossing, 113 miles away. After just a few riffling bends, we beached at the Mexican village of Boquillas. Three kids offered to watch our boats so we could walk up the steep bank into the village. "How much?" Ann asked.
A little boy with big brown eyes and a smile replied, "One dollar," then added, "One dollar *each*."

From a distance Boquillas has the look of ancient stone ruins. Its stark, dusty homes occupy a bench high above the river. Saddled burros waited at some houses. Children peeked out of doorways and pursued us with pretty cloth bracelets to sell. Kids seemed to be everywhere, though I saw no clue of how anybody's life could be supported; soil and water were lacking for even a garden.

Back on the water, we faced the headwall of Boquillas Canyon, and the river entered it as if passing through a door in some great fantasy dwarfing the Pyramids. Inside, the river led us effortlessly onward, the rocky sides climbing high, the isolation hushing, enchanting, promising. This is the only river in the United States that offers a view of the Chihuahuan Desert. The canyon floor was lined with impenetrable thickets of giant reed, an exotic that looks like bamboo. These have displaced the native common reed and the lanceleaf cottonwood and willows. I tried to walk across the fifty-foot-wide reed belt to reach a cave up above. I scraped and staggered, one step up, half a step back. I fell into a hidden ditch, not thinking enough about rattlesnakes. Then, cursing my goal of reaching the dusty cave, I cut my leg on a spear of broken reed and spent the rest of the canoe trip guarding against infection from the polluted water.

Without such reed thickets, and in fact without any plant life at all for miles at a time, the Mexican side of the river was mowed by horses, cows, and goats in an open, unregulated, denuded range—a mix of federal, private, and communal, or *ejidos,* land. Several times a year the Park Service rounds up trespassing cows on the American side. Rather than being shot, the cows are impounded, vaccinated, and advertised to Mexican owners, but few claim their animals because of the expense of picking them up. With all this costly effort, the problem of cows wading across the ankle-deep river and trashing its northern shore is only minimally controlled.

A sandy campsite lured us in for the evening, and hikes up side canyons showed us sotol with fringed or toothed leaves, ocotillo with dead-looking stems but scarlet flowers, prickly pear cacti almost as large as tennis rackets, and a brushscape of other cacti so dense that cross-country travel quickly filled my trousers with jagging spines.

At night, all the hardships turned to pure rapture when a full moon shone white light into the canyon. Fairy-tale landforms jutted upward in black and gray. A roughly textured cliff climbed to the right, and a shiny, moonlit wall of polished rock rose to the left. Stars sprinkled a fissure of sky between canyon faces, and a fuzzy mane of clouds drifted by.

On the next day we saw two Mexicans preparing candelilla—a plant dug up in large quantities by the roots, then boiled with sulfuric acid to render a wax that is smuggled north and used in cosmetics, paint remover, and chewing gum. "No English," they responded when I spoke.

On the third day we cruised under the bridge at La Linda, past a fluorspar plant, and entered the wilderness of the Lower Canyons with its desert vistas, whitewater, and a soothing solitude. Low water exposed a streamside of gross algae and, underneath, an anaerobic pudding of stinking black sludge. Throughout Big Bend National Park, fecal coliform counts in the water are high, and heavy metals contaminate the flesh of fish and birds.

Several days later we portaged the sharp pitch of Upper Madison Falls, a train wreck of scattered boulders. From our campsite we climbed to Burro Bluff, straight up for more than 1,000 feet, and thrilled to a bird's-eye view of the canyon in which the rapid was reduced to a rock-and-water schematic.

At riverfront springs we made our first stop for drinking water, having used up the twelve gallons we brought with us. Then, at San Francisco Canyon, a herd of javelinas snorted down to the river. The fifty-pound beasts were one-third head with no neck to speak of—cute, wary, piggish rooters of the Chihuahua. Meanwhile, hundreds of Big Bend turtles populated stones at water level throughout the trip. White-throated swifts jetted by with a *"whoosh,"* but as fast as we could look up, they were gone.

On the last day we drifted slowly out, and ten minutes after we had disembarked at Dryden Landing a Border Patrol officer dusted up in a four-wheel-drive vehicle. "Did you get out of your canoe a mile up-stream?" he inquired. Apparently when I had stopped to look at a rapid at a common fording spot, I had tripped an electronic sensing device.

We visited with the officer, and eventually our hired shuttle driver ar-rived. Ann and I packed up, and the next day we rolled on to the lower Rio Grande. That 624-mile stretch includes two reservoirs, five cities on the American side with counterparts in Mexico, and long, brushy agri-cultural reaches without main roads. Where Amistad Dam floods the Rio Grande, silt and pollution settle in a 50-mile-long septic tank that releases blue-green water, though it turns gray-green before long.

At Del Rio, population 30,000, we left behind the views of distant mountains and entered the Coastal Plain, though desert conditions per-sisted. Large canals shunted water to farmlands near and far. Eagle Pass had a bustling downtown. Remote ranching country led to Laredo, the second-fastest-growing urban area in the United States in 1991. The streets of Laredo appeared not as they do in song but principally as car-congested commercial strips. As on the fringes of other Texas border towns, the development there constantly redefined a new apogee of bad taste in discount store architecture and cinder block fundamental-ism. But the interesting downtown was packed with Mexican shoppers, and a square of parkland bordered by a church lent an isolated sense of heritage to this town, founded in 1755. "It gets pretty hot here," one Mexican American man offered. "Up to 105. You have to get a bathing suit on and go to the beach. Except there is no beach. This place is a hole." Border Patrol officers bicycled the riverfront, where a big park lay devoid of people. I snooped along a Rio Grande frontage thick with reeds and brush where a tributary entered through a rank sewer pipe as tall as a man. Six boys swam in their underwear on the Mexican side at Nuevo Laredo, whose population of 350,000 discharges untreated sewage directly into canals and the river. Later in 1994, a swimmer here was killed by the amoeba *Naegleria,* which enters through the nose and in six days causes death when it penetrates the brain.

Downstream another 80 miles, Falcon Dam blocks the Rio Grande, accumulating water one final time for irrigation canals. Roughly 10 per-cent of the flow is left in the river. A little farther, at Los Ebanos, four

Mexican men—three of them quite old—gripped a rope strung across the river and pulled in unison to operate a hand-powered ferryboat. The three-car barge served laughing, chatting Mexicans and picture-taking tourists.

Along this lower river, the oasis of Bentsen–Rio Grande Valley State Park and Santa Ana National Wildlife Refuge hosts one of the continent's most exceptional migrations of birds, including species of the Mexican subtropics. In groves of cedar elm, hackberry, mesquite, and acacia we saw the cardinal-like pyrrhuloxia; the chachalaca, with its comically screeching voice; and the brilliantly colored green jay—its body green, tail yellow, breast black, and head blue, and, as if that weren't enough, its forehead unbelievably spangled with a star-splash of white. Two flyways converge here, enabling Santa Ana to claim 325 bird species—more than almost any other refuge in the nation. Three kinds of cat prowl in this fragment of riparian growth—the ocelot, jaguarundi, and bobcat.

These myriad life forms depend on the corridor of the lower Rio Grande, yet farms on the velvety brown soil usurp the riverfront in a deathly comprehensive way. Ninety percent of the valley has been cleared for crops. Piecing together at least a shred of interconnected habitat, the Fish and Wildlife Service is creating the Lower Rio Grande National Wildlife Refuge by buying property along a 200-mile stretch of river. In 1994 the refuge amounted to about 70,000 acres in scattered parcels—half of what the agency planned to protect and a fourth of what Audubon Society activists say is needed. But federal cost-cutting measures after 1994 may spell doom to this effort, which is essential to so much life. Much of the refuge describes an unimpressive weed-edge of fields or an eddy of willow and tamarisk in corners too tight for turning around a tractor. Yet even a minimalist corridor will be helpful to the region's host of subtropical and migrating birds and wildlife. Cyndy Chapman of the local Audubon group said, "The hallmark and rewarding thing about this project is the cooperation we're getting from cities, counties, and individual groups to protect small areas, many of them to be linked together."

We entered Brownsville, the last city on the American side. Matamoros occupies the Mexican side here, and both cities do a heartless job of trashing the river and sprawling across the flats. The assault on the ecosystem is equivalent to Sherman's march across Georgia, except that the damage here is permanent. As a big selling point, subdividers advertised "aqua potable." Machines dispensing filtered drinking water sat outside the grocery stores, $1 for five gallons. Valley International

Bail Bonds occupied a prominent storefront. The river lay brown and still, and shopping carts bristled with muddy straw in eddies.

When we were there at the bottom of the river, an anemic flow of about 200 cubic feet per second oozed through the final miles of the fifth-longest river in America. In naming the Rio Grande the most endangered river of the country in 1993, American Rivers called this reach a "conduit of disease." Hepatitis was rampant on the Mexican side, and toxics were present in alarming levels. Though banned for use in the United States, DDT is still produced by American chemical companies for sale in Mexico. It is returned to us, not only on the Mexican produce we eat but also in the Rio Grande, now a pariah of rivers.

Leaving the cities behind, anxious for the journey's end, Ann and I drove eastward toward the mouth of the river. City sprawl thinned to scattered houses. Then a plain of grass stretched out across the Gulf flats. Between dunes, the road finally stopped point-blank at a six-foot surf.

On the beach we walked south toward the mouth of the Rio Grande. We felt reinvigorated by the sea and by the sweet, warm wind of the Gulf Coast, yet somehow we sensed we were still in a war zone of some kind. A man came running up the beach from Mexico.

"How far to the Rio Grande?" I asked, pointing the way he had come.

"River," he said, and made the shape of an arc with his hand.

"Is it close?" I asked, holding my hands together.

"Yes, close!" He smiled and ran on northward.

There at Boca Chica—the "little mouth"—the river entered the sea as a quiet stream of brown flatwater reaching the end of a twisted, troubled journey. Two men lounged in a large rowboat on the Mexican side, waiting for customers. A man fished while his wife stood by the truck and their daughter splashed knee-deep. When I asked if they had caught anything, the woman held up a plastic bag containing five fish. "We come here all the time," she said. "From Brownsville."

"The river is small," I commented without judgment.

"Yes, the river is no problem. It's easy to cross."

A brown pelican glided above the surf. Mist from the springtime wind dampened my face, and waves rolled in the Gulf as far as I could see.

Chapter 8

Brilliant Waters of the Sierra Nevada

Imagine a river born beneath perpetual snowbanks at 11,600 feet, one that flows across whole basins of white granite, then over hundred-foot waterfalls. The stream broadens in a forest of girthy conifers, finally cutting through golden-glowing canyons to foothills of oak and a velvety tan grassland. This describes the Kings River of the Sierra Nevada in California, but fourteen other magnificent or once magnificent rivers share similar features where they flow from the "Range of Light," as pioneer preservationist John Muir called his favorite mountains. Though occupying a small region 400 miles long and 70 miles wide, the streams of the Sierra Nevada are alluring in their passage from sky-reaching mountains down to billiard-table flats. Here are the West's most-floated whitewater, the deepest canyon on the continent, and the greatest vertical drop of any river in North America.

Undeniably distinct as a mountain range, the Sierra is part of the larger Pacific Mountain System province defined by geographer N. M. Fenneman. As a region of rivers, the Sierra is in a class by itself because of its numerous and extraordinary streams. This chapter also includes the rivers after they leave the mountains and cross the Central Valley,

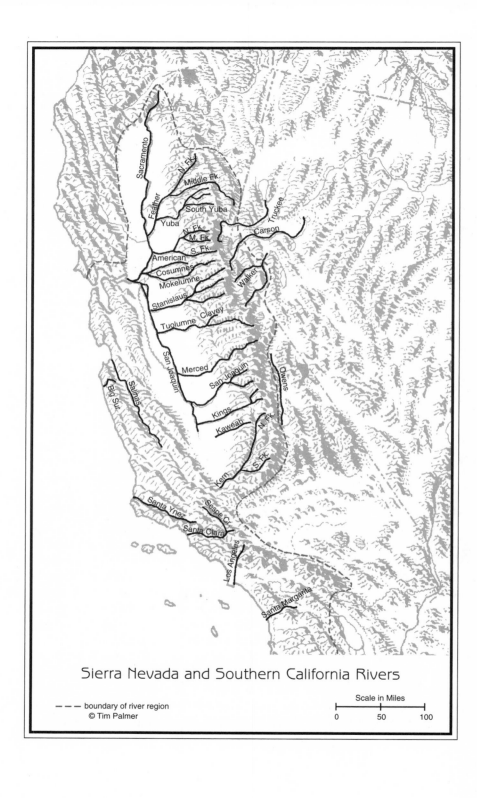

Sierra Nevada and Southern California Rivers

– – – boundary of river region
© Tim Palmer

Scale in Miles

0   50   100

and briefly addresses the small streams of coastal California below San Francisco Bay.

Occupying the eastern side of California, the granitic and volcanic peaks of the Sierra run roughly north–south, encompassing a whole range of superlatives. Here are the largest continuous mountain block in America and our highest peak outside Alaska. As the largest organism on earth, one sequoia tree stands thirty-six feet in diameter. Mapped on Erwin Raisz's *Landforms of the United States,* the Sierra stands out as our most extreme, extensive area of mountainous topography. Only the North Cascades—much smaller in extent—have a similarly rugged texture. Our longest protected wilderness runs along a 145-mile crest of the Sierra, and straddling it lie four of only sixteen areas in the country outside Alaska where a person can be more than 10 miles from a road. Remnants of some of the range's sixty glaciers remain at latitudes as far south as Norfolk, Virginia. And this country produces rivers as remarkable as its mountains.

To the north, the Sierra melds into the Cascades at Lake Almanor, which was enlarged by damming the North Fork of the Feather River. At the southern end of the range, the Sierra trails off into the desert at the Tehachapi Mountains—a transverse range that runs westward until it is welded into the Coast Range. At the explicit eastern boundary of the Sierra, the fault-block escarpment veers skyward from the edge of the Great Basin desert. In the west, the mountains roll down to foothills and then to the Central Valley—the largest expanse of flat land in the entire western cordillera between the Great Plains and the Pacific.

For 400 miles the cigar-shaped Central Valley is flanked by the Sierra on the east and the Coast Range on the west. Alluvial runoff brought by Sierra rivers filled the center of the Valley with sediment thousands of feet deep. Now the combination of fertile soil, hot summers, mild winters, and flatness makes the Valley the richest and largest tract of farmland in the West, a landscape of former wetlands and savanna transformed into an agricultural machine. The Valley is the terminus of most Sierra rivers, and its hydrology can be pictured as two major streams colliding head-on in the center. The Sacramento flows from the north, the San Joaquin from the south, and their sea-level confluence creates the Sacramento–San Joaquin Delta. A unique feature in the geography of rivers, this is America's largest inland delta, not counting Alaska, and is composed of a thousand miles of sloughs in an empire of marshes, now gridded by canals and levees. Much of the Delta lies well below sea level owing to wind erosion, compaction, and oxidation of organic peat soil during a century of farming. Only precarious levees keep the waters of the rivers and the ocean at bay, a situation with a finite future because the farmed land continues to disappear at the rate of three inches per year. From the Delta, the water drifts out to San Francisco Bay—that is, the water that remains after pumps lift millions of acre-feet per year to farms and cities of southern, central, and coastal California.

Flowing to San Francisco Bay through the Coast Range, the consolidated rivers have deposited their sediment to form one of the few large flat areas on the West Coast (others are at Los Angeles, the Columbia River, and Puget Sound).

Back up where all these rivers begin, the genesis of the flow is snowfall. Some of America's deepest snowpacks occur here when Pacific storms blow in from the ocean and the air—saturated with water vapor—encounters the 8,000- to 14,000-foot incline of the Sierra. As the clouds ramp upward and cool, the vapor condenses and drops. Four hundred inches of snow typically fall each year. By springtime, twelve-foot depths of dense, consolidated snow mantle the high country and then yield prodigious runoff to create many rivers in the rugged, fractured topography. In this "Mediterranean" climate, nearly all precipitation falls from November through April, but the snowpacks conveniently delay the runoff until the growing season and the hot months of May, June, and July. Heavy winter rains pummel the lower lands, sometimes flooding valley rivers. The lowest flows occur in late fall. Since 1976, droughts have visited with increasing frequency, interspersed with a few very wet years.

Rivers dropping through whole zones of climate in a matter of miles present one fascinating family of plant life after another. At alpine elevations, the Sierra blooms in a ground cover of wildflower color. Downhill lies one of the greatest mixes of conifers on earth—eighteen species grow in the Sierra—which in turn yields to an ecosystem of oaks, chaparral, and, finally, sensuous hills of grass on the western side of the mountains.

The pattern of watersheds here is simple: the Sierra rivers flow either east or west. The eastern slope quickly drains to the Basin and Range province of the desert. But 90 percent of the Sierra's land mass lies west of the crest, and an even greater percentage of the runoff flows in that direction. The Sacramento River absorbs a lineup of Sierra rivers in the north, and the San Joaquin picks up the southern Sierra rivers—what remain after a gauntlet of dams and canals. No river boldly transects the Sierra, though the Middle Fork of the Feather nominally crosses the range with braided strings of headwaters flowing through the meadows of Sierra Valley, which merge with the Basin and Range province to the east.

Stratified by elevation, several types of river reach inhabit the Sierra. Up high, waters cross the exposed granite of this largest of all American batholiths and compose pure mountain streams in alpine settings of glaciated geography and rocky canyons. At middle elevations, the Sierra rivers become jewels of the evergreen forest, still spraying over waterfalls and rapids but growing in size, with their gradient relieved in serene, parklike interludes. Dense growths of subalpine fir, whitebark pine, red fir, Jeffrey pine, sugar pine, white fir, lodgepole pine, sequoia, and ponderosa pine shade the middle elevations. In the foothill canyons, the rivers' gradient eases from that of waterfalls to that of the rapids beloved by whitewater boaters. The banks here rise up to tawny grasslands, scattered oaks, and chaparral of scratchy, dense, heat-tolerant shrubs. Finally the rivers reach the Central Valley, where they once drifted across flats bordered by willows and cottonwoods but are now constrained by levees and crowded by farmed fields.

A wholly different type of stream flows from the eastern side of the Sierra. These small rivers drop radically from high country and through Jeffrey pine groves to sage flats of the Basin and Range province. Outside the Sierra, southern California's rivers likewise compose a separate type, rising in the oak woodlands of the Coast Range, which lacks snowmelt but is soaked by heavy rains in winter. These small rivers have cut rocky courses through oak and chaparral, and nearly all are tapped for farms or cities. Some coastal streams approach the Pacific among redwood and fir forests, some in cascades and narrow canyons, some across sandy estuaries, and some through pavement and culverts.

The Sierra rivers typically flow directly out of the mountains. Just one waterway—the upper Kern—flows for many north-south miles within the heart of the Sierra, much like the Greenbrier in the Appalachians and the Salmon River in the Rockies. In their volume of flow the Sierra rivers rate as the smallest of any major river region in America, but the watersheds are even smaller and, in fact, produce an extraordinary output of runoff given the acreage involved.

The Sacramento River (22,680 cfs) is the largest river in California. Though not in the Sierra per se, it picks up the runoff of the northern range along a 380-mile course that could be a keel of the northern Central Valley. The river begins in the Cascade Mountains in a corridor now crowded by Interstate 5. This upper section quickly terminates in Shasta Reservoir, behind one of the largest Bureau of Reclamation dams. Most of the Sacramento has been riprapped and leveed in deference to farmland, and only one natural section of riparian forest remains—a 54-mile highlight between Redding and Red Bluff. Finally, at its bottom, the Sacramento has the second-longest tidal reach on the West Coast—83 miles from Sacramento to San Pablo Bay, an arm of San Francisco Bay.

As in the Rockies, the greatest precipitation falls to the north, and so the Sierra's northernmost river, the Feather, is California's fourth-largest. (The Klamath, described in chapter 9, is second-largest, followed by the Colorado in the desert region.) The Feather's average flow of 9,424 cfs is by far the highest within the Sierra Nevada. The northern Sierra's American River (3,942 cfs) is followed in volume by the adjacent Yuba (3,147 cfs), though that riverbed is robbed of its flows more than any other in the Sierra when the water is diverted southward.

The Tuolumne River, as the geographic centerpiece of the Sierra, carries 2,514 cfs, followed in size by the San Joaquin (2,386 cfs), originating in high parklands. This river later mirrors the Sacramento by flowing northward through the Central Valley, picking up tributaries and growing to 4,783 cfs by the time it reaches the Delta. The Kings carries 2,177 cfs, the Stanislaus 1,529, and the Merced 1,304. The Mokelumne and Kern each flow at 990 cfs.

The central cultural identity of the northern Sierra goes back to the gold rush. In the 1800s, rivers from the Feather down through the Stanislaus were dug up, mined with high-pressure hydraulic hoses, sluiced, denuded, and dammed—totally trashed. Lacking gold, Sierra rivers of high country and the south remained an enclave of mountain scenery. But throughout the Sierra, the modern cultural context is quite different. No collection of streams in America gets more recreational use. When people think of Sierra rivers now, they think about rafting on whitewater, going trout fishing in shorts and sandals, and swimming in clear pools rimmed by hot, sunny rocks crawling with sunbathers. No towns lie along the steep-walled rivers of the Sierra, but once one reaches the Central Valley, a different image takes over. A farmscape even more thorough than that of the Midwest shoulders the waterfronts with levees, diversions, ditches, mile-long fields, and polluted runoff.

Even in their mountain strongholds, the Sierra rivers possess just a fraction of their old wealth. The density of dams here is greater than anywhere but New England, and the reservoirs are larger. The American and Stanislaus bear twenty-seven and sixteen dams, respectively, in basins that are small relative to other hardworking rivers in the country. California's 1,336 sizeable dams were built at sites as high as 9,128 feet above sea level (Middle Fork Bishop Creek). However, the big projects typically lie in the foothills, at the 500- to 1,000-foot elevation, to maximize water collection.

As the rivers flow through the foothills and enter the Central Valley, sizeable diversions bend water away from every stream and into a water-tank, pipe-fitting triumph of engineering. Rivers have been connected into networks of conduits and tunnels and dams transporting water to neighboring basins for hydropower, irrigation, or city supplies. The Middle Yuba, for example, is diverted to the South Yuba and then farther south to the basin of the Bear River, whose water is diverted yet again to the American River, a total transaction difficult to imagine when viewing the intervening mountains and canyons from an airplane or on the ground. The Tuolumne and Mokelumne are piped from the mountains and across the Central Valley and the Delta to the San Francisco Bay Area, 140 miles and several watersheds away. With the largest use of energy in the state, the Sacramento is pumped uphill 3,000 feet for sluicing to southern California. Feather River water is displaced 430 miles to serve cities in the South.

Water withdrawals deplete 70 percent of the Sacramento's normal spring runoff and 90 percent of the San Joaquin's. Salinity of the Delta thus increased by a factor of 5 to 15 during the 1987–1991 drought; the chinook salmon, striped bass, and American shad fisheries nearly vanished. The diversions caused a $3 billion loss of income for fisheries in San Francisco Bay between 1960 and 1990, and other losses included a decline in quality of drinking water for 20 million people served by the Delta.

Ninety percent of the stream mileage statewide suffers from diversions of one kind or another. More than 80 percent of the water used in the state goes to agriculture; half of the total goes to livestock and animal feed. The federal water projects offer water to agribusiness at subsidies of 92 percent and greater. But 45 percent of that water has gone to grow surplus crops, defined as crops for which farmers receive government subsidies intended to curtail production. To support such a twisted agricultural economy and costly welfare state masked as agribusiness, the San Joaquin, Kings, and Kern Rivers are totally dried up in the Central Valley. The southern coastal rivers also suffer terminal withdrawals for crops and cities.

While diversions have starved the rivers, the broader riparian zone in most of the Central Valley has been eliminated by levees. Built along virtually all the valley and lowland waterways, the levees cordon streams from their historical riparian systems. Sierra streams in flood once nourished much of the state's original 5 million acres of wetlands, but levees, diversions, and drains have now cut this acreage to less than 300,000.

Much of the water that's left in Central Valley streams is not of usable quality. Though Sierra water is excellent in the mountains, pollution takes over down below. Agricultural runoff, including silt, pesticides, fertilizer, nitrates, and phosphates, plagues all the major lowland channels. The San Joaquin has been called the "lower colon" of California—a cesspool of polluted farm waste not subject to water quality laws because agriculture is exempt from regulations. These lower-elevation rivers once offered an Eden of biological assets as they flowed through fertile areas of mild climate, historical winter range for wildlife, and essential habitat for migratory waterfowl that "darkened the sky," as early settlers claimed. The problems of rivers now go far beyond wildlife to include the whole skein of the Central Valley, plagued with groundwater overdraft, salinization, selenium poisoning, pesticide saturation, and air pollution so bad it inhibits the growth of crops.

Another threat to natural waters in California is new land development in the foothills, the Central Valley, and the Coast Range. The state's population perpetually booms, gaining over 800,000 more people per year in the early 1990s, an annual increase greater than the population of San Francisco. An exodus of the white, upper, and middle classes to neighboring states causes new, unwelcome problems in those areas. The vacated space is immediately backfilled by immigrants from Latin America and Asia, by illegal immigrants from Mexico, and by children, reflecting the high birth rates among new immigrants. Local, state, and national governments do almost nothing to address the population explosion that has already put this garden state into an economic, social, and environmental tailspin.

California also has the nation's strongest environmental lobby, and though environmental conditions there do not rank well relative to other states, protection policies score highest in the nation, according to the *Green Index*. Friends of the River and local groups have protected most of the remaining rivers from new dams since the loss of the Stanislaus in 1982, and conservation groups have averted many assaults on waterways accompanying state administrations hostile to environmental protection in the 1980s and 1990s. Championed by Congressman George Miller, a step toward reform of federal water projects came with a rewriting of the Central Valley Project Act in 1992, reallocating some water from agriculture to neglected instream flows.

To look at the individual rivers of the Sierra, I begin in the north with the Feather. Crowded by a road and a railroad, the North Fork's canyon is dammed and diverted for hydropower, but the Middle Fork remains in wild splendor, with remote and rugged canyons, granite walls, and wooded mountainsides. Clean water plunges over hundreds of rapids in one of the most difficult whitewater rivers in the West. America's tallest dam, 770 feet high, blocks the main stem at Oroville—centerpiece of a state water project that delivers the river to southern California.

To the south, miners excavated the Yuba more than any other river during the gold rush. Devastating effects remain, and large dams and diversions affect even the headwaters, but superb sections of undeveloped river have recovered. The North Yuba flows through a forested corridor, with heavy rapids accessible by Highway 49. The remote Middle Yuba suffers from extreme withdrawals for hydropower. Though its flows are also depleted, the South Yuba below Spaulding Dam includes 40 miles of intriguing Sierra river in canyons still wild yet crossed by five roads providing access for recreation.

The American River basin borders the Yuba, followed southward by the small Cosumnes, one of few rivers in California without any dams. Its lower reach through the Central Valley supplies vital habitat to sandhill cranes and waterfowl. Next, the Mokelumne drops from the Sierra crest at Ebbetts Pass through canyons with waterfalls and granite cliffs interspersed with reservoirs and diversions that lead to cities on the eastern side of San Francisco Bay.

The Stanislaus, with stunning reaches still surviving on its North, Middle, and South Forks, offers a wealth of mountain riverscape, from alpine heights down through green wilderness and vertical-wall gorges, but dams on each branch impound stellar sections and manipulate flows. New Melones Dam rises 620 feet on the main stem. The most contested dam in American history, in 1982 it flooded the West's most popular whitewater and the deepest limestone canyon on the Pacific Coast. As the reservoir's water was drawn down during drought years of the early 1990s, the river remarkably reemerged, leading to renewed efforts to keep the reservoir level low.

The extraordinary qualities of the Sierra rivers accumulate to the south as the mountains rise taller. The high country of Yosemite National Park produces the Tuolumne, cascading through its Grand Canyon—a name that reflects no understatement. O'Shaughnessy Dam then floods the river through Hetch Hetchy Valley. This eulogized place was the subject of John Muir's greatest battle, marking the birth of river conservation in America, though the fight was lost. Below the dam, 18 miles of magnificent whitewater offer one of the premier river trips in America and one of California's finest trout fisheries. Within this reach, the Clavey River flows into the Tuolumne after its own tumultuous course through rugged country of the Sierra's lower elevations. This is one of few small rivers that remain undammed in the Sierra. An irrigation district has proposed two hydroelectric projects on the wild Clavey, and while the Federal Energy Regulatory Commission rejected the plan in 1994, it could surface again. The sprawling New Don Pedro Reservoir impounds the Tuolumne's foothill reaches, followed by slow windings through farmland to the San Joaquin.

Next to the Niagara at its falls, the Merced may be America's most-photographed river. At Yosemite it crashes over waterfalls 600 and 320 feet high, then riffles through a valley bordered by smooth granite walls rising 3,000 feet, a place regarded by many as the ultimate in American scenery. Yosemite Creek, a Merced tributary, plunges 1,430 feet over an upper falls linked to a 679-foot middle falls and a 320-foot lower falls, all totaling 2,429 feet—the seventh-highest in the world. A turbulent reach of the foothills Merced tours a springtime landscape of vivid green, succeeded by the tan grass of summer. McClure Reservoir floods a lower section, followed by a flattened runout to the San Joaquin.

The 350-mile San Joaquin begins by flowing across the high granite wilderness of Kings Canyon National Park. Dammed below the park, this once-great artery of the Central Valley is reduced by irrigation diversions to absolutely nothing in some places. The river reappears with return flows of agricultural wastewater. After drifting north in multiple channels to the Delta, much of the flow is pumped back southward for farm and city uses. Salmon runs, trout habitat, and a fabulous riparian corridor along the San Joaquin have been lost, but not irrevocably so. The Natural Resources Defense Council sued the Bureau of Reclamation to prepare an environmental impact statement concerning the diversions from Friant Dam, the key storage facility. With increased water efficiency and concern for water quality, part of the San Joaquin could be restored as a lifeline to the Central Valley.

Next comes the incomparable Kings. No other river in North America offers as much vertical drop without dams blocking its flow; from its upper channels, the Kings descends 11,260 feet before its first impoundment. The Middle and South Forks cut through the continent's deepest canyons, with peaks in two reaches averaging 6,500 to 7,700 feet above the canyon floor. The Middle Fork's remote Tehipite Valley, with a granite dome over 3,000 feet tall, is the closest thing to another Yosemite since Hetch Hetchy Valley was flooded. The South Fork of the Kings rises in similar high country and flows through the idyllic Cedar Grove of Kings Canyon National Park. Along the impressive rock-walled main stem, Spanish Mountain rises 8,240 feet directly over the northern side of the river (Hells Canyon of the Snake River, for com-

South Yuba River above Purdon Crossing

South Fork American below Kyburz

North Fork American below Iowa Hill

American River in Sacramento

Tuolumne River below Tuolumne Meadows

Kings River below Converse Cr.

North Fork Kern, West Wall Rapid

West Fork Carson below Hope Valley

Kings River below Garnet Dike

Hot Creek, Owens River tributary

parison, drops 7,900 feet below the summit of He Devil Mountain). The upper main stem is California's largest designated wild trout fishery and a risky run even for expert kayakers. Below that stretch, one of the most popular whitewater rivers in the state curves through oak groves and grassland to Pine Flat Reservoir. The lower Kings riffles into the Central Valley but ultimately loses its water to irrigation ditches. The river once ended in the 700-square-mile Tulare Lake, complete with a commercial fishery, but the lake bed is now irrigated in a seemingly endless grid of cotton—a surplus, heavily subsidized, pesticide-laced crop that has displaced one of the West's great wetlands.

Through Sequoia National Park, the five forks of the Kaweah River flow similarly to the King's upper reaches and then drop into a main stem through chaparral to Kaweah Reservoir. Below the dam, the river is diverted until nothing remains.

As the southernmost Sierra river, the 155-mile Kern is born of runoff from Mount Whitney—at 14,494 feet, it is the highest American peak outside Alaska. Here is the longest river within the mountainous area of the Sierra, though its volume ranks tenth owing to the drier climate of the south. The rare, brilliantly colored golden trout survive only in high mountain streams here. Following a ruler-straight fault line through 30 miles of canyon as deep as 4,000 feet, the North Fork accumulates runoff and then roars through a reach called the Forks of the Kern, one of the premier Class V wilderness whitewater runs in the nation. Lower sections drop over big rapids accessible by road. The South Fork of the Kern threads together a fascinating integration of five biological zones, ranging from alpine to Mojave Desert, and at a Nature Conservancy preserve it waters one of the few sizeable cottonwood forests remaining in California. After the flatwater of Isabella Reservoir, the main stem resumes with lively whitewater and then a boulder-strewn gorge along Highway 178. Like the San Joaquin, Kings, and Kaweah, the lower Kern is trained into engineered ditches, right-angled turns, and absolutely square ponds—a hydrologic system that looks like the back of an old radio. Finally, the water disappears at corporate farms that stretch beyond the horizon line in the southern San Joaquin Valley.

Rivers of the eastern Sierra begin in the north with the Truckee, flowing from heavenly peaks down to the eye-dazzling wonder of Lake Tahoe. Even with the nation's most strenuous effort to protect water quality, this lake of the richest blue imaginable is being degraded by excess nutrients, resulting from erosion caused by land development and road cuts, and by nitrate air pollution in the car-plagued basin. Flowing at a mere 240 cfs at the lake's outlet, the Truckee is still the largest river on the east side of the Sierra. Downstream from Tahoe, Interstate 80 shoulders the Truckee through incised gaps that exit the Sierra and spill out to Reno in the desert region, where the river ends in Pyramid Lake.

To the south, the Carson flows from the Sierra crest and through steep canyons; its East Branch offers one of the region's few multiday float trips with intermediate whitewater. The Walker River drops steeply off the east slope from Sonora Pass.

Six small streams of the eastern Sierra feed the landlocked Mono Lake, and to its south the Owens River picks up dozens of bubbling tributaries as they leap off the two-mile-high Sierra escarpment. Once the Owens enters the desert region, Los Angeles pipes the entire river south.

Outside the Sierra, all the rivers of California south of San Francisco are small and short, with the exception of the lower Colorado, at the Arizona border. Not even a sizeable creek flows eastward from the Coast Range to the Central Valley, but dozens drop from the Coast Range to the Pacific. The largest of these, the 150-mile Salinas River of John Steinbeck stories, averages 590 cfs, but its flow is entirely diverted in the irrigation season, leaving a waterless riverbed full of dirt bike and dune buggy tracks.

The Big Sur River flows from forest and chaparral and then through the southernmost redwoods at the coastline at Big Sur. San Luis Obispo Creek's 43-cfs flow is blocked for water supplies in a pattern that has systematically dammed coastal streams from there southward. One of the few unimpounded streams in southern California, Sespe Creek plunges through wild country of the Los Padres National Forest. In the center of the city, the Los Angeles River may be the victim of America's longest paved streambed. One of the first water sources for southern California, the small river lies bone dry most of the time. Recurrently proposed for damming near San Diego, the Santa Margarita River's main stem flows for 27 miles through chaparral and sycamores to the Pacific.

Returning to the Sierra for a more detailed view of the region's riverscape, I set my sights on the tempting headwaters of the American.

The American River

Trapper Jedediah Smith called this waterway the Wild River, a name that described it simply and well. It was later renamed the American—which now reminds me of the values and complexities of rivers nationwide. While the broad Hudson may have represented the national image of rivers in the eighteenth century and the Mississippi, with its belching steamboats, symbolized rivers in the nineteenth century, the American could be the emblematic stream of today, with all its varied recreational use, from mountaintop to valley bottom. This river is central to California history, crucial to water supplies in a thirsty state, and vital to ecosystems in troubled times. Through short trips spanning many years, I've come to know the American.

Pyramid Peak towers over the basin like the father or mother or God of it all. Breaking camp along the South Fork one mid-December, I set out for the mountaintop, and the granite slabs and fir groves of Pyramid Creek occupied me in a wandering sort of admiration for half a day. Then, climbing by foot and hand, I ascended alongside the whitewater curtain of Horsetail Falls, hundreds of feet high and inclined slightly off the vertical so that water fizzed against its granite wall from brink to base.

Facing dead-of-winter darkness at 5 P.M., I camped above a rivulet at the base of rocky scree that soared upward, promising hard work and biting winds. Normally my route would resemble an Antarctica of ice and snow in December, but this was looking like another drought year in California. Drifts had blown into pockets, but most of the mountain bared its rock—dry and icy cold. The whole view upward appeared not like a smooth epidermis of earth but more like a grainy photograph, with millions of rocks everywhere speckling the scene.

After thirteen hours of darkness in my tent, I squirmed out of my down bag, bundled up, gobbled some breakfast, and pointed myself toward the summit of the Pyramid. A landmark of the northern Sierra, the peak stands three-sided above all other mountains and feeds the American River its water. On a rare, clear day when the yellow shroud of Sacramento's car exhaust doesn't block the view, Pyramid punctures the eastern skyline. Now, looking the other way—down from the summit—I saw the river basin like the fanned tail of a ruffed grouse fluttering away from me. The South Fork entrenched itself in the country through which I had come. The Middle Fork gathered waters and tore away to the west. In remote country, the North Fork crashed through canyons that looked extremely promising as an uncivilized enclave where the real world might survive. Beyond my view, all the forks joined in a main stem that bisected the Sacramento urban area just before meeting the Sacramento River, which sloshed tidally out to San Francisco Bay.

From the top of Pyramid, the morning sun cast stark shadows that heightened the rough topography. The troughs of the streams jogged left and right at every entering tributary; the effect was not the sinuous course of a mature river but a zigzag of youth and indecision. Green slopes lay rumpled like an all-cotton sheet that had been rolled into a ball after washing and then laid out loosely to dry. The high country where I stood soared upward from the forest in dusted snowfields; I was on a big wave that was rising to break above an incline of spumy surf.

To see the American close-up, I first followed the course of the South Fork, beginning in a forest of white fir. The mountain stream swished over granite slabs and, at Lovers' Leap, curved beneath a polished granite dome soaring hundreds of feet. A plunging succession of drops repeated themselves mile after mile, where Highway 50 offered glimpses of green and white water.

At the village of Kyburz, the Silver Fork enters from the south, a magnificent stream of clear water, conifers, and small falls accessible by a narrow mountain road. This and all other large tributaries to the South Fork are impounded near their headwaters. The Pacific Gas and Electric Company releases water from the dams to generate power downriver.

Eleven miles below the confluence with the Silver Fork, Highway 50 bends away from its river valley and opts for a gentler ridge route to the Central Valley. Alone now, the river enters a boulder-plugged gorge followed by the slender Slab Creek and Chili Bar Reservoirs. Below them begins the great, watery playground of the American.

In foothills country, the American from Chili Bar to Coloma ranks among the most popular whitewater runs in the West; rafters wait in lines to run the rapids on hot summer weekends. Avid boaters paddle here all year long, taking advantage of mild winters. Drawing from 10 million Californians in the Sacramento region and San Francisco Bay Area, this river brings whitewater joy to more than 130,000 people per year.

I had rowed my raft on the South Fork below Chili Bar but made my first canoe run in 1987 with a friend, Nancy Mertz, who guided there and knew the river well. Leading the way in an inflatable kayak, she announced the larger drops: Meatgrinder, Racehorse, and Triple Threat. No longer dressed in the blackened green of a conifer forest, the foothills sprawled and curved upward in tawny annual grasses, brown by May. The original deep-rooted native grasses had stayed green in summer, but they were displaced after settlers herded cattle into this country. The chaparral of California buckeye, manzanita, toyon, deer brush, poison oak, and weak-limbed gray pine now texture hot hillsides above the riparian thicket of willow and white alder. The interior live oak, blue oak, and black oak form forests rich in acorns favored by deer and acorn woodpeckers. Farther up on north-facing slopes, clusters of ponderosa pine endure, once plentiful at this low elevation but failing to regerminate in the baked soils after the original forests were sawed up during the mining days.

Eventually Nancy and I arrived at Troublemaker, the big challenge. In my sixteen-and-a-half-foot Mad River canoe, I hugged the left shore to avoid a nasty hole. I caught an eddy against the bank and reentered the current just below the hole, circumventing rather than confronting the chief hazard of the day. To prolong my brief stay at this point of terrific power, I caught another eddy behind the famed Troublemaker Rock, which lurks midstream to snag survivors of the hole. Nancy, beaming, had also made a successful run.

We passed Coloma State Park, the site of Sutter's Mill. There John Marshall found gold in 1848, igniting the gold rush, which forever altered the face of this paradisaic state and set it on the course of perpetual development that to this day chews up natural assets. The reach above and below Coloma was threatened in the 1970s by power and water supply dams that are not likely to be revived, given modern recreational activity.

Several years after my Chili Bar run I canoed the lower South Fork, teaming up with my old friends Grant Werschkull and Marty Booth, both accomplished kayakers. On a hot summer evening we drove up from Sacramento and dipped our paddles into the coolness of the river. We surfed on waves and played in the rapids to our hearts' content. At the largest drop, where the river consolidates into a flume between truck-sized rocks, I slipped through easily, only to get my canoe recirculated in a grabby, mouthy hole farther downriver. In no time the hydraulic had plucked me out of my thigh straps and sent me on a long, stony swim before I could tug my flooded craft ashore. Darkness arrived as we skated our boats across flatwater where the South Fork and the main stem form a two-pronged reservoir behind Folsom Dam.

The Middle Fork is the lesser-known American. The big day of infamy here occurred on the principal tributary, the Rubicon River, where the Placer County Water Agency's Hell Hole Dam burst while under construction in 1964. A seventy-five-foot tidal wave carrying boulders and earthen dam debris in abrasive suspension scoured the canyon for 34 miles and ripped up the Middle Fork as well; the effects are still evident. Twice dammed in its headwater sections, the fork also includes an intense rafting reach, the unrunnable Ruck-a-Chucky Falls, and then water that is calmer but still spiced with fright and trouble at Murderers Bar Rapid.

The American River's canyons are gradually reclaiming themselves from a gold-mining industry that popular history romanticizes but that in fact destroyed everything in its path with all the romanticism of genocide. The Indians were killed, and then the native landscape was destroyed as well. Old photos show the valley at Kennebeck Bar stripped, flumed, and packed with shacks in 1857; today the site is a gravel bar with a clear-water river running through it and slow-growing riparian vegetation. Once housing 10,000 people, the Middle Fork's canyon now houses next to none, and though these rivers still offer only a fraction of the natural wealth they once possessed, the recovery under way shows one of the more remarkable natural comebacks of rivers in America.

The North Fork endures as the American's fabulous wonderland of Sierra canyons—remote, shadowy-deep, hidden from sun, armored in granite, softened here and there with great forests but then tearing through foothill gorges. Any crumb of doubt that the American is an extraordinary place is lost like a stone skipped in a depthless pool here. This wild stream remains undammed down to Clementine Reservoir, near the Middle Fork confluence.

When I caught my first view of the North Fork, it happened to be March, when twelve feet of snowpack had just begun to melt in the high country. From Donner Pass, where Interstate 80 crosses the Sierra, I skied southward to the flanks of Anderson Peak and camped in a hut managed by the Sierra Club. The next day I plunged 2,000 feet down through glades and timbered slopes, emerging on the banks of the American. Gurgling with snowmelt, the river shone almost black. The snow had piled up to make a miniature canyon where six feet of compacted crystals walled in the stream. Wolverine tracks lured me up the mountain valley until evening approached and I had to climb back to the hut for shelter from the chilling night.

Below those headwaters, 40 miles of wild canyons are cut 1,500 to 3,500 feet deep at Royal Gorge and Giant Gap. Some sections have difficult trail access; most require a bruising scramble through boulder fields and brush, with cliff-bound pools mandating swims for any sort of travel. Native rainbow trout thrive in this important wilderness fishery, and deer find needed winter range in the canyon.

At the Iowa Hill Bridge anybody can drive to the river and camp, and for years squatters dredged for gold and people littered the banks. With strange visitors and gunshots in the night, the place seemed to belong to social misfits at the fringe of California society. I remember camping there and feeling bothered, then irritated, then scared. But it isn't that way any longer. In 1978 Congress designated the North Fork above there as a National Wild and Scenic River, stopping construction of a 550-foot-high dam proposed at Giant Gap. State and federal agencies improved recreation management. The Chamberlain Falls whitewater run below Iowa Hill became a favorite of expert kayakers and rafters in the spring. Half a million people now come to the North and Middle Forks' canyons to hike, swim, boat, fish, and revel in the recovered natural beauty of these places that were once so rapaciously mined.

This and other canyons of the Sierra foothills are more ruggedly wild than picturesque. Narrow channels are powerful, water jetting over boulders and unsorted rocks of all shapes and sizes. Lacking much soil, the chaparral vegetation includes buckeye and thickets of poison oak with roots like ganglia gripping onto boulders.

Rafting here one spring with Otis Wollan, Eric Peach, and other friends, I flushed airborne over the six-foot-high Chamberlain Falls and splashed down in green depths bordered by white rock. We scrambled up Indian Creek to a waterfall and swam for cool relief on the ninety-degree day.

The river flows through a series of easier rapids before ending in the 5-mile-long Clementine Reservoir, built in 1939 solely to catch sediment from the mined watershed above. The North Fork–Middle Fork confluence lies beyond, followed in 3 miles by the Auburn Dam site.

A recurrent threat for thirty years, Auburn was once planned as a 685-foot-tall concrete edifice to flood 48 miles of the North and Middle Forks for irrigation supplies. A lawsuit by the Environmental Defense Fund and the Natural Resources Defense Council stopped construction in 1974, and a year later an earthquake further stymied the plan. Simply digging a foundation had already cost taxpayers $250 million, the result being no more than a lot of torn-up earth. Though the dam was redesigned for safety, costs escalated so much that Secretary of the Interior Cecil Andrus in the late 1970s declared that the dam would have to be reauthorized by Congress, a group then disinclined to spend the needed $3 billion. Water costing $350 to $900 per acre-foot to develop would be sold to irrigators for as little as $3.50 per acre-foot, with taxpayers paying the difference.

Facing no chance of the project's passage, the dam builders redressed Auburn as a flood-control panacea following high water in 1987. A "dry" dam would be filled only during floods but would have the capacity to be expanded in the future. Friends of the River, California's statewide river protection organization, battled the plan and defeated it by a wide margin in Congress. Studies continued regarding other dams and alternatives to protect the area from floods less expensively. The 1994 election brought conservative members to Congress who curiously put austerity aside and vowed to build the dam at any cost, and it appeared that the thirty-year-old battle would be fought again. The California Planning and Conservation League and Friends of the River argued for designation of a national recreation area to protect the canyons and promote use of the river without damming it.

Down below the Auburn site the principal storage dam on the American is Folsom, on the main stem at Sacramento's urban edge. The Bureau of Reclamation manages this large reservoir for irrigation of Central Valley farms and for flood control. It cut off 125 miles of once-productive salmon habitat on the forks of the American—mileage that may have supported 129,000 fish annually before the mining and dams.

Below Folsom the American is centerpiece to one of the great urban river parks in the country. A bicycle trail follows its shores for 23 miles from Nimbus Dam—an afterbay just below Folsom—to the mouth of the river. A riparian zone that was once miles wide through today's city is hemmed in by levees, but a sizeable belt still allows for willows, silver maples, box elders, and Fremont cottonwoods. Deer, foxes, beavers, muskrats, and otters have returned to the American, with downtown Sacramento to the south and endless suburbia to the north. Fall-run chinook still spawn in the river below Nimbus, though the numbers of salmon drop lower and lower because of Delta diversions.

The idea of a city greenway began in the 1950s when a few people saw the potential for a parkway where the levees enclosed a corridor unsuitable for building. This stretch of the American is now among the most-used river segments in America; more than 5 million people per year boat, bike, run, walk, and rollerblade along the waterfront here. When I have lived in Sacramento from time to time, Mark DuBois, his wife, Sharon, and I have taken our canoes out to the river—a five-minute drive from their house—and put them in for an evening float, or embarked at dawn for the sunrise show of great blue herons, green herons, mallards, pintails, and spotted sandpipers. On the hottest afternoons, Mark and I have taken our boats to San Juan Rapid and surfed on waves for an hour, soaking up the coolness of the moving water— "river magic," Mark calls it. Sacramento is one of few cities where people can enjoy a river so well. California's capital, with its sprawling suburbs, is the only urban area along the entire course of the American and its tributaries, and here people have made respectable use of a great riverway running right through town.

Having traveled from Pyramid Peak to the river's end near sea level, the quiet waters of the American spill into the larger Sacramento River and then drift out to San Francisco Bay.

Chapter 9

A Land of Rivers in the Northwest

A land of rivers lies along the Pacific coast from San Francisco Bay northward, a region blessed by abundant water and by a topography as rugged and wrinkled as any in America. Rainfall and rivers, mountains and forests—these are synonymous with the Pacific Northwest. Photographs of this region show misty waterfronts, conifer foliage dripping rain onto a spongy duff of rotting wood and humus, and mad, roily flows in streams dumping into a wave-tossed Pacific streaked with gray sunset light.

The river-enabling belt of forty inches or more of annual rainfall begins north of San Francisco Bay and extends inland for 130 miles on average, covering the Coast Range and the interior valleys and topping the crest of the Cascade Mountains. It swings northward, following the Pacific arc all the way through south central Alaska. The rivers of northern California appear in this chapter with those of Oregon and Washington because all have headstrong, clean waters flowing from evergreen mountains, the whole group drenched in the north Pacific's winter storms.

Northwest Rivers

The region's legendary natural bounty is emblematic of an unspoiled environment. But the legend is no longer fact; in reality, people have cut all but about 10 percent of the original forests, dammed the rivers, depleted the fisheries, and accommodated runaway urban growth, especially in western Washington. Yet those changes have happened even more elsewhere, and enough remains in the Northwest to keep the legend alive as one stands beneath shadowy limbs of arrow-topped firs at the banks of a wild waterway in glacial runoff.

The rivers here drain not one but two great mountain ranges, and the river assets are thus doubled. The Coast Range of California and Oregon ascends without an inch of hesitation from sea level—much of the West Coast has no coastal plain but rather a ragged and sometimes vertical edge of uplifted cliffs and terraces, owing to seismic activity where the Pacific plate slides beneath the North American plate in a demolition derby of tectonics. America's longest, slenderest, and youngest large mountain range, the coastal mountains often top out within 10 miles of the sea. In Washington, bays and low-lying land extend inland for 5 to 20 miles, and the range reaches a climax with the Olympic Mountains. In British Columbia and southern Alaska, the Coast Range continues as an archipelago of mountaintop islands sprinkled in the sea.

On the landward side of northern California's coastal backbone lies a jumbled mix of ragged ridges and summits collectively known as the Klamath Mountains. These include the Yolla Bolly, Salmon, Marble, and Siskiyou subranges. Spanning 80 miles from east to west including the Coast Range, these constitute the widest and most continuous mountain mass of the region and one of the wider bulks of unbroken mountains in America.

East of the Coast Range lies an interior valley—a trench discontinuously appearing from the Vale of Chile to the Matanuska Valley of Alaska. This lowland complex holds some of the best farmland, largest cities, and longest rivers in the Far West. As part of this, the Central Valley of California reaches north to Redding (see chapter 8). The cross-grain of the Klamath Mountains interrupts the lowland for 230 miles, but it resumes in the Willamette Valley of Oregon, with its northbound river of the same name. In Washington, the weight of glacial ice depressed the interior valley, resulting in the saltwater intrusion of Puget Sound.

To the east of the interior valley, peaks of the Cascade Mountains gleam as a north-south chain of volcanoes from Mount Lassen in northern California to the Canadian border. While most of the Cascade mass describes a subdued, rolling terrain saturated with conifers, breathtaking cones of great volcanoes accent the range. These rise as the most archetypal mountains in America, with contoured stars of snowcaps on top and radial patterns of rivers flowing from the peaks. From south to north, the stratovolcanoes include Lassen, Shasta, the Three Sisters, Jefferson, Hood, St. Helens, Adams, Rainier, Glacier, and Baker. Eleven volcanoes rise above 11,000 feet, and all yield fascinating rivers. Dramatic geologic activity appears here more than anywhere in the contiguous forty-eight states—Lassen erupted early in this century, and St. Helens dramatically exploded in 1980. River valleys south of Washington's Mount Rainier tend to be narrow and eroded deeply by water; to the north they are broad, U-shaped valleys carved by glaciers. The North Cascades of northern Washington sport volcanic peaks but also an enormous uplift of granite and high plateaus cut by glaciers—one of the most extreme masses of topography and stormy weather in America.

As the one large, contiguous area of moderate and heavy precipitation in the whole American West, this region attracted the first pioneers. Infected with "Oregon fever," they were drawn to the Willamette Valley. But farmland has not been the Northwest's strongest suit. Along with southeast Alaska, this region breeds the greatest temperate forests on earth, once as thick as fur on a beaver's back: Sitka spruce, western hemlock, mountain hemlock, Douglas fir, grand fir, white fir, noble fir, subalpine fir, Pacific yew, western white pine, lodgepole pine, ponderosa pine, and the tallest of all trees—the sky-scraping coast redwood. Seventeen conifer species thrive along the northern California coast.

The unruly geology of earthquakes and volcanoes and the month-after-month monotony of winter rain and snow make inevitable an extraordinary system of rivers, something like an Appalachia with evergreens, snowcaps, and clearcuts instead of strip mines. The rivers crest with the rains of winter and the snowmelt of early spring; sun-drenched summers cause low flows in autumn, a time when high-flowing rivers still emanate from the glacier-fed northern slopes of the volcanoes. The rivers flow westward in a roundabout course as the Pacific Coast watershed system.

Only three rivers transect the enormous bulk of the 560-mile-long Cascades in the United States. The little-known Pit River, which rises at the edge of the Basin and Range province, flows westward between Mount Shasta and Mount Lassen, then joins the southward flow of the Sacramento River. Klamath River headwaters rise east of Crater Lake, contributing to a river that crosses Cascade lowlands north of Mount

Shasta. Finally, the Columbia is born a river of the Canadian Rockies, S-bends across the desert, and then divides the Cascades at the Oregon-Washington border.

Many rivers begin at the Cascade summits and flow westbound for the Pacific, but with the exception of rivers homing toward Puget Sound, few make a direct beeline to the sea. Instead they join interior rivers that shunt the water north or south just before it encounters the Coast Range. These younger mountains rose in the rivers' way and forced them to go around. Causing the range's buildup, the Pacific plate moves northward along the North American plate by two inches per year and in the process drags the mouths of some rivers radically north. The Eel, for example, used to enter the ocean far south of its present outlet.

While only three rivers transect the Cascades, seven cut across the 1,240-mile-long Coast Range between Mexico and Canada. The Sacramento reaches the Pacific through the Sacramento–San Joaquin Delta, so wide and low it is unrecognizable as a gap in the mountains. The other six rivers all lie in the Northwest. North of the Sacramento's mouth by 260 miles, the Klamath cuts a staggering path south, west, south, west, north, and finally west again through the Klamath and Coast Ranges. In Oregon the Rogue begins at the Cascade crest, flows down its western slope, and then crosses the Coast Range through narrow mountain breaks. Just to the north and somewhat less spectacularly, the Umpqua does likewise. Rising on the eastern fringe of the Coast Range, the small Siuslaw filters all the way across the coastal mountains in a convoluted path north of the Umpqua. The mile-wide Columbia rolls through its gaping, straight-line schism in the range, a massive trench shouldered by the gleaming slopes of Mount Hood to the south and Mount Adams to the north, all of which can be seen in one eyeful from the rim of the gorge. To its north, the Chehalis makes a humble crossing of the Coast Range by drawing tributaries from the eastern flank of the Cascades and winding through lowlands. The Strait of Juan de Fuca then truncates the Coast Range, separating the Olympic Mountains from Canada's Vancouver Island. The Strait would be a river mouth draining the streams of northwestern Washington if sea level were substantially lowered.

Without exception, rivers of the West Coast south of Canada are dwarfed by the Columbia. This same giant of the Rocky Mountains and desert regions gains even greater strength as it nears its conclusion in the Pacific surf; its flow of 265,000 cubic feet per second makes it the fourth-largest river in America, fifth-largest on the continent. As the region's second-largest river, the Willamette averages 37,400 cfs northward through the developed heart of Oregon. The Klamath of Oregon and northern California flows at 18,110 cfs. The Skagit of Washington's North Cascades ranks fourth in regional size, with a flow of 16,700 cfs. The Santiam in Oregon's central Cascades carries 7,821 cfs, and just to the south the Umpqua flows with 7,517. The Eel of California averages 7,412, while the Rogue of Oregon carries 6,149. Northern California's Smith runs at 3,891. Washington's Yakima, the most sizeable river from the eastern Cascades of Washington, carries 3,640 cfs. The Quinault (2,861 cfs) flows from the Olympic Peninsula—the most water-productive real estate for its size in America.

Sizeable streams are never far away, so a culture of northwestern rivers exists in people's minds and daily lives. With many rivers surviving undamaged relative to those of other regions, northwesterners are aware of their waterways as threads stitching the environmental and social fabrics together. A few waterways served as highways of exploration, settlement, and transportation. Lewis and Clark's account of descending the Columbia introduced white America to the Northwest. Hydroelectric development, destroying some rivers as natural entities, became a building block of the industrial society, especially in Washington. Many writings of the region, including modern novels such as Tom Robbins's *Another Roadside Attraction* and Ken Kesey's *Sometimes a Great Notion,* depend on the full-bodied rivers as their backdrop. And always people fished in the rivers—first the Indians, then the settlers. Today, angling for steelhead, salmon, and trout is the passion of a sizeable population. And whitewater boating could be a national sport if the Northwest were a country. An imaginary account of just such a scenario was written by author Ernest Callenbach, whose delightful novel *Ecotopia* describes an environmentally conscious majority in the Northwest seceding and creating a utopian nation based on ecology. The regional newspaper *Cascadia Times* reports with fine journalism on the environment of the Northwest from California to Alaska.

Environmental consciousness in the Northwest runs high relative to that in other regions, but still not high enough to avert the loss of most of the Columbia River salmon in return for cheap hydroelectric power that subsidizes the aluminum industry, and not high enough to have saved more than a small percentage of the old forests that healthy streams depend on.

More than anything, the culture of rivers in the Northwest is a culture of salmon, a creature that embodies the very nature of rivers. One journalist went so far as to define the Northwest as anyplace a salmon can go. This is a purely rhetorical line—salmon exist as far south as

Monterey Bay in the middle California coast, as far north as the Arctic Ocean, and as far inland as Sawtooth Valley, at the heart of the Rocky Mountains. But these fish are indeed a cultural signpost of the region. Many Indian tribes revered the fin-backed, oceangoing "people" of the rivers and built intricate societies based on these fish. Because of the easy food supply the salmon represented, native people enjoyed enough leisure time to create fabulous artworks. After the rush for gold, the salmon-fishing and packing industry was the next great commercial enterprise in the West, and the results were no less rapacious.

After a century of overfishing, damming of rivers, diversion of the flows, and clearcutting of watersheds into raggy scraps, many salmon and steelhead runs now face extinction. The anadromous fish in each stream differ genetically; many subspecies are already gone forever. These problems, documented well in the writings of Anthony Netboy, were foreseen by some people, but they were not listened to. Concern finally grew after 100 years of unconscionable neglect. In April 1991, biologists Willa Nehlsen, Jack E. Williams, and James A. Lichatowich published their alarming "Pacific Salmon at the Crossroads" in the *Journal of the American Fisheries Society*. Of 214 native, naturally spawning runs of Pacific salmon, steelhead, and sea-run cutthroat trout in California, Oregon, and Washington, 101 were at a high risk of extinction, 58 were at moderate risk, and 54 were of special concern. At that time the federal government had listed only one run under the Endangered Species Act. The authors recognized eighteen stocks that may already have become extinct.

Overfishing could be reversed by tightening regulations, but more fundamental problems resulted from people's belief that the Columbia existed to be tamed. In 1843 John C. Fremont wrote of running "wild-looking rapids" at a turbulent drop called the Cascades. This became the cemented-over site of Bonneville Dam. Many other impoundments followed, including The Dalles Dam, flooding Celilo Falls, which existed up until 1957. This spectacular twenty-foot drop, sheer in some places but in others tumbling down, had been an Indian fishing site for thousands of years. Many tribes had congregated at the fruitful place to catch chinook, sockeye, and coho salmon. Today the background of basalt rocks lies unchanged, but the dam has reduced the river to half-mile-wide flatwater, deeply burying the ledges that had made the falls a sacred place. Celilo's spectacle of turbulence and river life is now difficult to imagine alongside that sea of a reservoir.

The hydroelectric industry built dams on Washington's Elwha and other rivers illegally, without fish ladders, which give spawning salmon a chance to return upriver. Even where ladders exist on the Columbia and lower Snake Rivers, up to 95 percent of the young salmon smolts moving out to sea perish—killed when they are swept through turbines or delayed in the flatwater of the reservoirs. Modification of the dams and of their management could remedy many problems, but the reforms have not occurred because hydropower interests, chiefly the aluminum industry, reign politically and have little regard for other uses of this public resource in the Northwest.

Even without dams to contend with, the fisheries of coastal rivers face extreme losses through clearcutting, which silts the streams, destroys gravel spawning habitat, lowers flows through much of the year, aggravates floods, and raises water temperatures to suffocating levels. Artificial hatcheries, built so that the wild fish could be replaced, don't solve the problems but accentuate them by weakening the gene pool of native fish, introducing diseases, and stealing the wild fish as brood stock for hatcheries. In some areas wild salmon are nothing but a hazy memory of people old enough to remember the undammed rivers.

Intense pressure for reform in the 1990s resulted in small gains, with programs attempting restoration on streams such as the Nooksack and Yakima in Washington, but the big picture remained bleak. The Bonneville Power Administration and Army Corps of Engineers, controlling the giant hydroelectric dams of the Northwest, gave lip service and money to "mitigation" of fish losses but failed to enact meaningful change to the hydropower system that destroys so many fish. Reform of logging practices and protection of the few remaining old-growth forests were intensely debated and some timber stands were saved, but the shift in management necessary to sustain wild fisheries seldom occurred because of the power of politicians elected with the support of the logging industry. None of this is hopeless, however. Viable solutions are economical, as described by Governor Cecil Andrus of Idaho before his term expired in 1994, in the work of biologists and economists employed by Indian tribes, in the plans of state fisheries agencies, and in the agendas of conservation groups. What is needed is the political will to alter the way some people have profited from subsidized hydroelectric power while causing the demise of the fish.

Attempting to cope with the alarming loss of the Northwest's unique river wealth, conservationists in these states have organized four of the most active river conservation groups in America: Friends of the River in California, the Pacific Rivers Council and Oregon Natural Resources Council in Oregon, and the Rivers Council of Washington. The inclusion of 1,238 miles of northern California rivers from the Smith through the Eel marked one of the landmark gains of the National Wild and

Scenic Rivers System in 1980. This established a safeguarded rivers region of unprecedented significance by enrolling three large adjacent basins. Pushed by river conservationists in 1988, Congress incorporated parts of forty-four Oregon rivers, totaling 1,442 miles, into the system. Efforts to protect a comparable group of Washington's finest streams were stymied by industry and private-rights groups.

While dams block many northwestern streams, the mileage is not comprehensively dammed, as it is in a basin such as the Tennessee. Farmers divert water in the Northwest, yet with plentiful flows few of the waterways shrivel up as they do in the desert and the Great Plains. Urbanization extracts a toll, but its effects are not yet overwhelming, and it's possible that rivers here can have a better future than those in other regions.

To look at the individual rivers of the Northwest, I begin just north of San Francisco Bay. The Russian River riffles southward though an interior valley of oak woodlands in the Coast Range and then bends toward the Pacific with an average flow of 2,435 cfs. Crowds of people enjoy canoeing here; liveries rent thousands of boats. The Russian was once a steelhead and salmon river of world renown, but its fishery was decimated by water pollution and gravel mining. Friends of the Russian River, led by veteran river conservationist David Bolling, seeks to restore lost qualities to this once-great waterway. Where it meets the Pacific at Jenner, the Russian shapes one of the finer natural beaches at a river mouth.

Streams to the north include the Gualala, Navarro, Big, and Noyo Rivers, flowing through the cutover redwood forests of California's Coast Range. Each of these small rivers once flowed as a gem, past old-growth waterfront. In a few isolated sections, such as at Hendy Woods State Park on the Navarro, ancient redwoods survive. On the drier eastern side of the Coast Range, Putah Creek, Cache Creek, and Stony Creek drain to California's Central Valley, all of them dammed and diverted, though Cache Creek can still be paddled in the winter rainy season, when bald eagles roost there by the dozens.

Farther north, the Mattole River flows from one of the wettest enclaves facing the Pacific and out through a secretive valley tucked between steep ridges of the Coast Range—a place that felt like Shangri-la when I first visited it. One of the last pure native stocks of salmon in California survives here, but just barely, because of damage from logging and grazing in the watershed. Residents banding together as the Mattole Restoration Council pioneered a program of local involvement in habitat restoration.

Next comes the Eel River, its Middle Fork a superlative California river flowing through a mountain range of evergreens, oaks, and velvety sweeps of grassland, also with spacious gravel bars, beaches, and narrow-slotted rapids. A 30-mile section offers one of the longer wilderness runs in the state, a trip that stretches to 77 miles when linked with an excellent reach of the main stem. The neighboring South Fork drifts past some of the state's finest redwood groves. The main stem includes good whitewater, though its upper reaches are diverted to the Russian. Instead of exiting directly from the Coast Range, the Eel runs for many miles down an interior valley that parallels the main range, much as do the Greenbrier in the Appalachians and the North Fork Kern in the Sierra. The river wanders through a picturesque savanna of oaks and grassland and over immense gravel bars and finally concludes in marshes at an undeveloped Pacific shore. There are times when this river dries up to a small stream on a plain of gravel, times when it riffles like good music, and times when it spills out of its banks and floods, hissing, to the tops of alder trees. The Eel's enormous winter flows often peak at 100,000 cfs, and they reached 752,000 in 1964—35 percent higher than the record flow of the Klamath, though the Eel's watershed is one-fourth the size. Because the river drains the fractured geology of the Franciscan Complex at the collision zone of the Pacific and North American plates, its flood flows are among the siltiest anywhere—fifteen times siltier than those of the muddy Mississippi.

East of Crater Lake in Oregon, the Williamson River forms the genesis of one of the great western rivers—the Klamath. Wetlands of the upper river may be the most important stopover site on the Pacific Flyway but have been depleted by irrigators who receive a $20 million-a-year subsidy. Salmon and the shortnose sucker are extinct or endangered here because of dams and habitat loss. Below Klamath Lake the river runs for 263 miles, including a 188-mile section that is the least-developed long reach of river on the West Coast. It is also the third-longest undammed reach, interrupted midway by the thundering rapid of Ishi Pishi Falls. Historically one of the nation's finest steelhead rivers, the Klamath transects mountains that have a splendid diversity of plant life. Among all northwestern streams, this one crosses the Coast Range the most dramatically as it curves mazelike within the mountains, much as the Salmon does in the Rockies. The river flows through an Indian reservation and enters the Pacific at a rare natural mouth unencumbered by the usual boat harbors and jetties. The Russian, Mattole, Eel, and Klamath all share the unusual quality of having undeveloped outlets to the sea. Walking along the spits of sand where these four rivers spill into the Pacific has led me to marvel at the satisfying completion of the hydrologic cycle as runoff joins the oceans again.

The Klamath's largest tributary, the 170-mile Trinity, flows with several branches and includes excellent canoeing and also sections with severe rapids. Gold miners dredged the river heavily, and the Bureau of Reclamation diverts the flow from Lewiston Dam to southern California, a problem that legislation in 1992 sought to address by letting the Trinity keep more of its own water. As an exceptional Klamath tributary, the Salmon River rises at the only glacier in the California Coast Range and then flows with green tinted riffles, wild shorelines, and frothing big rapids.

Like the Klamath, the Smith River starts in Oregon. It benefits from 100 inches of rain annually and flows with three branches as California's only completely undammed river system and one of the finer free-flowing systems nationwide. The Smith has one of the highest volume-to-length ratios in America; a 49-mile stretch from the Middle Fork headwaters to the mouth delivers 3,891 cfs to the ocean. Excellent whitewater in its upper reaches, especially on the North Fork, flattens out to gentle flows at one of the country's finest riverfront redwood groves, in Jedediah Smith State Park. The clear water in this comparatively undisturbed watershed still offers good salmon and steelhead habitat. With most of its length protected as a National Wild and Scenic River and a national recreation area, the Smith ranks as one of the most safeguarded watersheds in America outside the national park and wilderness systems.

To the east, in the southern Cascade Mountains of California, the Mc-Cloud River, near the volcanic cone of Mount Shasta, is a wild stream of tingling-cold, transparent springwater that is bordered by ferns and lush evergreens as it foams down to the Sacramento. As a group, all these waterways of northern California constitute the most extraordinary region of long, undeveloped, undammed rivers in America outside Alaska.

In Oregon, twenty-three named rivers flow from the Coast Range to the Pacific, many of them exquisite in their geography of forested gorges. But all of them have been heavily logged. The Chetco remains a superb stream, running for 45 miles to the sea. Its upper wilderness reaches receive 100 inches of rain per year, making it a good salmon and steelhead river. The Illinois, with one of the premier wilderness whitewater descents in America, flows across the Coast Range to the

Rogue River. North of there, the Elk River churns off the Coast Range through a storybook forested gorge, perhaps the finest salmon and steelhead stream of its size on the West Coast.

Farther north, the Umpqua River drains the Cascades with its stellar 106-mile North Fork. This legendary steelhead stream also has fine whitewater, but logging has taken its toll on the river, especially along the small tributaries so important to spawning fish. Sea-run cutthroat trout here have been proposed for listing as endangered; because of habitat loss, no adult fish were counted in 1993. The main stem Umpqua, along with its South Fork headwaters, flows for 223 miles without dams—the longest unimpounded reach in the Northwest. With a few short portages, the main stem offers 113 miles of canoeable water to the ocean; it is the only coastal river in the region that can be run for so long without encountering dams or long, difficult rapids. Near the river's mouth, seals swim up between steep mountainsides enclosing a 20-mile fjord.

Between the Umpqua and the Columbia, many creeks and small rivers drain from the Coast Range to the Pacific. The Suislaw was the home of 220,000 coho salmon a hundred years ago—more coho than now survive on the entire Oregon Coast. Postlogging landslides in 1980 caused massive siltation of this historically great stream.

To the east of Oregon's Coast Range, the Willamette River flows from Cascade branches and into an agricultural valley extending from Eugene north to Portland. Once heavily polluted, the Willamette has benefited from government and industrial cleanups treating sewage and pulp mill waste, and the river now forms a parkland centerpiece in Eugene, Corvallis, and other communities. For 169 miles, from its Coast Fork above Eugene to the backwater of a dam above Oregon City, no impoundments block the Willamette. This stretch offers one of the finest long, gentle-water cruises in the West. Just above Portland, a forty-foot waterfall has been crimped and ringed by a dam, and the river below is girded with old industries in an intensity of development seldom seen in the West. Willamette tributaries from the Cascades include the beautiful and undammed North Fork of the Middle Fork Willamette and the much-floated McKenzie. The Santiam and its forks are dammed in places but free-flowing in others. The South Santiam at Cascadia State Park remains a highlight, as does the undammed Little North Fork with its exquisite Opal Creek headwaters. The Clackamas, with its tributary, the Collawash, flows through excellent rapids to the lower Willamette. Running to the Columbia, the Sandy River drops from the snowy flanks of Mount Hood as a popular recreational stream

Klamath River below Weitchpec, CA

Umpqua River above Reedsport, OR

Illinois River, OR

Rogue River source, OR

Rogue near Natural Bridge, OR

Rogue, Mule Cr. Canyon, OR

North Santiam River above Detroit, OR

Salmon River above Wemme, OR

Wahkenna Falls Cr., Columbia Gorge, OR

Columbia River below Bonneville Dam, OR, WA

Calapooia River, OR

Cispus River, WA

North Fork Sauk, WA

Middle Fork Snoqualmie, WA

within a half-hour drive of Portland. Its tributary, the Salmon, swishes through old-growth forests as a northwestern gem.

The east side of the Oregon Cascades yields far less water, and much of the runoff sinks directly into the plumbing of cavitated lava. The Deschutes of the desert grows from these Cascade spring flows and tributaries. Outstanding among these is the Metolius, one of the largest spring-fed rivers in the United States, beginning beneath the snowy splendor of Mount Jefferson. Its cold, transparent water seldom reaches more than 44 degrees Fahrenheit and flows with absolute steadiness year-round. The White River plunges from Mount Hood's glaciers in a spectacle of forests and rapids to the Deschutes, and the Hood River's headwaters drop from the sublime Lost Lake at the base of Mount Hood and then down through orchard country to the Columbia.

The Columbia, a 1,248-mile river with 60 percent of its length in the United States, first flows through the Rockies and the desert and then ends as the artery of the Northwest. Antecedent to the Cascade uplift, the river cut down while the mountains rose up, leaving the scenic legacy of a 50-mile-long gorge where the river lops the Cascades in two. Columbia tributaries on the Oregon side leap over the blackened basalt cliffs; only the Sierra's Yosemite Valley surpasses this gorge for an abundance of tall waterfalls. Multnomah Creek, with one of the highest falls in America, drops 610 feet after flowing through a fairyland of old-growth fir where moss makes even dead trees look alive in shaggy green. Through most of the gorge, the Columbia lies impounded behind Bonneville Dam, built at the head of tidewater. Pulsing outward, the tidal Columbia flows for another 140 miles as the longest sea-level river on the West Coast, passing Portland on the way. With the turbulence of big-river water meeting the ocean, the 5-mile-wide mouth of the Columbia is one of the most dreaded graveyards of Pacific shipping. To see this colossal meeting of fresh water and saltwater, to be almost *in* it, one can walk at low tide on a narrow rock jetty at Fort Stevens State Park, with one side exposed to the sea and the other facing the mouth of the river.

Hundreds of rivers and streams network the Olympic Peninsula and the Cascade Mountains of Washington, where the riverine nature of the Northwest intensifies under heavier rain and snow. The Humptulips, Quinault, Queets, Hoh, Bogachiel, and Sol Duc drain the western slope of the monumental Olympic Mountains. As a source of five rivers, Mount Olympus rises 7,965 feet within 35 miles of the ocean and collects 250 inches of precipitation from the heaviest rains and snowfalls on the continent (the most rain in the United States, however, falls on Mount Waialeale, on the island of Kauai, which receives an astonishing

486 inches). The Northwest's mossy-rock rivers of ancient rainforests flow from the security of Olympic National Park onto national forest, timber industry, and tribal lands, where clearcutting has been as rapacious as anywhere. The effects are evident in silted and eroded streams. Protected in the park, the beautiful upper Dosewallips River drains the eastern Olympics, and the Elwha flows north toward Puget Sound. Federal agencies have recommended the removal of two large Elwha dams so that salmon can return to one of their finest historical habitats. Budget cuts for environmental programs may prevent this from happening, though long-term economic benefits clearly lie with the dam removal.

Flowing from the Washington Cascades directly south to the Columbia, the Washougal, Wind, White Salmon, and Klickitat Rivers cut through narrow-slotted volcanic gorges. Indians on the Klickitat still dipnet for salmon, though remaining stocks are a ghost of the old-time runs. Draining the Cascades' eastern slope in Washington, the Yakima River pulls in the Tieton and Naches Rivers and then flows through the most intensively farmed valley on the entire east side of the Cascade-Sierra complex. Once the Columbia's second-largest producer of salmon, the Yakima has lost nearly all its runs—victims of irrigation diversions. Yet a watershed organization there strives to bring the fish back and has become a model of cooperation among diverse interest groups. To the north, the Wenatchee River flows with popular whitewater, and farther up, the splendid Stehekin of the North Cascades drops off snowy peaks into Lake Chelan. The Methow River leaves the eastern side of the North Cascades through a sparkling valley of orchards and whitewater near the Columbia. The sluggish and agricultural Okanogan, its valley gridded with apple orchards, flows south from Canada at the border of the Northwest and Rocky Mountain regions.

The more populated western side of Washington's Cascades breeds the Lewis River in the south, then the Toutle from the erupted slope of Mount St. Helens, where viscous mudflows delivered volcanic debris at a grandiose scale. The emerald beauty of the Cispus flows from Mount Adams to the Cowlitz River, which, along with the Ohanapecosh, Nisqually, Puyallup, Carbon, and White, extend in a glistening radial pattern from the majestic monolith of Mount Rainier. Twenty-four glaciers here drain into rivers of chalky white, silty tan, and crème de menthe—variations of color caused by rock dust pulverized under the moving ice.

To the north, the Snoqualmie, with its Middle Fork, flows from a stunning landscape with rocky peaks and verdant shores, but in between them the timber industry has voraciously clearcut squares as big as whole mountainsides. After plunging over one of the region's highest waterfalls—often reduced to a trickle by hydropower diversions—the main stem Snoqualmie traverses an agricultural valley of riparian charm, picking up the Tolt River east of Seattle before meeting the Skykomish River. This fine stream accumulates scenic tributaries such as the Miller and Beckler Rivers, then adds the superlative whitewater of the North Fork Skykomish before winding out past forests, farms, and towns. The Snoqualmie and Skykomish create the short tidal flow of the Snohomish. As the next river to the north, the Stillaguamish drops beautifully from North Cascade peaks to Puget Sound.

Rising in British Columbia, the Skagit is a landmark in the northwestern riverscape. Now heavily dammed, the upper river once ranked among the most spectacular wild streams anywhere. Below three reservoirs, the Skagit flows for 100 miles, and along with the Willamette and Umpqua, this river offers one of the longer canoe trips possible in the Northwest. From the south the river picks up the wild, rapid, undammed Cascade and Sauk Rivers; the North Fork of the Sauk sports waterfalls and one of the most exquisite wilderness trails I have hiked through cathedrals of ancient forest along a stream. With many of its hillsides clearcut, the middle and lower Skagit drifts into a farmed and settled valley and then to Puget Sound.

In far northwestern Washington, the Nooksack plunges off the snow-cone of Mount Baker and through rainy forests with primeval green undergrowth and giant trees in a few pockets that the timber industry has missed. Through the emerald fields of farm country, the lower river meets saltwater at Bellingham Bay, near the Canadian border.

From the Nooksack down through the Russian, each northwestern river tells a story of this great landscape, but to carefully explore a river encompassing all the changing scenes of the Cascades, the interior valley, and the Coast Range, I chose the Rogue.

The Rogue River

After a walk of 2 miles, Ann and I arrived at the springs. The largest ran crystalline over dark volcanic rocks in a flow too wide to step across. A varied thrush and a winter wren fed in the brush nearby, and the cool backcountry trench lay thick with mountain hemlock, subalpine fir, and lodgepole pine. Beneath the mat of needles and duff lay volcano-spewed pumice—a rock so filled with air bubbles that it floats. Robustly artesian, the springs rose in effervescent mounds. Nobody had trampled on the luxuriant carpet of moss. Carefully stone-stepping, we reached down and fingered the ice-cold water. Then we dipped our hands and drank at the source of the 216-mile Rogue.

A legendary wild river of the Northwest, this Oregon stream, known for its past wealth of salmon and steelhead, includes whitewater considered classic by river runners. The spring where we drank is probably the main outlet of Crater Lake, a circle of water 6 miles across and 1,931 feet deep. The bluest-blue and cleanest large lake in America, Crater is the child of an earthshaking eruption that occurred 6,600 years ago when the 12,000-foot-high Mount Mazama literally blew its top off. Like the explosion of Mount St. Helens, only much, much larger, the eruption decapitated this Cascade peak, and its base sank inward much as a half-eaten scoop of ice cream sinks into a cone on a summer day. The cone of Mount Mazama then filled with water. Surrounded by cliffs up to 2,000 feet high, Crater Lake has no surface outlet but seeps away underground, and hundreds of its springs feed the Rogue River.

From the source, 51 miles of continuous trail hug the Rogue and allow for a week-long hike at the headwaters. Fallen timber riddles some sections; others drop through gorges and waterfalls with roads nearby. The trail and the river offer views of marshy meadows, pools of transparent water with reflections of forest etched on the surface, and shoreline rocks shagged in yellow-green moss. In old-growth enclaves, sugar pine and Douglas fir tower 200 feet into the sky; mountain hemlock, western white pine, and ponderosa pine thrive as well. In the autumn the water reflects the pink, red, and green foliage of dogwood mixed with the starry red leaves of vine maples, all color-enhanced by the conifer background.

Had we remained at the river's edge, I might have thought that substantial ancient forests of the Pacific Northwest had been spared. In fact, the cut zone presses hard against the river. I saw the skylight created by clearcuts through the wooded "beauty strip" along the water; just a few hundred feet away lay a patchwork quilt of ragged logging jobs. A spaghetti-like tangle of logging roads had been dug into the mountainsides and up tributary valleys.

The Rogue's otherwise fabulous course through the lava landscape includes cauldrons big enough to sit in. Natural pipes and tunnels were left underground as "tubes" when still-liquid lava drained away beneath an air-hardened crust. At Rogue River Gorge, the water jets past basalt blockages and slices through a fifteen-foot-wide slot in the Cascade landscape. At Natural Bridge, the river's entire 300-cfs flow boils into a sinkhole and vanishes; with a dark rumble, it is gone. Along with the

Lost River of West Virginia and the Lost River of Idaho, this is one of few sizeable streams that go subterranean and then reappear. For 200 feet the river thrashes underground, hisses through fractured rock, and blows cold air to the surface.

The thin corridor of scenic river ends abruptly above Prospect where a Pacific Power and Light Company dam sluices the Rogue off to a power plant, leaving a depleted river to limp down to the mud-ringed backwater of Lost Creek Dam. The Rogue had no storage reservoir on its entire length when I first visited there while working as a carpenter's helper at Crater Lake National Park in 1967, but the plans for Lost Creek had been drawn. After the great flood of 1964, few people spoke out against damming of the Rogue; few realized the effects an impoundment would have on the biological health of the river, not just here but all the way to the sea. The Army Corps of Engineers finished construction in 1977, and the 327-foot-high dam flooded 10 miles of the Rogue at the Cascades' lower slopes. When I last visited, in October 1993, the level of the reservoir was so low that a red-dirt "bathtub ring" rose 200 vertical feet between flatwater and forest.

The dam's altered flows wreak havoc on the downstream riparian corridor. "The entire ecosystem has changed," said Jim Leffmann, the Rogue River manager for the federal Bureau of Land Management, the agency responsible for large sections of downstream riverfront. "Gravel bars are becoming grown over, and native plants that could withstand floods are being replaced with noxious invaders such as purple loosestrife, jimsonweed, and star thistle. These are nearly useless to wildlife." Beaches at the lower river are disappearing year by year because of the dams upstream, which stop the sand-depositing flood flows and trap silt in the reservoirs.

Below Lost Creek Dam, the Rogue resurrects itself as a riffling northwestern melody for 36 miles. Oaks and ponderosa pines shade the shores; drivers tool alongside on Highway 62 through farms and forests. When the Army Corps of Engineers planned another dam on Elk Creek, which joins the Rogue from the north, Oregon conservationists fought the project for a decade and lost. But in 1987, one year after construction began, a court order finally stopped the Corps. Unnecessary for flood control, the dam would have eliminated 25 miles of spawning habitat of imperiled salmon and further degraded the Rogue downstream, according to Forest Service and Bureau of Land Management studies. Oregon Governor Barbara Roberts, the Oregon Department of Fish and Wildlife, and many of the state's newspaper editorial boards favored removal of the one-third-completed dam. The Corps favored the far more expensive alternative of completion of the project and its use as a dry dam, to be filled only during floods, but in 1995 the agency recommended that the dam not be completed. If dismantled, Elk Creek would represent the largest demolition of a dam in America.

Six miles below Tou Velle State Park, Gold Rey Dam blocks the river. This antiquated twenty-foot-high structure once produced hydropower. Water flows over the top of the dam, flanked by a poorly functioning fish ladder, trash on the ground, and abandoned buildings, giving a ruined look to the place. A movement grows to get rid of the dam altogether.

Below Gold Rey, grasslands peppered with oaks and red-barked madrones announced hotter, drier country; we had left the Cascades behind and entered the interior valley of the Rogue. An 8-mile section of river included two rapids followed by 16 miles of riffles and pools, with Interstate 5 and local roads set back along both sides of the river. A gray haze of car exhaust and smoke from wood-burning stoves in the Medford area filled the valley.

The last of four dams blocked the Rogue at Savage Rapids, just above the town of Grants Pass. This diversion structure, about twenty feet high, was built by the Grants Pass Irrigation District in 1921 to deliver water to 7,300 acres. The dam's fish ladder worked poorly—one reason that four major stocks of steelhead, coho salmon, and chinook salmon will likely be added to the endangered species list. Up to 27,000 more fish could return to the upper river each year if the dam were removed, and the National Marine Fisheries Service has offered to pay for pumps to bring water to farmers' fields. Squeezed between two costly alternatives, the irrigation district was required by the state to either fix the fish passage for $17 million or remove the whole obstruction for $11 million. Most of the farmland had been converted to urban development; cemeteries and golf courses are now the big water users. The district favored removal and the switch to pumping, but their plan was fought by landowners who liked the flatwater view. If Savage Rapids and Gold Rey Dams are both eliminated, the middle and lower Rogue could be America's finest example of a newly reclaimed river and would run freely for 161 miles to the ocean.

To see the Rogue's longest section without dams, Ann and I put our boats into the water just below Savage Rapids Dam and set out for the Pacific. Our two-week route would take us 112 miles through the Coast

Range on a river of nominally surviving salmon and steelhead, lively rapids, rugged mountain views, and campsites on sandy beaches rimmed by the richly blended forests of the Pacific slope. Choosing from our four boats, we decided to take Ann's kayak and my fourteen-foot Avon raft with rowing frame and oars. That way we could carry adequate provisions and each guide our own boat.

On a surprisingly hot October first, the coolness of the river came as a relief. Its low-flow odor of algae and slight fishiness contrasted with the dusty scent of autumn in a crackling, dry woodland, the oaks turning orange, the ash yellow. Not long after entering the water we drifted through the fringe of Grants Pass, where homes were set back behind big lawns. Since it had taken us all day to shuttle the van and load our gear, we soon needed to camp, and we settled on a site just above a bridge where we could hide in the willows. Early the next morning fishermen tramped through our camp, inviting themselves to breakfast.

A river town through and through, Grants Pass has a waterfront park that's crowded on weekends, and the municipal mallards, mergansers, and Canada geese flock up in bunches of a hundred. Below town we drifted through long pools and chattering riffles, the peace of the place blemished only by jet boats powering up and down the river, each packed with sixty or so tourists sitting in broad rows across the sled-like craft. These boats gave the impression of covering half the river's width as they roared around bends and broke into view, bank-to-bank wakes streaming behind. Increasingly, landowners, fisheries interests, floaters, and other people enjoying the river have questioned the effects of the big boats and their three-foot-high wakes pounding the shore hour after hour, year after year. About 11 percent of the area's salmon spawn during the jet boat season, and all the juvenile salmon and steelhead try to survive near the shorelines during the tourist months, when boat-induced waves break against the banks. Twenty years after this all started to be a problem, federal agencies began studies to document jet boat effects. New regulations may be in order, but they are certain to be resisted by the industry, which now says it hosts 80,000 people on the middle river and 55,000 on the lower Rogue. In 1993 the Oregon Natural Resources Council and a property owner sued the Bureau of Land Management to restrict jet boat use.

Ann and I beached for lunch at the mouth of the Applegate River, a landmark because it represents one of the last major dam fights in America that river conservationists lost. The Corps impounded the Applegate in 1980 to provide flood control for a lot of undeveloped land

and thereby line the pockets of speculative developers. During a county referendum in 1976, dam proponents plastered billboards with the slogan "Protect 170,000 jobs." That many jobs didn't exist in all of southwestern Oregon, and none of them depended on the new reservoir, but the propaganda had the desired effect.

The Rouge filtered around islands near the mouth of the Applegate, where there were gravel-bottomed spawning beds for salmon. At dusk we settled into camp on a thin strip of rocky beach. In the morning men casting lures drifted by in dories, and after we launched we passed a lot of people casting from shore. A hot spot of river resorts, the Rogue has rustic and refined accommodations catering to salmon and steelhead anglers, and several lodges are accessible only by boat below Grave Creek. This is one of the most active river corridors in America for river-related tourism.

At our first canyon, inappropriately named Hell Gate, the heavenly Rogue narrowed and dropped us through rapids. Chunky gray bedrock typical of the Coast Range rose from the banks. Later, six muskrats nibbled on algae at a cluster of rocks in a calm pool. We flushed through a flume called Galice riffle, then beached our boats and bought bread at the Galice store. Farther downriver, we pitched our tent on a gravel bar overlooking swift water while clouds thickened to gruel in the western sky.

In a pelting eight-hour rainstorm the next day, we bumped ashore at the Grave Creek access, where most people begin their Rogue River trips and where Ann's friend Beth Jacobi awaited us in the cozy shelter of her truck. With her kayak, she would join us for the rest of the journey to the ocean. Meanwhile, a hired driver would shuttle Beth's pickup down to Gold Beach.

The Forest Service required permits to run the "wild" Rogue from June 1 to September 15 in order to limit the number of people to 12,000, split between commercial outfitters and all other boaters. But even with the permit program, 120 people crowd the river each day. Exempt this late in the season, we simply checked in with ranger Jeanne Klein and piled Beth's gear into the raft. We ate lunch in the cramped shelter of her truck while raindrops beat like mallets on the roof. Then we pulled on our paddling jackets, zipped up our Gore-Tex, and launched into a blurry gray world of water.

Peering through the wet curtain—a real beauty of a storm, breaking a long siege of drought—I piloted my raft over big waves at the centerline of Grave Creek Riffle, then pivoted at the lip of Grave Creek

Falls. If it weren't for the fact that I had confronted this blind drop sixteen years before in a frighteningly smaller boat, I would have been
scared. Now I remembered Bob Peirce's simple advice: "Point the raft
straight and keep it moving." In this rainstorm, I missed Bob's presence.
He had been fifty years old on that earlier trip and had been boating
in Oregon for twenty years. One of the originators of the Oregon state
scenic rivers system and an authoritative guide to the Northwest, he
also joined me on other Oregon trips in the 1970s. Bob's current business of guiding treks in Nepal prevented him from being with us now.

My raft tilted over the steep drop and buoyed up on the wave beyond. Ann and Beth disappeared like soaked driftwood in foam at the
base but quickly reemerged, relief and then delight shining on their
faces. They played in the rapids while I drifted alone, mesmerized by
the rainy wilderness of pine, oak, myrtle, and madrone in shades of
gray-green behind a streaked atmosphere. We dropped deeper and
deeper into the Rogue's crosscut of the Coast Range.

Being swallowed once again in these mountainous folds reminded
me of my first visit here. In 1967 I had hitchhiked down from Crater
Lake and, on a Saturday morning, climbed into a pickup driven by a
man who pulled a dory. Launching at Galice, he invited me to ride in
the bow to Grave Creek. There I set off to hike the 40-mile-long Rogue
River Trail. Walking at a brisk pace, I covered the 24 miles to Marial by
the next afternoon, enjoying the magic of that remote canyon. Twenty-
five years later, with a hundred pounds' worth of additional gear, I traveled at a more reasonable pace, taking four days to raft what I had
walked in one.

We next approached the roar of Rainy Falls, a ten-foot drop that can
be boated, though the odds on having a clean run versus getting really
trashed are random. We opted for a skinny channel to the right that had
been blasted out as a fish ladder to allow salmon and steelhead to pass
the falls. In a passage too cramped for rowing I stood at the bow,
pushed off from rocks with my feet and the butt of an oar, and eventually rattled back into the main channel.

The following days offered a waking dream of river and Coast Range
scenery. Tan, sandy beaches reclined beneath rocky rises and playful,
exciting rapids. Remarkably mixed, the forests include broad-leafed
trees from the warmer climes of the California coast along with conifers
of the Northwest; the Rogue's forest presents one of the finest cross
sections of the plant kingdom on the Pacific Coast. Pacific madrone and
white oak dominate dry areas. Oregon ash and bigleaf maple thrive in
moist reaches. Douglas fir, western hemlock, and sugar pine shade

mountainsides. Along the river I found Pacific yew, canyon live oak, golden chinkapin, tanoak, and Oregon myrtle.

One day we went 3 miles. One day we didn't go anywhere. Twelve groups passed us one day and other days we saw almost no one. We strolled on the trail I had hustled across years ago. Great blue herons, mergansers, and kingfishers indicated that a lot of small fish must live in the river, yet I knew that the salmon runs were dangerously small due to logging-induced losses of spawning habitat. After the enchanting Horseshoe Bend, we breezed through small rapids and bypassed campsites that tempted me even though we had just broken camp a mile before. We toured Winkle Bar, where writer Zane Grey's log cabin still stands.

Below there the Rogue narrowed and accelerated in a heart-thumping crescendo. Ahead lay Mule Creek Canyon, one of the more extraordinary river passages commonly boated. Rock walls rose to fifty feet, and the inner canyon narrowed to twenty. Boiling-milk rapids guarded the entrance as if to foreshadow some frightening event to come. Then the narrowing hallway sucked me in. A glaringly low afternoon sun obliterated detail and added partial blindness to the adventure. At one place the walls compressed to nearly a raft's length where the Rogue sudsed green and white. None of it proved difficult, but all of it was sensational and insanely exhilarating as the river dug downward into the Coast Range's rocky spine.

Beyond the canyon, a drift offering welcome breathing time delivered us to Blossom Bar, the largest rapid. I savored the rocky drop, entering left, pulling right, catching eddies, then waiting for Ann and Beth, who also eddy-hopped like kids in a rocky playpen.

For two nights we camped at a beach below Blossom Bar, once again in the range of jet boats—four of them roaring daily upriver to the base of the rapids. A man chattered away on a loudspeaker. The sound of the boat and its public address system echoed from canyon walls long before it arrived and long after it left, creating the strange effect of being in an auditorium with a rock-and-roll band's amplifiers making noise but nobody on stage.

Another two lazy days took us to Foster Bar, a boat ramp where most people take out, but we continued on to an Indian-summer campsite. The next day we bought frozen juice at the Agness store and soon reached the mouth of the Illinois River. Excited by what I glimpsed from the raft, I grabbed my mask and snorkel to check out whole schools of four-inch-long fish in the clear water where the tributary spilled quietly into the Rogue. Though the lower river is still one of the

greatest whitewater runs in America during the high waters of springtime, the upper Illinois endures clearcutting, erosion from logging
roads, and irrigation withdrawals; the steelhead of this river, which for
so long were synonymous with wildness, are now up for listing as endangered.

Below the Illinois the Rogue runs bigger in a larger valley, with fair-
way-sized gravel bars and views to higher mountains. Sitting back at
our campsite in an unroaded canyon, I reflected on my surroundings
as the finest of the Northwest: green river in green forest, ten-story
conifers down to water's edge, slap of the beaver, hiss of the otter, track
of the bear at the edge of the woods.

After two days of muscling into stiff headwinds, we spilled out into
an open valley where the river split around islands. Suddenly I found
myself face to face with a seal—bald headed, oval faced, whiskered. Its
big eyes met mine for long seconds of connection. The seal disappeared without a splash, then resurfaced to stare some more, and I felt
as though I had found a long-lost relative.

Cows had taken over the best campsites, but finally we found a
gravel beach for our last night out. Downriver, a flat-topped rock rose
at the water's edge, 100 feet high, reminiscent of the sea stacks in the
ocean that lay so close—just how close we had not guessed.

In the middle of the night the wind howled me awake. I crawled out
of the tent to check the gear. What I found was water flooding the
kitchen site! Still miles from the ocean, we hadn't thought about the
hazards of tides on a river that had been flowing when we made camp.
"Ann!" I shouted for help. "Beth!" We hustled the gear up to higher
ground.

The riparian habitat of the lower river had been grazed to stubble,
and cows even browsed on the willow-covered islands. But we also
saw beavers, otters, seals, and an eagle—a picture-book sampling of
riverine wildlife, all dependent on the aquatic heartbeat of this river.
Knowing that the Rogue has only a fraction of its earlier health owing
to clearcut swaths, four dams, diversions, grazing, development, overfishing, and jet boats, I still gazed in awe at what remained, a glimpse
of what so many rivers in America once offered. I spotted a big fish
surfacing—a lonely chinook on its way home to create a much-needed
new generation.

Beyond the Highway 101 bridge, I could see through a gap to the
west and sensed the emptiness that lay beyond—the sea, though full
of life, seemed like an infinite stretch of nothingness. The wind blew

stronger. The water tasted faintly of salt where we beached for the last time.

I had hoped to raft into the Pacific and bob around in big water for a while, but it was a goal I immediately abandoned on arrival—the mouth of the river was far too rough. Beyond the Gold Beach harbor, the Rogue crossed the last of the Coast Range, and then a rock jetty extended into the sea and funneled the water into a violent surf with five-foot breakers. Ann, Beth, and I walked as close to the water as we could and then sat on misted rocks, where we watched the collisions of waves throwing water high into the air.

Chapter 10

The Wild Rivers of Alaska

Alaska ranks as the preeminent wild river region not only of the United States but of the world. Here and in northern Canada, hundreds of rivers flow from unspoiled landscapes.

Going to the north is an opportunity to go back in time. On hundreds of streams in this region we may as well have returned to the nineteenth century, the Stone Age, or the Ice Age. Some of the rivers suffer the effects of energy development, logging, mining, homesteading, and a recreational boom, but even so, a trip in Alaska can resemble a journey to the Rockies with Lewis and Clark in 1805. It's like canoeing the Tennessee before the Tennessee Valley Authority, exploring the Colorado River before the first drop was diverted, or following the salmon down the Columbia before the first dam was built. The land is extreme—as lightly peopled and as distant from cities as nearly anyplace on earth. Cold, dark, rugged, wet, icy, incredibly buggy, the land flames to the whim of volcanoes, shakes to seismic upheaval, and suddenly disappears beneath glacial surges. All these attributes help to keep the rivers wild and natural.

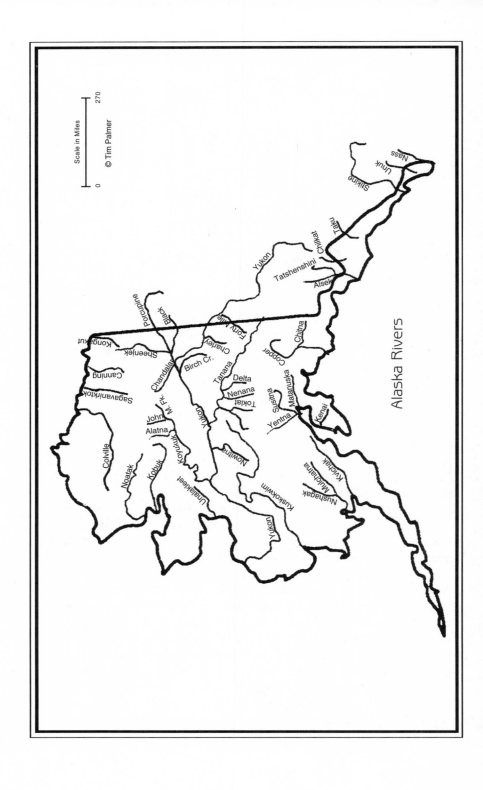

Alaska Rivers

The United States bought Alaska from Russia and later made it a state, but most people have never really adopted it as a part of the country. Geographic data about the nation often exclude Alaska; to include it skews the numbers radically and changes our overall impression of America. For example, consider the map of the forty-eight states, but then add 20 percent more acreage. If Alaska is superimposed on the rest of the United States, Ketchikan overlays Jacksonville, Florida, while Attu settles on San Francisco (the bulk of the state extends only from Chicago to Denver, Manitoba to Arkansas). Here lies 29 percent of the nation's Wild and Scenic Rivers System, 40 percent of its National Park System, 86 percent of its National Wildlife Refuge System, and most of its remaining wilderness.

Every page out of the DeLorme Atlas of Alaska is frameable as abstract art, breathtaking in its presentation and even more striking when one considers what's really on the ground: here the crowns of North America's highest mountains, steep and snowy; there the largest nonpolar ice mass—white oceans of ice and then white rivers of it churning past outcrops of rock. The potholed wetlands of the tundra show as thousands of blue dots speckled on muskeg green, eventually collecting into streams. The crooked coastline of jagged cliffs and embayments taper into rivers bordered by emerald forests. Rushing streams originate on brown volcanoes thrown up in cones that pierce the clouds.

Alaska is the second-least-populated state and by far the lightest in density: one person per square mile, compared with the national average of sixty-nine. But the people, counting millions of visitors each summer, affect the landscape proportionately more than they do elsewhere because the land is so fragile.

And the rivers—nothing else in America remotely resembles the 365,000-mile-long rivers estate of Alaska, almost devoid of the dams, levees, diversions, and urbanized floodplains that leave naturally functioning waterways elsewhere as a dim memory from earlier generations. This one state contains more rivers, and more large ones, than any other region by far. Considering the climatic limitations of the far north, Alaska also has a remarkable variety of river types. These relate closely to the moods of landscape in the state's four landform provinces.

The Pacific Mountain System province of Alaska embraces rainy, snowy glacial peaks from the southeastern panhandle and across southern Alaska. Here the St. Elias Range of Canada reaches 18,000 feet and the adjoining Wrangell Mountains of Alaska reach 16,000 feet—the highest continuous mass of mountains on the continent, higher than the Alaska Range were Denali (Mount McKinley) taken out of it. To the north a trough of disconnected lowlands arches through the Copper River lowlands and the Matanuska Valley to Cook Inlet at Anchorage. North of the trough but still in the Pacific Mountain System, the Alaska Range incorporates Mount McKinley, the continent's highest peak at 20,320 feet, and mountains sweep southwestward across the 1,000-mile-long Aleutian chain of volcanic islands to Attu, far out in the Pacific. North of the Pacific Mountain System, Alaska's interior province presents an 800-mile-wide swath of plains, plateaus, deltas, and low mountains, 200 to 800 miles from north to south. A land of immense rivers and wetlands as big as some states, this paradoxical northern desert receives only six to twelve inches of rain per year but is saturated with water owing to rivers flowing from its high borderlands and to permafrost. This year-round ice just beneath the soil prevents water from soaking into the ground. To the north of the Interior province, the Brooks Range—the largest of all east-west mountain ranges in America—rises as 600 miles of high country, 80 miles wide, nearly treeless, and mostly lacking glaciers in the dry climate north of the Arctic Circle. Finally, the Arctic Coastal Plain province flanks the northern slope of the mountains as a maze of marshes, lakes, and waterlogged tundra perched on permafrost.

Though distinctly Alaskan, these four provinces correspond to the familiar geography of the West. The three zones of the Pacific Mountain System reflect the Coast Range, interior valleys, and Cascade Mountains of the Northwest. The Interior province corresponds to the West's desert region between the Cascade-Sierra mountain block and the Rocky Mountains. The Brooks Range represents an extension of the Rockies, and the Coastal Plain is America's Great Plains of the Arctic.

Draining to Alaska's three watersheds—the Gulf of Alaska at the southern end of the state; the interior's Yukon and Kuskokwim Rivers, which flow west with other streams to the Bering Sea; and the Arctic Ocean to the north—each province produces distinctive types of rivers unlike any others in America. In the southeast, plentiful water plunges off glacial slopes at the Alaska–British Columbia border and then flows through a narrow belt housing the largest temperate rainforest on earth. Much of this area can be described as an extraordinarily rugged mountain range carved by glaciers and wild rivers, then flooded in its lower reaches by the combined effects of a rising ocean and a depressed landscape. Fjords are the result. The sea-level passage of the Portland Inlet at the southern boundary of Alaska and British Columbia, for ex-

ample, extends inland for 100 miles with a nearly uniform width of
only 4 miles, fed at its head by the Nass River of Canada. Scores of
rivers end similarly, with sea-level fjords backed by ice-water runoff in
valleys inhabited by grizzlies and thick with Sitka spruce, western hemlock, and an impenetrable shrub aptly named devil's club. A few large
rivers cut through the Coast Range, and networks of streams decorate
even small islands in the southeast Alaskan archipelago, where rainfall
reaches 100 inches and in some places 200 inches per year. Salmon and
eagles populate these rainy rivers.

Leaving the panhandle and curving north and west to the main body
of Alaska, I see a second type of river—enormous ones fed by glacial
runoff, rain, and snow, describing much of the river mileage through
the Pacific Mountain System. The Alsek, Copper, and Susitna flow in
swift braids out to ocean inlets. So many of the rivers through this region look perpetually angry; the Copper River's tributary the Tazlina,
for example, has milky gray or brown water running hard and opaque,
shearing erosive banks. The silty water bulldozes whole trees on the
forceful blades of its icy flow. Hundreds of smaller streams are similar
to the parent rivers: swift, gritty, cold, and wild. Many are conduits for
salmon swimming up to clearer spawning waters. In between the large
rivers, steep streams plunge off the mountains everywhere in a rush to
myriad ocean embayments.

Virtually hundreds of waterways here and at the Alaska Range, farther inland, begin as rivers of ice. The glaciers plow their way down
valleys until they reach an elevation where the ice breaks up and water
runs in silty flows of glacially ground rock. The characteristic pattern of
shallow, many-braided rivers results from a surplus of rock, gravel, and
silt eroded by the glaciers but left where the flow is inadequate to carry
the debris downstream.

The Yukon River, along with its tributary the Tanana and the more
southwestern Kuskokwim, dominates the interior of Alaska. Some of
the region lies so low that it cannot be eroded any more; rather, it
builds up as a peneplain, an inland delta with the silt deposits of a mature, flattened landscape. Boggy rivers commonly snake through tundra lowlands as well, and clear water from nonglacial areas lie like jewels amid the interior mountain ranges, dwarfed by the big mountains
to the south but nonetheless rising in the style of miniature Rockies.

The Brooks Range rivers run swiftly from big, eroding, treeless
mountains. Southbound streams consolidate in spruce-lined corridors
leading to tundra plains of the Interior. Lacking glaciers and flowing
mostly through limestone, these mountains produce clear-water rivers

with few steep rapids. Finally, the north slope rivers begin as braided outwashes of the Brooks Range but then slow to a potholed, marshy meander across the nearly flat Arctic Plain until they reach the bays, lagoons, and frozen edges of the Arctic Ocean.

The types of rivers in Alaska include waterfall plunges from mountains to sea, glacier meltwater torrents, silty Mississippis of the north, braided channels on cobble bars, boggy meanderings in the muskeg, and gravel-bottomed clear water through spruce forests and rolling mountains.

With heavy runoff all over the Pacific Mountain System and with long rivers snaking across the Interior, Alaska has more than its share of unusually large rivers, even considering the state's epic size. Here are found seven of the twenty largest rivers in America and three of the largest ten. Alaskan rivers in aggregate discharge a third of the nation's stream flow from a fifth of the nation's land area. Only in Alaska does one find a "creek" (Beaver) that runs for 259 miles. Far and away the largest river, the Yukon carries 225,000 cubic feet per second—the fifth-highest volume in the country. The Kuskokwim, which empties into the same bulging delta at the western limits of the state, carries a flow of 67,000 cfs. The Copper, draining the Wrangell Mountains and the southeastern Interior, flows with 59,000. The Stikine, mostly in British Columbia, fans with 56,674 cfs into the sea at the southeastern coast of Alaska. The state's fifth-largest river, the Susitna, flows with 51,000 cfs down the southern center of the state. The Tanana—a Yukon tributary from the east central region—contributes 41,000 to the big river. The Nushagak, in the rainy southwest, drains to Bristol Bay with a flow of 36,000 cfs. The Alsek, incorporating the Tatshenshini as a Canadian tributary, averages 33,320. From Yukon Territory and the eastern Brooks Range, the Porcupine brings 23,000 cfs to the Yukon. The Kvichak, a neighbor to the Nushagak, carries 18,060—the tenth-largest river in Alaska but still larger than the Colorado.

Even more striking than the size of Alaskan waterways is their wildness. The longest undeveloped, undammed, unroaded reach of river in the other 49 states is a 260-mile reach of the Colorado in its Grand Canyon stretching from Lee's Ferry to Lake Mead, but dozens of rivers of greater wild mileage flow in Alaska. Even the Yukon—the north's equivalent of the Mississippi—is essentially wilderness for nearly 2,000 miles from its British Columbia headwaters. Only three bridges cross the whole river; only one bridge crosses in Alaska. Twenty-five dirt-street villages sit above the banks in Alaska, but only two of those villages can be reached by road.

Though the state's highway system accesses many rivers, invariably leading to people pressure, the great majority lie beyond the asphalt and gravel. Alaskans and visitors, however, now travel in airplanes and motorboats to the most remote outposts. All-terrain vehicles and snow-mobiles proliferate in the bush, and four-wheelers (all-terrain vehicles) cause a damaging scribble of long-lasting ruts, even in national parks. Pressure on the wildest places increases, easily damaging a fragile balance where wildlife responds to the slightest disturbance. Even in affecting rivers as massive as the Yukon, new technology and increased effectiveness of the commercial fishing industry deplete the runs of salmon and threaten the web of life dependent on them.

Hunters, anglers, boaters, and hikers infiltrate deeper and deeper into the wilds as bush pilots take more people to more places. At the remote Kongakut, Hulahula, and Sheenjek Rivers of the Brooks Range, recreational use increased by 500 percent between 1985 and 1990. The area's 1,794 visitors don't constitute a large number relative to use elsewhere, but in the spare ecosystem of the far north, they make a difference. "The farther north you go, the longer it takes for the land to recover," said Tom Edgerton when I interviewed him as the recreation planner for the Fish and Wildlife Service's Arctic National Wildlife Refuge. Wildlife is easily stressed in the open country, and the fisheries are easily depleted where the growing season is so short. A twelve-inch-long Arctic grayling in a Brooks Range river might require a decade to grow that large, while trout elsewhere need just a few years. Some species are limited in their ranges and vulnerable to any change; the Angayukaksurak char, for example, lives only in the northeastern Brooks Range rivers. These cross the Arctic National Wildlife Refuge, which is threatened by proposed oil drilling.

The effect of hunters, anglers, and boaters is coupled with larger intrusions on northern rivers. The Alaska Pipeline is the best-known example of energy development opening up wild country and razing habitat; its legacy includes the Exxon *Valdez* oil spill in Prince William Sound. A whole host of new roads, mines, pipelines, harbors, and railroads are proposed by Alaskan politicians anxious to sell off the wealth of the state as fast as possible; the political climate has not changed much since Ramparts Dam was proposed on the Yukon in 1963. That reservoir would have flooded one of the continent's most critical waterfowl strongholds with a reservoir the size of Lake Erie, all to produce hydropower that had no buyers. Alaskan politicians fought for the dam, arguing that the region had only a few flush toilets and that it would be difficult to find an equivalent area with so little to lose through flooding. In one of the early successful dam fights waged by conservationists and Department of the Interior personnel who were concerned about wildlife, the dam was stopped, as was a 1980s plan funded by the state to dam the Susitna. Facing a different type of threat, rivers of the southeast have been degraded and continue to be lost to clearcutting in Tongass National Forest, where the Forest Service allows enormous cuts no matter how little money the government receives for selling off the world's greatest temperate rainforest for export to Japan. The agency planned to cut 91 percent of our best forest acreage, eating up U.S. tax dollars and leaving Alaska's most productive ecosystem in ruins so that the trees could be shipped to Asia. This all continues because Alaskan politicians insist on it.

Perhaps most pressing on the rivers of Alaska in the 1990s, the Submerged Lands Act gave ownership of navigable riverbeds to the state, which could open up waters to placer mining even more than they already are. Even national parks are threatened. Placer miners excavate with bulldozers and sluice the riverbed for gold, killing whatever is there, causing siltation for miles downstream, and causing long-term damage to the morphology, or shape, of the riverbeds. Sad, muddy evidence of the problem exists today even on the Fortymile River and Birch Creek, both in the National Wild and Scenic Rivers System. Riverbed mining could end up proving that statehood for Alaska was the worst thing that ever happened to its streams, but conservationists, including Jack Hession of the Sierra Club, are trying to get federal and state agencies to cooperatively manage the waterways to regulate the mining.

Though the politicians from our largest state consistently define the right-wing fringe favoring liquidation of natural assets as fast as possible, conservation groups such as the Northern Alaska Environmental Center, Southeast Alaska Conservation Coalition, and Alaska Clean Water Alliance push for reform while some tribes likewise strive to protect their lands. But, making efforts more difficult, Congress has established a system of native development "corporations" designed to encourage the tribes to sell natural resources or land to pay off debts incurred while trying to make the difficult adjustment to modern ways of the white world.

Protection of thirty-three rivers and major tributaries plus twenty-eight smaller tributaries in the National Wild and Scenic Rivers System marked a rare positive step toward protection of some good streams. A total of 3,284 miles were designated; however, 73 percent of that mileage was already included in national parks, refuges, or other safeguarded areas under the Alaska Lands Act of 1980. That milestone law of the Jimmy Carter era was passed in spite of opposition by the state's congressional delegation, which subsequently worked with Republican administrations to sabotage proper implementation of the law.

Two other notable successes for the rivers of Alaska resulted from nationwide or international campaigns in the early 1990s bypassing the Alaska delegation. A proposal to open the Arctic National Wildlife Refuge to oil and gas drilling fell to defeat in Congress, forestalling drilling in the eastern wilds of the northern slope, an activity that would have threatened wilderness rivers (the refuge was not permanently protected, and it faces a much more serious threat in the Republican Congress of 1996). In a milestone of North American conservation, the British Columbia government, led by Michael Harcourt, in 1993 stopped a copper mine proposal for the Alsek and Tatshenshini basins, which drain to the mouth of the Alsek in Alaska. The site was surrounded by the world's greatest parkland and wilderness complex. Exposing the threats of acid mine drainage to one of the great remaining salmon rivers and of new roads and an open-pit mine in superlative habitat, conservationists convinced British Columbia's government to set the Tatshenshini area aside as a provincial wilderness park. The Alsek is the only large river system in North America to be completely protected from source to mouth.

All three of these victories, however, demanded concerted national campaigns to overcome local elected officials. To protect anything here usually requires making it a nationwide priority of the entire conservation movement. Until Alaskans follow the lead of British Columbia and elect a different brand of politician, or until a nationwide movement is sparked to reform management of the federal lands and the waters of Alaska, little success in safeguarding the fragile wilderness of these rivers can be expected.

Everywhere else across America, bold arguments can be articulated to save what is natural because it is so scarce. The enormity of what is at stake in Alaska leads, ironically, to an argument of scarcity as well. No other place else exists in the world with the size and wild quality of Alaska. Here is the last chance to avoid the problems encountered everywhere else, and our last chance to save meaningful pieces and whole ecosystems.

To look at some of Alaska's rivers individually, I begin with the Unuk River, the southernmost among five rivers that completely cross the Coast Range in southern Alaska. Braided, gravel bottomed, littered with fallen timber, it bursts out of the mountains and crosses the protected

forests of Misty Fiords National Monument. To its north the Stikine—
the major river of the southeast panhandle and the fifth-largest river on
the western coast of North America—courses across British Columbia,
where it plunges through one of the ultimate whitewater canyons on
the continent. Then it streams evenly but powerfully from the village
of Telegraph Creek to the river's mouth at Wrangell, Alaska. This 130-
mile-long roadless reach offers one of the finest big-water trips anywhere, with a river pushing through a wilderness of ancient forests,
misty mountains, and low-lying glaciers. Near Juneau the Taku River,
combined with tributaries in British Columbia, cuts across the Coast
Range for 100 miles; it was one of the first great salmon rivers in Alaska
to be exploited by overfishing. At Haines, the Chilkat washes out from
Coast Range snowcaps in braided flows where rich salmon waters remain ice free in the fall and draw the world's largest concentrations of
bald eagles, with 3,000 at a time flocking here to feed.

Farther northwest, the Alsek picks up the Tatshenshini from British
Columbia and Yukon Territory, drains the largest nonpolar ice field in
the world, and cuts through the heart of the St. Elias Mountains. People honor the 130-mile-long trip on the Tatshenshini and lower Alsek
as one of the world classics, a Pantheon of the northern riverscape with
scores of glaciers in view, icebergs calving into the river, and Mount
Fairweather rising 15,318 feet up above the mouth at the Gulf of
Alaska. Long considered unrunnable, the upper Alsek is now kayaked
from its high reaches north of the Coast Range, but it requires an arduous portage across the 12-mile-wide Tweedsmuir Glacier, which
pinches the river shut against rock walls in Turnback Canyon. Some
boaters hire a helicopter shuttle across the glacier, even though it's in
a Canadian national park.

Other waterways in this region rank as some of the shortest large
rivers found anywhere, disgorging the runoff of glaciers that reach as
low as sea level. The Glacier River, for example, comes to life at an icy
headwall and runs for only a few miles before reaching the ocean. The
Edwardes River consists of braids so plentiful that from an airplane they
look like strands of hair running for 10 miles to the sandy shoals in the
Gulf of Alaska. The Seal River—really just a slough—cuts across a 2-
mile-wide peninsula of glacial debris at sea level. The glaciers themselves can be thought of as solid rivers extending inland for many
miles. The permutations of waterways in wet southern Alaska stretch
the imagination about what a river can be.

Another 250 miles west of the Alsek, the Copper River enters the Gulf
of Alaska as another giant of the north crossing the coastal mountains.

One of Alaska's road-accessible rivers, it drains from hundreds of streams in the Wrangell Mountains where waters plunge from Mount Sanford. This volcanic peak looks like a Cascade mountain of Oregon but rises twice as high, 16,237 feet above sea level. The Chitina (CHIT-na), up to a mile wide, is the major Copper tributary. When combined with its tributaries the Nizina and Kennicott, the Chitina offers a wilderness river trip that is rare in Alaska because it can be reached at either end by road. The Gulkana—a Copper tributary to the northwest—flows from the wild country of south central Alaska, attracting sockeye salmon to headwater lakes.

The Matanuska River drains Alaska's only farming valley, northeast of Anchorage, where a short growing season is compensated for by long hours of summer sunshine. North and west of it the Susitna, with its beautiful tributary the Maclaren River, rips down from the Alaska Range and the Talkeetna Mountains. A wide, winding Susitna funnels into raging flows in Devils Canyon, then broadens across bars to enter Cook Inlet west of Anchorage.

The Coast Range tapers down to the ocean southwest of Anchorage, where the clear rivers of the Kenai Peninsula gleam out in satiny flows from inland lakes. The Kenai River, with its gentle waters, may be the most-floated stream in the state.

North of Cook Inlet, the Alaska Range bends southwestward and tracks out to sea, spawning big rivers on the Alaskan Peninsula and short, voluminous flows off the seaward face of the land. The McNeil River, on the western side of Cook Inlet, draws dozens of brown (grizzly) bears that can be watched at close range as they fish for salmon at rapids.

One of the greatest expanses of wild and unpeopled rivers in the world flows in southwestern Alaska. Hundreds of streams in the region's remote mountains and on a 200-mile-wide delta made by the Yukon and Kuskokwim are rarely visited by white people, though native villages appear here and there. While glaciers occupy most of the mountain valleys in southeastern Alaska, and while the Interior and Brooks Range provinces are relatively dry, the southwest breeds rivers without restraint. Some are giants: the Nushagak flows to Bristol Bay, and the Kvichak is known as the world's largest producer of sockeye, or red, salmon. The Aniakchak flows from an active volcanic crater with cinder cones and hot springs in headwaters within a 6-mile-wide caldera. Flanked by 6,000-foot peaks with glacier-sculpted waterfalls and cirques, the Tlikakila flows from the Chigmit Mountains to Lake Clark west of Cook Inlet, the only distraction being constant air traffic on a flight line from Anchorage to the south. Rivers of southwestern Alaska drain from active volcanoes, 60-mile-long lakes, 10,000-foot-high mountains, and wetlands spanning thousands of square miles. Many of the finest remaining salmon rivers in the world wash out to untracked Pacific shores.

Farther north, the Kuskokwim rises only 55 miles from the Tanana River, west of Fairbanks, but flows for 680 miles in a Pacific-bound course paralleling the Yukon, its basin a similar lowland of spruce, bog, tundra, and soggy delta.

The Interior province—encompassing more than half of Alaska—is the kingdom of the Yukon River, whose waters begin in British Columbia only 15 miles from the Pacific but journey 1,980 miles to reach it. Its lower 1,310 miles in Alaska drain 35 percent of the state. This is the longest, least-developed wild river in America and in the world (another logical choice—the Northwest Territory's Mackenzie—has a dirt road near much of it). The Yukon also supports large salmon runs and the longest migrations of these fish. After a low dam on the upper river at Whitehorse and a mountain-bordered descent through the Yukon Territory, the river picks up the forested Fortymile River of east central Alaska. The Yukon then draws in the beautiful clear water of the Charlie National River and enters the Yukon Flats. This 50- by 100-mile bottomland of sloughs is one of the greatest nesting and breeding habitats for waterfowl in North America. The Wild and Scenic Birch and Beaver Creeks join from their headwaters in scenic uplands, which rise 4,000 feet above the interior plain. The river traverses the Yukon Flats National Wildlife Refuge, where the 460-mile Porcupine River enters from the northeast—a historical transportation route draining the vastness of Yukon Territory and the eastern Brooks Range. Below the Pipeline Road in central Alaska, the Yukon cuts through the steep upland of the Ramparts, where a dam was proposed in the 1960s.

The Yukon's principal tributary, the 620-mile Tanana River, flows in from the south via multiple braids southeast of Fairbanks. The Delta River swings through the Alaska Range with a choice section of wild river accessible by roads south of Fairbanks, then joins the Tanana. This river absorbs the Nenana after that large tributary's vigorous push northward, then incorporates other wildlife-rich rivers of Denali National Park: the Toklat, Teklanika, and McKinley. Below the mouth of the Tanana, in lowlands stretching farther than the eye can see, the Nowitna joins the Yukon from the south. One of the most meandering large rivers anywhere, it runs for 140 miles in its lower reaches to cover

Alsek River below confluence with the Tatshenshini River

Susitna River from Denali Hwy.

Copper River below Chitina

Nenana River above Denali National Park

Toklat River in Denali National Park

Clearwater Cr. near Denali Hwy.

Sheenjek River and aufeis

Sheenjek River near Table Mt.

a straight distance of 30 miles. This is America's second-longest National Wild and Scenic River, with 225 of its miles so designated.

The 470-mile Koyukuk, a hefty river with a flow of 14,540 cfs, joins the Yukon after a wilderness journey through the southwestern Brooks Range. Also joining the lower river, the Andreafsky's two branches rate among the Yukon's finest wild streams for king and chum salmon.

Taking stock of the lower Yukon basin, geographer Wallace Atwood reported that the Yukon is "the one great drainage system on the continent where continental ice has not disturbed the orderly sequence of events." Strange as it may seem at our northernmost large river, the continental glaciers did not invade Alaska's Interior province, the mountain glaciers did not overflow into the Yukon valley, and headwaters survived unchanged by the ice-end lakes, altered flowages, and captured streams found in the Columbia, Mississippi, and St. Lawrence basins.

The Yukon finally ends at the Bering Sea, after flowing through one of the few remaining large unspoiled river deltas in the world. One of the greatest concentrations of North American waterfowl nests there. With the Kuskokwim just to its south, the Yukon is one of only three river complexes in America big and silty enough to form substantial deltas in the ocean (the others are the Mississippi-Atchafalaya and the Apalachicola of Florida). Native villages near the Yukon's outlet perch on higher ground surrounded by water, much as the Cajun communities sit along the bayous of Louisiana. But the health of this northern river contrasts markedly with that of the heavily stressed Mississippi.

The Brooks Range province is far drier than southern Alaska but still produces a fine network of rivers flowing either north or south. In the southeastern Brooks Range the Coleen, Sheenjek, and Chandalar drain the highest mountains. To the north the Kongakut, Canning, and others run across the Arctic Coastal Plain to the Beaufort Sea. The Utukok is the principal calving ground of the Arctic caribou herd.

The south central Brooks Range is highlighted by the Koyukuk, including its outstanding North Fork; by the Alatna, with its headwaters at the photogenic Arrigetch Peaks; and by the John River, beneath 6,000-foot summits. All traverse high, barren ground, then widen to spruce-lined ribbons through foothills and tundra. In the southwestern Brooks Range, the Kobuk (15,270 cfs) drains to Kotzebue Sound.

The 350-mile Colville River forms the artery of the north central Brooks Range. By far the largest river on the Arctic Slope, it picks up dozens of north-flowing tributaries and carries them east and north to the Beaufort Sea and the Arctic Ocean. Finally, flowing through mountainous landscapes more than any other Brooks Range river, the Noatak runs west to Kotzebue Sound on the northwestern edge of Alaska, winding for much of its 450 miles with impressive views of high country. The Noatak is the longest river in the National Wild and Scenic Rivers System (330 designated miles) and the most popular stream of the Brooks Range for canoeing. Nearly all the watershed lies within parklands or preserves managed by the National Park Service. The Noatak is one of the largest watersheds in America virtually unaffected by human development, but the same wildness resonates at many of the Alaskan rivers, including the Sheenjek.

The Sheenjek River

The real challenge as I flew above the river was deciding where the pilot should land. He gave me two choices: a gravel bar and a gravel bar. But one lay farther upstream; my reason for going upstream—almost to the Arctic Ocean divide—was that I wanted to hike in the nearby Romanzof Mountains, the highest peaks of the Brooks Range. My reason for landing 10 miles lower was that the river down there carried enough water to float my raft.

I tried to grasp the consequences of each alternative from my speedy vantage point 500 feet above ground. Even in that dry year of 1990, the upper Sheenjek carried enough runoff to float a boat, provided the water all flowed in one channel. But there at its mountain source the river fanned into braids; twenty of them now sieved through the valley's gravel floor. Obviously, I would have inadequate flow for continuous cruising, but could I limp through by walking here and there? By tugging on the raft? By anything short of carrying it?

Only with difficulty did I avoid distractions. The bare limestone peaks of the Brooks Range roughened the skyline as far as I could see to the north, west, and east, not vertical uplifts but blunt, accessible crowns like cones of sifted flour. Double Mountain rose to 7,610 feet above sea level and several thousand feet above the valley, which for the moment appeared bowling-alley flat.

The bush pilot was losing patience, I could tell. "Take the upper one," I said, and on this act of faith favoring adventure over security, we banked, turned 180 degrees between rocky snags, and sank. Only 100 feet below us the river glistened, its braids criss crossing. A gravel bar perhaps 200 yards long lay just ahead. Slower than I had ever imagined it possible to fly, the pilot skillfully homed in on the bar. Then the rocks jumped up to greet us as the plane's fat tundra tires banged and bounced on stones the size of softballs, and we stopped—a successful flight in the Russian roulette of the bush plane. One day later a flaming exhaust system forced my pilot to land on an unknown gravel bar. If he had been carrying then the heavy load he carried with my gear, he might have had a difficult time.

It had taken nearly two hours to reach the upper Sheenjek from Fort Yukon, a bush town at the end of a two-hour flight from Fairbanks. I unloaded camping gear, food for four weeks, and my fourteen-foot raft with oars—quite heavy for such a small plane but the only boat I owned that could be rolled into a bundle. Rigid canoes can be strapped to the pontoons of seaplanes, but the obvious prerequisite is a lake, which I didn't have near the top of the watershed. Besides, safety regulations in the United States prohibit commercial aircraft from carrying passengers along with lashed-on canoes, effectively doubling the air fare.

The pilot flew away but three hours later returned with two of my friends, ferried in from the Indian town of Arctic Village. Jon Miller thus launched his vacation from Ph.D. research at Point Barrow and the University of Alaska, where he studied Arctic birds. Though he was a backcountry skier extraordinaire and savvy in the ways of wilderness, boating was new to him. Lou Brown worked for the Northern Alaska Environmental Center, but I had met her years before, when she worked for the Mono Lake Committee in the Sierra Nevada. Both were old friends, and I yearned to spend time with them again. Jon and Lou shared my enthusiasm for the adventure ahead.

At the door of the plane Jon tugged on the unlikely bag that contained his canoe—a collapsible variety whose aluminum frame and vinyl skin were disassembled and now looked like a squared-off backpack. Lou piled their camping gear alongside a willow shrub, severely stunted by the ten-month winters that predominate 150 miles north of the Arctic Circle. Though less than a hundred miles south of the Arctic Ocean, we would be floating away from it and toward the Porcupine and Yukon Rivers.

This time the pilot flew away for good, and Jon, Lou, and I sat down to plan our future together. We had wanted to hike for a week, but with the water level dropping daily, we decided to shorten our high-country exploration to three days. Then we would embark on the Sheenjek. We allotted three weeks to travel down to the Porcupine River, then down it for 50 miles to the Yukon. The entire distance lay in wilderness; only two log cabins appeared in 380 miles. The entire trip also lay within the Arctic National Wildlife Refuge and the Yukon Flats National Wildlife Refuge.

Our hikes in the Brooks Range took us across the tussock-covered tundra that lies just beyond the gravel bars, up steep slopes of wild-flowers and talus, and onto ridges and peaks. By myself one day, I belly-crawled to sneak up on caribou that grazed just beyond the ridge-line while the wind blew stiffly in my direction and hid my scent. I climbed up scree slopes of pure slate—broken daggers eighteen inches long and one inch square. From a peak 2,000 feet above camp I gazed across the Arctic divide to the Kongakut River's headwaters as they cut northward toward the Arctic Ocean. The salient feature was rocks; veg-etation consisted of little but lichen, which is what caribou eat. A golden eagle soared below me. I looked down the Sheenjek valley to the lacework of braids, silvery in the afternoon sun, and beyond to five sections of aufeis, or overflow ice.

In this broad, gently sloped valley, shallow water freezes solid to the riverbed in winter, forcing incoming water to flow over the top of the anchor ice. Then more water freezes, forcing the inflow to the edges, and higher, over additional ice. The final effect is a valley half a mile wide coated with a twelve-foot-deep pack of aufeis that never com-pletely melts. From the altitude and speed of the airplane it appeared that the river had cut channels through all five ice blocks.

The next day we rigged our boats and, with great anticipation, began floating. Jon and Lou's canoe slipped through narrow, shallow chan-nels; my raft bogged down on gravel. The water, too shallow for oars, was nonetheless swift, so I kneeled on the rear tube, sometimes strok-ing with a canoe paddle and sometimes kicking my way along as if on a scooter. I hopped off to push or pull over the shallows. With wet, rounded river stones serving as ball bearings of a sort, few of the rocky bars required great effort, though I jumped off thirty or forty times that first afternoon. Wet suit booties kept my feet nominally warm.

The temperature dropped when we entered the first field of aufeis. The river had melted through the solid sheet that still blanketed half the valley. More precisely, the river had *tunneled* through the ice pack, and then the ice overhead had caved in and later washed away to open the river's channel. Undeterred, the Sheenjek had snaked left and right, and walls of ice on either side had grown to be six feet tall, leaving us in a miniature canyon. Then the walls grew closer together. Then the bends became tighter, the current swifter, the future less certain.

Fascinated, but wary of this new sport I called "ice-canyon boating," I rounded a sharp bend to find that the ice up ahead blocked my path completely. The river ran directly under it, leaving a six-inch air space between the riffled surface of the water and the bluish turquoise chill of the ice pack. If swept up against the ice I'd be stuck, and if swept under it I wouldn't have a sporting chance of coming out the other end. None of this really registered at the time, but what I did know immediately was that I had to get out of there. In a current too swift to row against, I jumped off the raft and held it against the flow in thigh-deep water. During this consequential moment in life, I didn't want to slip. Jon and Lou eddied out up above, where they could get to shore at a melted refuge with an exposed bed of gravel. Seeking firm footing, I ferried the boat to the right side and into shallower water, then pulled it upstream to the shelter of the gravel bar, but not without noticing the ominous wall of ice, sections of which were prone to calving away.

Though it would not get dark that far north on August 5, we had a long carry ahead of us and decided to camp on the claustrophobic gravel bar, encircled by ice. We planned to portage the aufeis in the morning—we would have to carry our gear a full 300 yards before the river reemerged from its gloomy passage underneath. While we ate dinner, ice broke with the sound of a shotgun blast. A section of the bridge promptly slumped over the river, its bottom dragging in the current. The blasts continued, and once in a while I heard splashes as well.

Concerned that a cave-in down below might dam the river and flood our site, I obsessively stored my gear in the raft and slept beside it. Lacking the security my houseboat afforded me, Lou and Jon spent a cold night on the ice, avoiding the bridged portion over the river.

The ice rumbled and boomed and cracked all night. Arising in the morning, we found that the entire blockage had disappeared! The river channel lay wide open. We floated effortlessly through and considered our lives carefree.

With the shallow braids also behind us, we decided to linger again before leaving the high mountain country. Arctic loons landed in the eddy at our camp; merlins zipped through the sky up above. Tracks showed that a wolverine had ambled across the sand bar. Prints of moose, grizzly bears, and wolves decorated the mud and sand here and almost everywhere we stopped. Yet we never saw any of those animals. For a day we hiked to peaks above the river and felt that the whole world lay beneath us; the mountains, plains, and rivers of a continent shaped the great geography below.

The next day, near Table Mountain, we beached and climbed a hilltop for more perspective on the Sheenjek, now a substantial stream winding in S bends out of the Brooks Range. We picked cranberries and later dumped the delicious red fruit into muffin batter.

Disturbed that we weren't making as much downriver progress as I had expected, I took some time the following evening to unfold the topographical maps and scale the miles of the radically meandering river. I found that our mileage estimate—taken from a now-forgotten source—was wrong. Our trip would be 80 miles longer than we had expected! Jon and Lou were not concerned; they had packed extra food in case we decided to go down the Yukon River for an extra week to the pipeline road. In that event I had planned on buying food at Fort Yukon, where we would enter the Yukon River. Jon and Lou said they would share their extra food with me. Together we could buy provisions at Fort Yukon.

The following days brought lingering, cool drizzle, lively Class II rapids, and a river channel exiting the mountains and entering a long reach of swift water over gravel bars. Black spruce were common among the tundra of huckleberries, cranberries, grasses, and sedges. Our clear river had become silty with bank erosion, but now it became clear again, perhaps due to the water's filtering through the coarse gravel and cobblestone bars that lay everywhere. The Sheenjek was one of few undammed rivers I've seen become clearer as I advanced downstream.

At out next camp, a pair of caribou kicked up water with their hooves when they crossed the river. Claw-tipped, fifteen-inch-long grizzly tracks still greeted us on beaches, and I toted my twelve-gauge double-barreled shotgun loaded with slugs when bushwhacking away from the river. Mosquitoes and flies troubled us so little that we wore head nets only a few times. That late in a dry year the bugs, whose biomass surely exceeds that of all the caribou in the north, posed little problem. The huckleberries and cottonwoods had turned to autumn's red and gold. Along with a few rubber-boot tracks of boaters who had gone downriver before us, an airplane droning overhead every other day or so was the only evidence of people at the upper river. The outside world seemed distant, remote, a thing of the past—a lesser reality to what we now knew.

On day ten we spotted an incongruous hand-lettered sign that said, "Tame black wolf in area, don't shoot." Soon another sign announced the Haydens' camp: "Stop for coffee." As we pulled onto shore, three young Indians rushed up to greet us. "Hi; my name is Daniel." "I'm Richard." "I'm Susan." These three teenagers were as curious about our trip as we were about their fascinating life along the Sheenjek. Soon

Shannon, their mother, arrived carrying baby Judy, with Richard Senior carrying two-year-old Duane. I had to look twice at Richard before chuckling. He wore a Halloween wig of long black hair—this Minnesota native's nutty gesture at fitting in with the rest of his family, who all displayed such handsome Indian features.

"Come on up to the cabin," Richard and Shannon said, and, beaming, we accepted their invitation. We walked past twenty-two sled dogs, including several wolf-dog crosses with wild yellow eyes, each chained to a dog house, as we approached the Haydens' fourteen-foot-square summer cabin.

Richard Hayden had left Minnesota at the age of eighteen to become a fur trapper in Alaska. In 1969 he met Shannon, a Tlingit Indian living in Yukon Territory, and the two had moved to this wilderness to begin their family away from the roads, people, and development they had seen elsewhere. Three hours flew by while we talked about the 120 miles of trapline the family maintains by dogsled, the homemade parkas they sew, the long months alone, the hunger that comes in a lean winter, the correspondence courses the children take, the bush planes, which usually provide sole contact with the outside, and the dog food that is the family's big cash expense. Two dozen caribou per year constitute the family's primary food source. We accepted some dried caribou meat and set off again downstream, feeling fortunate to have met this family living at a subsistence level, the way everybody once lived.

The darkness of autumn had crept up on us; nighttime, which had scarcely existed when the trip began, arrived six minutes sooner each day. Sitting up late, we now saw the northern lights tracing a smoky bouquet of flowers into the sky, their white petals peeling off a core of turbulence, then dripping into a curtain of shimmering light.

We had entered the Yukon Flats National Wildlife Refuge, where birch and aspen grew on occasional dry slopes, white spruce clung to riverbanks, and black spruce reigned as the climax forest. We climbed the last bluff of the Brooks Range foothills and gazed out over the horizonwide flats to the south—a view of the Interior province of Alaska. Wetlands puddled the tundra as far as we could see.

On day thirteen we came to a sign marking Bill Russell's cabin, a stop we didn't want to miss. Back through the trees we found a log home inhabited by sixty-three-year-old Bill, a graying, crew-cut man who had lived there off and on for forty years. "Come on in," he barked. We entered the overheated cabin, today a bakery of homemade bread. For some years, Bill had left seasonally to work on the North Slope pipeline, where he made good money as a mechanic fixing anything that broke. Part of each year he stayed in Fairbanks, where his wife and a grown child live. Given Bill's sarcasm about current conservation initiatives—the wildlife refuges, endangered species protection, and other measures Lou worked on at the Northern Alaska Environmental Center, our conversation had its limits. But we chatted about other things. Our hospitable host served up homemade bread and later led us down to the logjam.

Just below Bill's cabin, low flows had left the preferred channel of the Sheenjek bone dry. Driftwood had congested the alternate channel, where only one jet of water made it through by taking a sharp right turn amid splintered snags of timber. With difficulty and the help of our burly host, we lugged our gear and then the fully inflated raft over 200 feet of hellish crisscrossed timber, the whole collaboration requiring two hours.

While we sat in camp the next morning, an Indian and a white man piloting a flat-bottomed boat upriver spotted us and cut the motor to ask if we wanted a beer. They were headed north to hunt moose.

An hour later a red fuel can came bobbing down in the current. Jon and I looked curiously at it, then paddled out and retrieved it. Knowing something was up, we all canoed a mile upstream and found the Indian, the white man, and Bill Russell standing in the tangled undergrowth alongside the log jam and tugging on a flexible cable. They had somehow attached the other end to the hunters' motorboat, though only one silvery shine of it was visible under three feet of water; the current had thoroughly crammed the boat into the logjam. With a short rope, Bill anchored his chain saw to a tree, threaded the cable onto a winch on the saw, and yanked the starter cord. I retreated to watch from behind a cottonwood in case the cable were to snap. It grew taut as a piano wire, the saw whined and hesitated, and then the boat budged. Its aluminum hull partly slid and partly bent around the log holding it in place but then slithered clear, the winch pulling the boat's dented body across the current to where the rest of us could get our hands on it and lug it ashore.

Back at camp we packed up and headed downstream again. The gradient was lower in this section, and we drifted in long meanders that took us farther back and forth than forward, as if we were floating on diagrams of sound waves. The only way I knew where we were was by watching a compass; one bend in the complex was aligned to the northwest, and when we pointed in that direction I spotted our location on the map. Three times a motorboat hummed near, then receded as the meanders of the river alternately brought it closer, then farther away. Finally our routes converged, and I spoke to the boaters, an Indian family bound upriver. "There's a big bear here," one of them said without expression.

"Where?"

"We saw it right here."

I think they were pulling my leg. "Those bears are everywhere," I acknowledged. They chuckled and motored on.

Here on the lower Sheenjek the willows were just beginning to brighten into autumn yellow. The fireweed had turned red, and edible rose hips hung on spiny twigs, the fruit of the harvest season. But then the raspy edge of autumn arrived with an angry sky and a windy day of rain, which we sat out. After the beebee shots of rain had stopped peppering my tent, I looked for fresh tracks. Moose, wolves, and a bear had all roamed the sandbars behind our tents.

The next day blustery headwinds brought puffy clouds and made rowing a chore. During intervals of calm I could see three-foot-long chum salmon migrating upriver, their shadows darting in the pools. Another week or two would surely bring grizzly bears, drawn to the riverbanks to gorge on the spawned-out salmon. The wind subsided and we hooked some fine-tasting Arctic grayling, imagining how fragile their population must be and how easily overfished the river could become when a lot more people begin to visit. It raised a good question: Do people like us belong there at all?

While we sat together at dinner that night, reveling in the wonder of everything we had seen, Jon calmly reported, "There's a fox behind you." Cavorting silently, the little creature galloped in light-footed leaps all the way around our camp, stopping to look at us once in a while. Returning to the raft, the red fox teased the slack bow line of the boat, batting it with a paw as a house cat might do. It walked straight toward us and stared with shining eyes. Then it ran down the gravel bar, took a sip of water, and glanced back at us one last time. Finally it waded into the river and swam across.

On day eighteen we reached the tan Porcupine River, said good-by to the sweet Sheenjek, and entered the larger flow. Just below the confluence, a wind-blasted gravel bar extended upriver and downriver for a mile and shoreward 300 feet, all of it carpeted in cobbles. While strolling there I spotted an oddly textured rock. I picked it up. Like all the other rocks, it was the size of my fist, but its flattened surface showed divots, as if a handful of human molars had been welded together. Ivorylike enamel swirled throughout. Enamel covered the sides, fluted in wavy roughness. Jon knew what it was: the tooth of a mammoth that had populated the north when the continental glaciers receded.

A long, weary day on the Porcupine took us to an island, where we camped amid driftwood debris. Unexpected visitors–two Athapaskan Indian men—arrived in a flat-bottomed motorboat. They already knew about us. "I hear you guys helped out my brother," one said, referring to the incident at the logjam. A trim, handsome young man with raven-black hair, Clifton seemed friendly, and the older, crooked-toothed "Uncle Eddie" was especially talkative.

"Help yourselves to our fire," I offered.

"Tell you what," Clifton said. "I'll fix you guys a good meal."

The menu was salmon and potatoes. The salmon was whole, uncleaned, and frozen solid as a brick. Clifton cut it into sections about two inches thick and put everything in a boiling pot. "You eat only the meat," he cautioned. I wondered about the safety of picking around the intestines—in fact, I probably didn't question it enough—but I didn't want to snub this generosity, and I reasoned that if the Indians and their families prepared fish this way, they must not get sick from it.

After dinner we sat and talked awhile, and then Clifton asked, "You guys mind if we sleep here?" Jon and Lou soon went off to camp. Clifton said, "I'll tell you something. I like talking with you. I fixed a good meal for you guys, so you sit down and have a beer with me, okay?"

We talked about Fort Yukon. It had never been an Indian settlement in the old days, only a trading post of the Hudson's Bay Company, which established a troubling legacy that continues today. I had already heard that outlying Indian villages, not allowing alcohol, expel their incorrigibles to Fort Yukon, where they begin families of their own. For years family difficulties there were aggravated by irresponsible U.S. Air Force men stationed nearby at the local DEW line base and who left behind half-white babies with single Indian mothers. "There are still good people at Fort Yukon, but a lot of them drink," Clifton said of his hometown.

After a pause, he gestured to our boats. "Tell me, why do you do this?"

The Indians' trip upriver was to cut wood. Clifton has always lived along the river; it was his highway, his food source, his home. How would he understand our fascination? Why *was* I doing this?

"It's a great river. It's full of life. It flows through a country that's different from what I'm used to. It gives me a way to see this place. By traveling down this river, for just a little while, we can be a part of this place. I love rivers and all they stand for. Life is short, and getting to see the Sheenjek is one of the pleasures of living. Though I don't stay here, all the rivers seem like home to me."

"Yes," Clifton said.

He popped open another beer. "I really love my wife, and we want to move back upriver with our kids. That's where I grew up. When we go up there, there's no alcohol. We trap and hunt."

"What a way to live," I said. "It sounds perfect."

"It is."

Against the protests of Clifton and Uncle Eddie, who had another six-pack to go, I left for my tent.

The final day on the Porcupine tested our ability to keep warm. I wore most of my clothes, with rain gear on top, but the dirty, sweaty dampness of it all made it even harder to fight the cold. Windy and cloudy, a temperamental autumn had arrived in earnest. Jon and Lou had been sharing their food with me for several days, and it was running low. I had a cube of shredded wheat, a slice of cheese, and some dried fruit for lunch on the river. We planned to finish the trip that day.

Our preferred takeout, a tiny creek called the Sucker River, lay 4 miles upriver from Fort Yukon, but we didn't know what it looked like. My map showed a cabin near its mouth, but we never saw it, so we kept going.

A stiff headwind thickened to a gale, throwing whitecaps upstream and stopping me dead. For half a mile I got out and waded knee-deep in the cold river, tugging the raft downstream with taut line digging into my shoulder. Lou got out of her canoe and helped by pushing. Jon managed to wrestle his streamlined boat into the wind. Concerned that we might miss the uppermost slough that exits to the Yukon, we hugged the left shore in a stinging rain. Missing the slough would mean joining the Yukon some miles below, creating epic difficulties in getting back up the swift, oceanic river and into town.

Rounding the Porcupine's final bend we were confronted by brown in-rushing currents; the Porcupine was so low that its slough, which I had expected to flow out to the Yukon, flowed *in*. The roily current was too much to row or paddle against, so we pulled the boats by rope along the muddy bank.

I struggled with the raft while rain beat down and the wind smeared moisture into my jacket. Drops splattering against my face dripped down my neck, and soon my shoulders felt the dampness of leaking seams. Negotiating a five-foot-high, crumbling mudbank above the swift current, I pulled on the raft's bow line, then had to climb onto a log overhanging the angry current to coax the lummoxing raft out around the snag. When Lou got a rubber boot stuck in twelve inches of mud and pulled her wool-socked foot loose, we all broke down in laughter. Pulling on the boats, we expended great energy, but somehow the experience itself was energizing, essential, vital, final. Then, I boated across a swift but small slough with some frenzied rowing, Jon and Lou followed, and we settled in on the tip of a peninsula where Indians occupy a fishing camp for part of the year. The spot offered trail access to Fort Yukon, two miles back upstream on the banks of the great river.

The next day I walked into town and, as an anticlimax to a thirty-three-day trip, hired David Arnold at the Sourdough Hotel to motor his flat-bottomed freight boat down to the mouth of the Porcupine slough to pick us up. He said he had to borrow a motor and thought he'd be there by one o'clock.

Waiting back at camp, I stared out across the Yukon, remembering the gravel-bottomed stream where we had started. Safe from the barbs of civilization, the Sheenjek, with all its snowmelt, in every summer, will flow again. And here the Yukon River could have been the Mississippi in the year 1750, with all its unchanged wildness. I was in a time machine for the great rivers of America; I had returned to what those lifelines once were. I gazed in wonder across the mile-wide water running strong, without a blemish, as all the rivers of America once flowed.

Appendix 1

The Largest Rivers in America

River	Location at Mouth	Average Volume at Mouth (cfs)	Length[a] (mi.)	Watershed Area (sq. mi.)
Mississippi	LA	593,000	2,340	1,150,000
St. Lawrence	Canada	348,000	1,900	396,000
Ohio	IL, KY	281,000	1,310	203,000
Columbia	WA	265,000	1,240	258,000
Yukon	AK	225,000	1,980	328,000
Missouri	MO	76,200	2,540	529,000
Tennessee	KY	68,000	886	40,900
Mobile	AL	67,200	774	44,600
Kuskokwim	AK	67,000	724	48,000
Copper	AK	59,000	286	24,400
Atchafalaya	LA	58,000	140[b]	95,100[c]
Snake	WA	56,900	1,040	108,000

(*Continues*)

River	Location at Mouth	Average Volume at Mouth (cfs)	Length[a] (mi.)	Watershed Area (sq. mi.)
Stikine	AK	56,000	379	20,000
Red	LA	56,000	1,290	93,200
Susitna	AK	51,000	313	20,000
Tanana	AK	41,000	659	44,500
Arkansas	AR	41,000	1,460	161,000
Susquehanna	MD	38,200	447	27,200
Willamette	OR	37,400	309	11,400
Nushagak	AK	36,000	285	13,400

[a]Including headwaters and sections in Canada.
[b]Below Mississippi diversion, without headwaters.
[c]Includes western tributaries but not the Mississippi.

Source: U.S. Geological Survey, *Water Fact Sheet: Largest Rivers in the United States* (Reston, Va.: U.S. Geological Survey, 1990).

Appendix 2

Long, Undammed Sections of Rivers

River	Location	Free-Flowing Mileage	Comments
Northeast Region			
St. John	ME	200	
Aroostook	ME	126	
Mattawamkeag	ME	110	Entire river
Hudson	NY	108	
Appalachian Region			
E. Br. Delaware/ Delaware	PA, NY	340	Entire main stem with 96 mi. tidewater
Licking	KY	316	
Clinch	VA, TN	230	
Susquehanna	NY, PA	221	

(Continues)

River	Location	Free-Flowing Mileage	Comments
Green	KY	208	
Rappahannock	VA	207	Includes 115 mi. tidewater
S. Br. Potomac/ Potomac	WV, VA, MD	202	
Laurel Fk./N. Fk. S. Br. Potomac/ S. Br. Potomac/ Potomac	WV, VA, MD	198	Entire 53 mi. of N. Fk. S. Br.
Flint	GA	197	
N. Fk. Holston	VA, TN	193	
S. Fk. S. Br. Potomac/ Potomac	WV, VA, MD	193	Entire 66 mi. of S. Fk. S. Br.
W. Fk. Greenbrier/ Greenbrier	WV	171	Entire river
Powell	VA, TN	170	
James	VA	143	
Allegheny	PA	135	
Yadkin	NC	135	
Sequatchie	TN	120	Entire river except mouth
Lost/Cacapon	WV	109	
Juniata	PA	107	
S. Fk. New	NC	101	Entire S. Fk.
Green	KY	101	
Coastal Plain Region[a]			
Mississippi	MO through LA	1,000	Entire reach bordered by levees
Brazos (lower)	TX	498	See Great Plains for other reaches
Ocmulgee/Altamaha	GA	416	Entire 154 mi. of Altamaha
Chickasawhay/ Pascagoula	MS	386	

Alapaha/Suwannee	GA, FL	341	Entire 205 mi. of Alapaha
Big Black	MS	340	Entire river
St. Johns	FL	325	Entire river
Pearl	LA, MI	303	
Oconee/Altamaha	GA	300	Entire 154 mi. of Altamaha
Downing Cr./ Lumber/Little Pee Dee/Pee Dee	NC, SC	290	
Cypress Cr./ Withlacoochee/ Suwannee	GA, FL	269	Entire 141 mi. of Withlacoochee system
Sabine (upper)	TX	264	
Suwannee	GA, FL	250	
Lynches/Pee Dee	SC	252	
Neches	TX	250	
Satilla	GA	242	Entire river
S. Fk. Edisto/ Edisto	SC	223	Entire river
Neuse	NC	223	
Pee Dee	SC	214	
Sabine (lower)	TX	189	
Black	SC	185	
Savannah	GA	170	Entire reach is tidal
Waccamaw	SC	164	Entire river, most is tidal
Hatchie	TN	163	
Ouachita	AR	160	
Roanoke	NC	155	
Flint	GA	153	
Withlacoochee (south)	FL	135	
Choctawhatchee	AL, FL	120	
Apalachicola	FL	120	
St. Marys	FL, GA	120	
Pearl (upper)	MI	116	

(Continues)

River	Location	Free-Flowing Mileage	Comments
Strawberry	AR	109	
James (lower)	VA	106	
Northeast Cape Fear	NC	103	
Midwest Region			
Gasconade	MO	336	Entire river
Duck	TN	275	
Bowstring/Big Fk./Rainy	MN	265	Entire Bowstring/Big Fk.
Minnesota	MN	240	
Little Fk./Rainy	MN	214	Entire Little Fk.
Red Lake	MN	190	
Turkey	IA	161	
Wapsipinicon (lower)	IA	158	
Buffalo	AR	148	Entire river
Buffalo	TN	147	Entire river
Current	MO	139	
Wapsipinicon (upper)	IA	135	
Harpeth	TN	102	
Great Plains Region[b]			
N. Fk. S. Loup/ S. Loup/M. Loup/ Loup/Platte/ Missouri	NE, KA, MO	996	Includes 280 mi. of Loup system; Missouri R. is channelized
Elkhorn/ Platte/Missouri	NE, KA, MO	915	Entire 273 mi. of Elkhorn
M. Loup (lower)/ Loup/Platte/ Missouri	NE, KS, MO	910	Includes 194 mi. of M. Loup/Loup
Platte/Missouri	NE, KA, MO	852	Includes 243 mi. of Platte
N. Loup/Loup/ Platte/Missouri	NE, KA, MO	835	Includes 119 mi. of N. Loup/Loup
Missouri	NE, KS, MO	654	Entire reach is channelized

White	NE, SD	646	Includes diversions
Little Missouri	WY, MT, SD, ND	560	Includes diversions
Cimarron	KS, OK	485	Includes diversions
Powder	WY, MT	385	Includes diversions
Musselshell	MT	314	Includes diversions
North Canadian	OK	307	Includes diversions
James	SD	232	Includes diversions
Brazos (middle)	TX	213	See Coastal Plain region for other reach
Cheyenne	SD	206	Includes diversions
Canadian (upper)	NM	206	Includes diversions
Niobrara (upper)	NE	203	From Box Butte Dam to Cornell Reservoir
Brazos (upper)	TX	202	Includes diversions
N. Loup (upper)	NE	189	
Canadian (middle)	TX	167	Includes diversions
Tongue	MT	163	
Missouri (upper)	MT	149	
M. Br. Loup/ M. Loup	NE	146	
Pecos	NM	140	Includes diversions
Milk	MT	127	Only diversion dams on a 390-mi. reach
Canadian (lower)	OK	124	Includes diversions
Niobrara (lower)	NE	121	From Cornell Dam to Spencer Reservoir
N. Fk. Dismal/ Dismal/M. Loup	NE	119	

Rocky Mountain Region
(See Elk, Little Snake, Yampa, and Williams Fk. Yampa in Desert region.)

Salmon/Snake	ID, OR, WA	446	Entire 406 mi. of Salmon
Yellowstone	MT	360	Only low dams for entire 700 mi.

(*Continues*)

River	Location	Free-Flowing Mileage	Comments
Yampa	CO	205	See Desert region for further mileage
Selway/ Clearwater	ID	203	Entire 103 mi. of Selway
Brushy Fk./ Lochsa/Clearwater	ID	186	Entire 86 mi. of Lochsa
N. Fk. Flathead/ Flathead	MT	173	Entire 118 mi. of N. Fk.
Trail Cr./M. Fk. Flathead/ Flathead	MT	142	
Colorado	CO	120	
Animas	CO, NM	110	Entire river
St. Joe	ID	110	Entire river
Desert Region			
Trail Cr./N. Fk. Elk/Elk/Yampa/ Green/Colorado	CO, UT	587	Includes Rocky Mountain region
Silver City Cr./ M. Fk. Little Snake/ Little Snake/Yampa/ Green/Colorado	WY, CO, UT	554	May include diversion dams Includes Rocky Mountain Region
Yampa/Green/ Colorado	CO, UT	547	Includes Rocky Mountain region
Bunker Cr./E. Fk. Williams Fk./ Williams Fk./ Yampa/Green/ Colorado	CO, UT	541	Includes Rocky Mountain region
Green	CO, UT	407	
White/Green/ Colorado	CO, UT	356	
Dolores/ Colorado	CO, UT	309	Includes 187 mi. of the Dolores
Rio Grande	TX	309	Excludes dried-up reaches
Little Colorado	AZ	289	

Colorado	AZ	275	Glen Canyon Dam to Lake Mead
Colorado (upper)	CO, UT	263	
Gila	NM	255	Includes diversions
San Juan	NM, UT	255	
N. Fk. John Day/ John Day	OR	252	Entire 95 mi. of N. Fk.
John Day	OR	243	Entire river except lower 12 mi.
S. Fk. John Day/ John Day	OR	229	Entire 48 mi. of S. Fk.
M. Fk. John Day/ John Day	OR	211	Entire 54 mi. of of M. Fk.
Grande Ronde	OR	192	Entire river
Owyhee	ID, OR	163	
E. Fk. Virgin/ Virgin	UT	134	
Bruneau	ID	121	
Black	AZ	113	
San Rafael	UT	110	
San Francisco	AZ	104	
Sierra Nevada Region			
Sacramento	CA	380	Includes 83 tidal mi.
M. Fk. Feather	CA	84	
N. Fk. Kern	CA	81	
S. Fk. Kings/ Kings	CA	59	
Northwest Region			
Castle Rock Fk./ S. Fk. Umpqua/ Umpqua	OR	223	Entire S. Fk. and entire 113 mi. of main stem
Klamath	CA	188	
Coast Fk./ Willamette	OR	169	To Oregon City dam backwater
Rattlesnake Cr./ M. Fk. Eel/Eel	CA	167	Entire M. Fk. Eel
Eel	CA	157	

(Continues)

River	Location	Free-Flowing Mileage	Comments
N. Fk. Umpqua/ Umpqua	OR	119	
Rogue	OR	113	
Trinity	CA	111	
Skagit	WA	100	
Alaska Region[c]			
Yukon	AK	1,947	From Whitehorse to mouth
Kuskokwim	AK	724	
Tanana	AK	659	
Stikine	Can., AK	379	
Susitna	AK	313	
Copper	AK	286	
Nushagak	AK	285	

[a]Many reaches in the Coastal Plain region are tidal, making dams unfeasible.
[b]Many of these reaches are undammed because of diversions and inadequate flows.
[c]Many other rivers and river combinations in Alaska are 100 to 1,000 miles long.

Note: Mileages are approximate as measured from DeLorme atlases or on U.S. Geological Survey maps at 7½ minute, 1:100,000, and 1:250,000 scales. Very low dams or weirs may exist on some of the rivers, but where known, even low dams are considered as dams. Comments indicate where an entire river is free-flowing; other mileages represent a section of the river. Combinations of rivers listed in the left column indicate uninterrupted stretches without dams.

Appendix 3

Rivers Canoed or Rafted by the Author

Northeast
Allagash, ME
Machias, ME
Penobscot, ME
Penobscot, E. Br., ME
Penobscot, W. Br., ME
Pomperaug, CT
Saranac, NY
Union, W. Br., ME

Appalachians
Allegheny, PA
Babb Cr., PA
Beaver, PA
Cacapon, WV
Casselman, PA
Cheat, WV

Clarion, PA
Codorus Cr., PA
Connoquenessing, PA
Cowpasture, VA
Cumberland, KY
Delaware, NY, NJ, PA
Delaware, E. Br., NY
Four Mile Run, PA
French Broad, NC
Gauley, WV
Green, NC
Greenbrier, WV
Gunpowder Falls, MD
Haw, NC
James, VA
Juniata, PA
Kettle Cr., PA
Licking, KY

Little Beaver, OH
Little Pine Cr., PA
Lost, WV
Loyalhanna, PA
Loyalsock, PA
Lycoming, PA
Mahoning, PA
Marsh Cr., PA
Monongahela, PA
Mormons, VA
Moshannon, PA
Muncy Cr., PA
Neuse, NC
New, VA, WV
New, S. Fk., NC
Ohio, PA
Patapsco, MD
Patuxent, MD

Penns Cr., PA
Pine Cr., PA
Potomac, WV, MD, VA, DC
Potomac, N. Br., WV, MD
Raccoon Cr., PA
Red, N. Fk., KY
Rivanna, VA
Roanoke, VA
Shenandoah, VA
Shenandoah, S. Br., VA
Sinnemahoning, PA
Sinnemahoning, Drift-wood Br., PA
Slippery Rock Cr., PA
Susquehanna, PA
Susquehanna, W. Br., PA
Tococsin Cr., MD
Tionesta Cr., PA
Youghiogheny, MD, PA

Coastal Plain
Ashepoo, SC
Atchafalaya, LA
Chipola, FL
Escatawpa, AL, MS
Everglades, FL
Neches, TX
Oklawaha, FL
Pithlachascotee, FL
Sabine, LA, TX
San Marcos, TX
Silver, FL
Suwannee, FL
Tangipahoa, LA
Trinity, TX
Withlacoochee, FL

Midwest
Bois Brule, WI
Current, MO

Eleven Point, MO
Jacks Fork, MO
Meramec, MO
Minnesota, MN
Mississippi, MN, WI
Namekagon, WI
St. Croix, MN, WI

Great Plains
Marias, MT
Missouri, MT
Niobrara, NE
Yellowstone, MT

Rocky Mountains
Animas, CO
Bear, UT
Bear Valley Cr., ID
Bitterroot, MT
Blackfoot, MT
Boise, ID
Boise, M. Fk., ID
Boise, N. Fk., ID
Boise, S. Fk., ID
Buffalo Fk., WY
Cache la Poudre, CO
Coeur d'Alene, ID
Dolores, W. Fk., CO
Elk, CO
Encampment, WY
Flathead, MT
Flathead, M. Fk., MT
Flathead, N. Fk., MT
Gallatin, MT
Granite Cr., WY
Green, WY
Gros Ventre, WY
Gunnison, CO
Henrys Fork, ID
Hoback, WY
Kootenai, MT, ID
Little Snake, CO
Lochsa, ID
Platte, N. Fk., CO
Payette, ID

Payette, S. Fk., ID
Priest, ID
Rio Grande, CO
Rio Grande, S. Fk., CO
Roaring Fk., CO
Salmon, ID
Salmon, E. Fk., ID
Salmon, M. Fk., ID
Salt, WY
St. Joe, ID
San Miguel, CO
San Miguel, S. Fk., CO
Selway, ID
Smith, MT
Snake, WY, ID
Taylor, CO
White, S. Fk., CO
Wood, ID
Yampa, CO
Yellowstone, MT

Desert
Colorado, CO, UT, AZ
Columbia, WA
Deschutes, OR
Dolores, CO, UT
Grande Ronde, OR
Green, UT
Imnaha, OR
Owens, CA
Rio Grande, TX
San Juan, UT
Snake, ID, OR, WA
Spokane, WA
Wallowa, OR
White, CO, UT
Yampa, CO

Sierra Nevada
American, CA
American, N. Fk., CA
American, S. Fk., CA
Carson, E. Fk., CA

Carson, W. Fk., CA
Cosumnes, CA
Feather, CA
Feather, M. Fk., CA
Feather, N. Fk., E. Br.,
  CA
Kaweah, CA
Kern, N. Fk., CA
Kings, CA
Merced, CA
Mokelumne, CA
Sacramento, CA
San Joaquin, CA
Stanislaus, CA
Truckee, CA
Tuolumne, CA
Woods Cr., CA
Yuba, CA

Northwest
Alsea, OR
Beckler, WA
Big, CA
Cache Cr., CA
Chetco, OR
Clackamas, OR
Dosewallips, WA
Eel, CA
Eel, M. Fk., CA
Eel, S. Fk., CA
Elwha, WA
Hoh, WA
Humptulips, WA
Illinois, OR
Klamath, CA

Klickitat, WA
Mad, CA
Methow, WA
Nooksack, WA
Nooksack, S. Fk., WA
Noyo, CA
Redwood Cr., CA
Rogue, OR
Russian, CA
Salmon, CA
Sandy, OR
Santiam, North, OR
Sauk, WA
Skagit, WA
Skykomish, WA
Smith, CA
Smith, S. Fk., CA
Snoqualmie, WA
Snoqualmie, M. Fk., WA
Tolt, WA
Trinity, CA
Trinity, S. Fk., CA
Umpqua, OR
Umpqua, N. Fk., OR
Willamette, OR

Alaska
Alsek
Chilkat
Chitina
Clearwater Cr.
Copper
Delta
Fortymile
Gulkana

Kennicott
Nizina
Porcupine
Sheenjek
Stikine
Yukon

Canada
Athabasca, AB
Babine, BC
Bulkley, BC
Columbia, BC
Elk, BC
Fraser, BC
Illecillewaet, BC
Kicking Horse, BC
Kootenay, BC
Maligne, AB
Michipicoten, ON
Nadahini, YT
Salmo, BC
Saskatchewan, N. Fk.,
  AB
Skeena, BC
Slocan, BC
Stikine, BC
Sunwapta, AB
Susqua, BC
Tatshenshini, BC
Telkwa, BC
Teslin, YT
Whirlpool, AB
Yukon, YT

Sources

Introduction

The following are some of the important sources for the introduction and general sources for *America by Rivers*.

American Rivers. *Outstanding Rivers List*. Washington, D.C.: American Rivers, 1991.

Atwood, Wallace W. *The Physiographic Provinces of North America*. New York: Ginn, 1940.

BioScience. Entire issue on Ecology of Large Rivers. March 1995.

Birdsall, Stephen S., and John W. Florin. *Regional Landscapes of the United States and Canada*. New York: Wiley, 1978.

Bolling, David M. *How to Save a River*. Washington, D.C.: Island Press, 1994.

Cassady, Jim, Bill Cross, and Fryar Calhoun. *Western Whitewater*. Berkeley, Calif.: North Fork Press, 1994.

Collins, Robert O., and Roderick Nash. *The Big Drops*. San Francisco: Sierra Club Books, 1978.

Conzen, Michael P., ed. *The Making of the American Landscape*. Boston: Unwin Hyman, 1990.

De Blij, H. J., and Peter O. Muller. *Geography Regions and Concepts.* New York: Wiley, 1992.

Fenneman, N. M. "Physiographic Divisions of the United States." *Annals of the Association of American Geographers* 18 (1928): 261–353.

Hall, Bob, and Mary Lee Kerr. *Green Index.* Washington, D.C.: Island Press, 1991.

Leopold, Luna. *The View of the River.* Cambridge, Mass: Harvard University Press, 1994.

Lewis, Peirce. "America's Natural Landscapes." In *Making America,* ed. Luther S. Luedtke. Chapel Hill, NC: University of North Carolina Press, 1992.

Lobeck, Armin K. *Things Maps Don't Tell Us.* New York: Macmillan, 1957.

Morisawa, Marie. *Streams: Their Dynamics and Morphology.* New York: McGraw-Hill, 1968.

Page, Lawrence M., and Brooks M. Burr. *Freshwater Fishes.* Boston: Houghton Mifflin, 1991.

Palmer, Tim. *Endangered Rivers and the Conservation Movement.* Berkeley, Calif.: University of California Press, 1986. The history of river conservation.

_____. *Lifelines: The Case for River Conservation.* Washington, D.C.: Island Press, 1994.

_____. *The Wild and Scenic Rivers of America.* Washington, D.C.: Island Press, 1993.

Peirce, Neal R., and Jerry Hagstrom. *The Book of America.* New York: Norton, 1983. Excellent analysis of and information on all the states.

Shimer, John A. *Field Guide to Landforms in the United States.* New York: Macmillan, 1972.

Thomas, Bill. *American Rivers: A Natural History.* New York: Norton, 1978.

U.S. Department of Commerce. National Oceanic and Atmospheric Administration. *National Estuarine Inventory Data Atlas.* Washington, D.C.: U.S. Department of Commerce, 1985. Information on tidal sections of rivers.

Van der Leeden, Frits, Fred L. Troise, and David Keith Todd. *The Water Encyclopedia.* Chelsea, Mich.: Lewis, 1990. Flow figures.

Western Writers of America. *Water Trails West.* New York: Avon Books, 1978. River navigation.

Maps

Bailey, Robert G. *Ecoregions of North America.* Reston, Va.: U.S. Geological Survey, 1981.

Dahl, Thomas E. *Wetland Resources of the United States.* St. Petersburg, Fla.: U.S. Fish and Wildlife Service, National Wetlands Inventory, 1991.

Hilt, Kerie J. *Surface-Water and Related-Land Resources Development in the United States and Puerto Rico*. Washington, D.C.: U.S. Geological Survey, 1982.

Raisz, Erwin. *Landforms of the United States*. Raisz Landform Maps (P.O. Box 773, Melrose, Mass. 02176), 1957.

U.S. Geological Survey. *Digital Terrain Map of the United States*. Washington, D.C.: U.S. Geological Survey, 1991.

Chapter 1: Rivers of the Glaciated Northeast

Appalachian Mountain Club. *The A.M.C. New England Canoeing Guide*. Boston: Appalachian Mountain Club, 1971, 1986.

Bachman, Ben. *Upstream: A Voyage on the Connecticut River*. Chester, Conn.: Globe Peqot Press, 1988.

Burmeister, Walter F. *Appalachian Waters: The Hudson River and Its Tributaries*. Oakton, Va.: Appalachian Books, 1974.

Butler, James, and Arthur Taylor. *Penobscot River Renaissance*. Camden, Maine: Down East Books, 1992.

Connelly, John, and John Porterfield. *Appalachian Whitewater*. Vol. 3, *The Northern Mountains*. Birmingham, Ala.: Menasha Ridge Press, 1987.

Foster, Charles H. W. *Experiments in Bioregionalism: The New England River Basins Story*. Hanover, N.H.: University Press of New England, 1984.

Gabler, Ray. *New England White Water River Guide*. Boston: Appalachian Mountain Club, 1981.

Jorgensen, Neil. *A Guide to New England's Landscape*. Chester, Conn.: Globe Pequot Press, 1977.

Kauffmann, John M. *Flow East*. New York: McGraw-Hill, 1973.

Lourie, Peter. *River of Mountains: A Canoe Journey Down the Hudson*. Syracuse, NY: Syracuse University Press, 1995.

McKibben, Bill. "A Refuge Without Borders." *Audubon,* January 1995. Connecticut River.

Weber, Ken. *Canoeing Massachusetts, Rhode Island, and Connecticut*. Woodstock, Vt.: Backcountry, 1992.

Chapter 2: Appalachian Rivers of Green

Audubon, Maria R., ed. *Audubon and His Journals*. Vol. 2, New York: Dover, 1897.

Benner, Bob. *Carolina Whitewater*. Birmingham, Ala.: Menasha Ridge Press, 1987.

Brooks, Maurice. *The Appalachians*. Grantsville, W.Va.: Seneca Books, 1965.

Burkhead, N. M., and R. E. Jenkins. "Fishes." In *Virginia's Endangered Species,* ed. K. Terwilliger. Blacksburg, Va.: McDonald and Woodward, 1991.

Burmeister, Walter. *Appalachian Waters: The Delaware and Its Tributaries.* Oakton, Va.: Appalachian Books, 1974.

_____. *Appalachian Waters: The Upper Ohio.* Oakton, Va.: Appalachian Books, 1978.

_____. *The Susquehanna River and Its Tributaries*. Oakton, Va.: Appalachian Books, 1975.

Davidson, Paul, Ward Eister, and Dirk Davidson. *Wildwater West Virginia.* Birmingham, Ala.: Menasha Ridge Press, 1981.

Gertler, Ed. *Maryland and Delaware Canoe Trails*. Silver Spring, Md.: Seneca, 1989.

Grove, Ed, Bill Kirby, Charles Wabridge, Ward Eister, Paul Davidson, and Dirk Davidson. *Appalachian Whitewater*. Vol. 2, *The Central Mountains*. Birmingham, Ala.: Menasha Ridge Press, 1987.

Gutheim, Frederick. *The Potomac*. New York: Holt, Rinehart and Winston, 1974.

Interstate Commission on the Potomac River Basin. *Healing a River: The Potomac, 1940–1990*. Rockville, Md.: Interstate Commission on the Potomac River Basin, 1990.

Palmer, Tim. *Youghiogheny: Appalachian River*. Pittsburgh: University of Pittsburgh Press, 1984.

Sajna, Mike, and Jim Schafer. *The Allegheny River: Watershed of the Nation.* University Park, Pa.: The Pennsylvania State University Press, 1993.

Sehlinger, Bob. *A Canoeing and Kayaking Guide to the Streams of Kentucky.* Birmingham, Ala.: Menasha Ridge Press, 1978.

Stanton, Richard L. *Potomac Journey*. Washington, D.C.: Smithsonian Institution Press, 1993.

Stolzenburg, William. "The Mussels' Message." *Nature Conservancy News,* November–December 1992.

Chapter 3: Rich Waters
of the Coastal Plain and South

Benke, Arthur C. "A Perspective on America's Vanishing Streams." *Journal of the North American Benthological Society* 9, no. 1 (March 1990).

Benner, Bob, and Tom McCloud. *A Paddler's Guide to Eastern North Carolina.* Birmingham, Ala.: Menasha Ridge Press, 1987.

Brooks, Paul. "Oklawaha: 'The Sweetest Water-Lane in the World.'" *Audubon,* July 1970.

Burmeister, Walter. *Appalachian Waters: The Southeastern Rivers*. Oakton, Va.: Appalachian Books, 1976.

Burroughs, Franklin. *The River Home*. Boston: Houghton Mifflin, 1992. The Waccamaw River, South Carolina.

Carr, Archie. "All the Way Down upon the Suwannee River." *Audubon,* March 1983.

Carter, Elizabeth F., and John L. Pearce. *A Canoeing and Kayaking Guide to the Streams of Florida*. Vol. 1, Birmingham, Ala.: Menasha Ridge Press, 1985.

Lydeard, Charles, and Richard L. Mayden. "A Diverse and Endangered Aquatic Ecosystem of the Southeast United States." *Conservation Biology,* August 1995. Alabama rivers.

McPhee, John. *The Control of Nature*. New York: Farrar, Straus and Giroux, 1989. The Atchafalaya River.

_____. *The Pine Barrens*. New York: Farrar, Straus and Giroux, 1978. New Jersey rivers.

Meyer, Judy. "A Blackwater Perspective on Riverine Ecosystems." *BioScience,* October 1990.

Schueler, Donald G. "Southern Exposure." *Sierra,* November–December 1992. Water quality in the South.

Shoumatoff, Alex. *Florida Ramble*. New York: Vintage Books, 1974.

Stine, Jeffrey K. *Mixing the Waters: Environment, Politics, and the Building of the Tennessee-Tombigbee Waterway*. Akron, Ohio: University of Akron Press, 1994.

Suwannee River Water Management District. *1994 Land Acquisition and Management Plan*. Live Oak, Fla.: Suwanee River Water Management District, 1993.

Van Doren, Mark, ed. *The Travels of William Bartram*. New York: Dover, 1955.

Chapter 4: The Midwest: Flowing against the Grid

Davis, Nora Deakin, and Joseph Holmes. *The Father of Waters*. San Francisco: Sierra Club Books, 1982. The Mississippi River.

Dennis, Jerry, and Craig Date. *Canoeing Michigan Rivers*. Davison, Mich.: Friede, 1986.

Featherstonhaugh, George H. "A Canoe Voyage up the Minnay Sotor." Reprint, St. Paul: Minnesota Historical Society, 1970.

Hall, Leonard. *Stars Upstream*. Columbia: University of Missouri Press, 1958. The Current River.

Hedeen, Stanley. *The Mill Creek*. Cincinnati: Blue Heron Press, 1994. An urban stream in Ohio.

Indiana Department of Natural Resources. *Indiana Canoe Guide.* Indianapolis: Indiana Department of Natural Resources, n.d.

Madson, John. *Up on the River: An Upper Mississippi Chronicle.* New York: Penguin, 1985.

Minnesota Department of Natural Resources. *Best Management Practices for Water Quality.* St. Paul: Minnesota Department of Natural Resources, 1992. Brochure.

Minnesota Office of Tourism. *Explore Minnesota Canoe Rivers.* St. Paul: Minnesota Office of Tourism, 1990. Brochure.

Minnesota River Citizens' Advisory Committee. *Working Together: A Plan to Restore the Minnesota River.* St. Paul: Minnesota Pollution Control Agency, 1994.

Missouri Conservation Department. *Missouri Ozark Waterways.* Jefferson City: Missouri Conservation Department, 1965.

Palzer, Bob, and Jody Palzer. *Whitewater, Quietwater: A Guide to the Wild Rivers of Wisconsin, Upper Michigan, and Northeast Minnesota.* Two Rivers, Wisc.: Evergreen Paddleways, 1983.

Raban, Jonathan. *Old Glory.* New York: Penguin, 1981. The Mississippi River.

Sevareid, Eric. *Canoeing with the Cree.* Reprint, St. Paul: Minnesota Historical Society, 1968.

Waters, Thomas. *The Streams and Rivers of Minnesota.* Minneapolis: University of Minnesota Press, 1977.

Williams, Ted. "The River Always Wins." *Audubon,* July 1994. Mississippi flooding.

Winckler, Suzanne. "Where the Untamed Hand of Nature Fits a Civilized Glove." *Audubon,* July 1983. Lower Minnesota River.

Chapter 5: Sky-Filled Rivers of the Great Plains

Aucoin, James. *Water in Nebraska.* Lincoln: University of Nebraska Press, 1984.

Bleed, Ann, and Charles Flowerday, eds. *An Atlas of the Sand Hills.* Lincoln: University of Nebraska, Institute of Agriculture and Natural Resources, 1990.

Farrar, Jon. "Platte River Instream Flow—Who Needs It?" *Nebraskaland,* December 1992.

Flowerday, Charles A., ed. *Flat Water: A History of Nebraska—Its Water.* Lincoln: University of Nebraska, Institute of Agriculture and Natural Resources, 1993.

Graves, John. *Goodbye to a River.* New York: Ballantine; San Francisco: Sierra Club Books, 1960. The Brazos River.

Gudgel, Duane. *Niobrara River Canoeing Guide.* Valentine, Nebr.: Plains Trading Company Archives, 1992.

Hesse, Larry W., Carl W. Wolfe, and Nancy K. Cole. "Some Aspects of Energy Flow in the Missouri River Ecosystem and a Rationale for Recovery." In *The Missouri River: The Resources, Their Uses and Values,* ed. N. G. Benson. American Fisheries Society, North Central Division, 1988.

Nebraska Game and Parks Commission. "Lillian Annette Rowe Sanctuary: Way-Station on the Platte." *Nebraskaland,* March 1989.

_____. *Nebraska Canoe Trails.* Lincoln: Nebraska Game and Parks Commission, n.d. Brochure.

Madson, Chris. "The Death of a River." *Audubon,* May 1982. Arkansas River.

Quammen, David. "Bin of Water, River of Corn." *Audubon,* September 1983. Norden Dam and the Niobrara River.

Chapter 6: Rocky Mountain Lifelines

Carrier, Jim, and Jim Richardson. *The Colorado: A River at Risk.* Englewood, Colo.: Westcliffe, 1992.

Fielder, John. *Colorado: Rivers of the Rockies.* Englewood, Colo.: Westcliffe, 1993.

Fisher, Hank. *The Floater's Guide to Montana.* Helena, Mont.: Falcon Press, 1986.

Foreman, Dave, and Howie Wolke. *The Big Outside.* Tucson, Ariz.: Ned Ludd Books, 1989. Sourcebook on wilderness areas.

Garren, John. *Idaho River Tours.* Portland, Oreg.: Garren, 1987.

Krakel, Dean II. *Downriver: A Yellowstone Journey.* San Francisco: Sierra Club Books, 1987.

Lewis, Dan. *Paddle and Portage: The Floater's Guide to Wyoming Rivers.* Douglas, Wyo.: The Wyoming Naturalist, 1991.

Palmer, Tim. *The Snake River: Window to the West.* Washington, D.C.: Island Press, 1991.

Thompson, Curt. *Floating Montana.* Lakeside, Mont.: Curt Thompson, 1993.

Webb, Walter Prescott. "The American West: Perpetual Mirage." *Harpers,* May 1957.

Wheat, Doug. *The Floater's Guide to Colorado.* Helena, Mont.: Falcon Press, 1984.

Chapter 7: Rivers of the Deserts and Drylands

Aulbach, Louis F., and Joe Butler. *The Lower Canyons of the Rio Grande.* Houston: Wilderness Area Map Service, 1988.

Big Bend Natural History Association. *A Guide to the Rio Grande.* Panther Junction, Tex.: Big Bend Natural History Association, 1989.

Crawford, Clifford S. (team leader for Middle Rio Grande Interagency Team). *Middle Rio Grande Ecosystem: Bosque Biological Management Plan.* Albuquerque: University of New Mexico, 1993.

Daton, David J., and John M. Anderson. *The State of the Rio Grande/Rio Bravo.* Tucson, Ariz.: University of Arizona Press, 1987.

Fradkin, Philip L. *A River No More: The Colorado River and the West.* New York: Knopf, 1981.

Horgan, Paul. *Great River.* New York: Rinehart and Co., 1954.

Huser, Verne. *Canoe Country Paddles.* Salt Lake City, Utah: Wasatch, 1978.

MacCormack, John et al. "Rio Grande." *San Antonio Express,* Special Report, October 17, 1993.

McNamee, Gregory. *Gila: The Life and Death of an American River.* New York: Orion Books, 1994.

Meloy, Ellen. *Raven's Exile: A Season on the Green River.* New York: Henry Holt and Co., 1994.

Nichols, Gary C. *River Runner's Guide to Utah and Adjacent Areas.* Salt Lake City: University of Utah Press, 1986.

Parvin, Bob. "Valley under Siege." *Defenders,* January 1988. The lower Rio Grande.

Porter, Eliot. *The Place No One Knew.* San Francisco: Sierra Club Books, 1963. Glen Canyon of the Colorado.

Russell, Martin. *A Story That Stands Like a Dam: Glen Canyon and the Struggle for the Soul of the West.* New York: Henry Holt, 1989.

Shupe, Steven J., and John Folk-Williams. *The Upper Rio Grande: A Guide to Decision-Making.* Sante Fe, N.M.: Western Network, 1988.

Zwinger, Ann. *Run, River, Run.* New York: Harper and Row, 1975.

Chapter 8: Brilliant Waters of the Sierra Nevada

California Resources Agency. Department of Fish and Game. *Lower American River: Waterway Management Plan.* Sacramento: California Resources Agency, 1977.

California Resources Agency. Department of Fish and Game. *North Fork American River Waterway Management Plan.* Sacramento: California Resources Agency, 1977.

Cassady, Jim, and Fryar Calhoun. *California White Water.* Richmond, Calif.: Cassady and Calhoun, 1984.

Harris, Thomas. *Down the Wild Rivers: A Guide to the Streams of California.* San Francisco: Chronicle Books, 1973.

Holbec, Lars, and Chuck Stanley. *A Guide to the Best Whitewater in the State of California.* Stanford, Calif.: FOR Books, 1984.

Hundley, Norris Jr. *The Great Thirst: Californians and Water, 1770s–1990s.* Berkeley: University of California Press, 1992.

Mandel, Stephanie et al. *The American River: North, Middle, and South Forks.* Auburn, Calif.: Protect American River Canyons, 1989.

Palmer, Tim. *The Sierra Nevada: A Mountain Journey.* Washington, D.C.: Island Press, 1988.

_____. *Stanislaus: The Struggle for a River.* Berkeley, Calif.: University of California Press, 1980.

_____, ed. *California's Threatened Environment.* Washington, D.C.: Island Press, 1993.

Palmer, Tim, and Ann Vileisis. *The South Yuba: A Wild and Scenic River Report.* Nevada City, Calif.: The South Yuba River Citizens League, 1993.

Planning and Conservation League. *Protecting Our Heritage: A Proposal for an Upper American River National Recreation Area.* Sacramento, Calif.: Planning and Conservation League, 1984. Booklet.

Rose, Gene. *San Joaquin: A River Betrayed.* Fresno, Calif.: Linrose, 1992.

Chapter 9: A Land of Rivers in the Northwest

Bennett, Jeff. *A Guide to the Whitewater Rivers of Washington.* Portland, Oreg.: Swiftwater, 1991.

Brown, Bruce. *Mountain in the Clouds.* New York: Simon and Schuster, 1982. Salmon and the Olympic Peninsula.

Cassady, Jim, and Fryar Calhoun. *California White Water.* Richmond, Calif.: Cassady and Calhoun, 1984.

Cone, Joseph. *A Common Fate: Endangered Salmon and the People of the Pacific Northwest.* New York: Henry Holt, 1995.

Dietrich, William. *Northwest Passage: The Great Columbia River.* New York: Simon and Schuster, 1995.

Hedgecock, Dennis, Paul Siri, and Donald R. Strong. "Conservation Biology of Endangered Pacific Salmonids: Introductory Remarks." *Conservation Biology,* September 1994. See entire special section.

McNulty, Tim, and Pat O'Hara. *Washington's Wild Rivers: The Unfinished Work.* Seattle: The Mountaineers, 1990.

Nehlsen, Willa, Jack E. Williams, and James A. Lichatowich. "Pacific Salmon at the Crossroads." *Fisheries,* April 1991.

Netboy, Anthony. *Salmon of the Pacific Northwest.* Portland, Oreg.: Binfords and Mort, 1958.

_____. *The Salmon: Their Fight for Survival.* Boston: Houghton Mifflin, 1974.

North, Douglass A. *Washington Whitewater.* Vols. 1 and 2. Seattle: The Mountaineers, 1988.

U.S. Department of the Interior. Bureau of Land Management. *The Wild and Scenic Rogue River.* Medford, Oreg.: U.S. Department of the Interior, ca. 1990. Map and brochure.

Willamette Kayak and Canoe Club. *Soggy Sneakers: A Guide to Oregon Rivers.* Seattle: The Mountaineers, 1994.

Chapter 10: The Wild Rivers of Alaska

Jettmar, Karen. *The Alaska River Guide.* Seattle: Alaska Northwest Books, 1993.

Kauffmann, John M. *Alaska's Brooks Range.* Seattle: The Mountaineers, 1992.

Mosby, Jack, and David Dapkus. *Alaska Paddling Guide.* Anchorage: J & R Enterprises, 1986.

Simmerman, Nancy Lange. *Alaska's Parklands.* Seattle: The Mountaineers, 1983.

Weber, Sepp. *Wild Rivers of Alaska.* Anchorage: Alaska Northwest Books, 1976.

Wild, Summer, producer. *Tatshenshini: River Wild.* Englewood, Colo.: Westcliffe Publishers, 1993.

Index

About the Author

Tim Palmer has been involved with rivers since 1970 as a writer, photographer, planner, conservationist, and consultant to citizen organizations. His slide presentations on river topics are frequently featured at conferences nationwide. Most of his eleven books address rivers; they include *Lifelines: The Case for River Conservation, The Wild and Scenic Rivers of America, The Snake River: Window to the West, Endangered Rivers and the Conservation Movement, Youghiogheny: Appalachian River, Stanislaus: The Struggle for a River,* and *Rivers of Pennsylvania.*

With a bachelor of science degree in landscape architecture, the author worked for eight years as a planner dealing with water and land issues before becoming a full-time writer. He has received the Lifetime Achievement Award from American Rivers in recognition of his writings on river protection, and he currently serves on the board of River Network, a national group based in Portland, Oregon. Over a period of twenty-five years the author has canoed or rafted on more than 230 different streams nationwide and has amassed an extensive collection of river photographs. Frequently based near Kelly, Wyoming, in the winter, he travels during the rest of the year. He is currently writing a book about the Columbia River basin.